Visual QuickStart Guide

ClarisWorks 4

for Macintosh

C. Ann Brown

 **Peachpit Press**

Visual QuickStart Guide
ClarisWorks 4 for Macintosh
C. Ann Brown

Peachpit Press
2414 Sixth Street
Berkeley, CA 94710
(510) 548-4393
(510) 548-5991 (fax)

Find us on the World Wide Web at: http://www.peachpit.com.

Peachpit Press is a division of Addison-Wesley Publishing Company.

© 1996 by C. Ann Brown

Editorial assistance, John Hammett and Emily Marks

Production, C. Ann Brown

ISBN: 0-201-88407-0

9 8 7 6 5 4 3 2

Printed and bound in the United States of America

 Printed on recycled paper

Contents

Chapter 4 **Spreadsheets**

Chapter 5 **Databases**

Chapter 6 **Drawing**

Chapter 7 **Painting**

Getting Started

■ What is ClarisWorks 4?

ClarisWorks is a full-featured software program that helps you:

▲ Create letters and reports using a simple-to-understand word processing program

▲ Compile a database or mailing list, make labels, or use data in a mail merge

▲ Use a Drawing or Painting module to make logos or include clip-art in the documents

▲ Whip up a spreadsheet, create a graph with the data, and incorporate the graphs into your word-processed report

▲ Use telecommunications to connect with the Internet, bulletin board systems, or other small businesses

▲ Share your files and data over a network

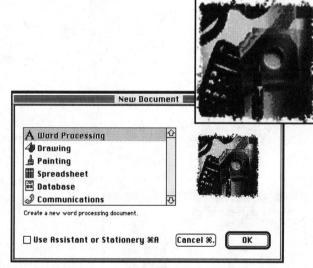

ClarisWorks 4 opening screen

How can just one program do all that work?

ClarisWorks is an integrated program that takes the place of multiple programs on your computer. Instead of your having to fit six very different programs together, you'll find that the Claris-Works' "suite" of programs works together smoothly. It is designed to make your personal and business life simpler.

✔ **Tip**: *ClarisWorks is so powerful you just might not need another software program—so be sure to sample each part of the program to find out just how flexible ClarisWorks is!*

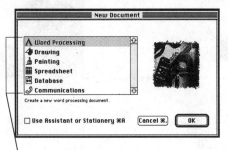

ClarisWorks program modes

One example of a ClarisWorks word-processed document

ClarisWorks 4 Assistants; notice that the box that says Use Assistant or Stationery has a check mark in it. When you click in that box, you will see all of the Assistants listed instead of the program mode list. This type of menu is called a scrolling list.

Program modes

ClarisWorks program modes are really independent but integrated programs. Each mode functions like a separate program but is designed to work effortlessly with the other parts of ClarisWorks.

Word Processing
▲ For writing letters, creating reports

Drawing
▲ For the architect in you, to design object-oriented graphics

Painting
▲ For the freehand artist, to paint and draw objects using the mouse

Spreadsheet
▲ For solving financial questions, helping to create mathematical solutions, and then making graphs of them

Database
▲ For keeping track of the names, addresses, and other important information about your friends, relatives, business associates, and students

Communications
▲ For dialing up the Internet, local bulletin board services (BBSs), or service bureaus with your computer modem

ClarisWorks Assistants

ClarisWorks uses special shortcuts called Assistants to automate tasks such as creating a mailing list, creating a checkbook layout, or designing a certificate. The Assistants and templates in Claris-Works save you time by providing a document set up to work for you, instead of your having to create the document from scratch.

What is ClarisWorks 4?

■ Just for beginners

A little basic Macintosh

If you have just purchased your first Macintosh, you probably have ClarisWorks 4 installed on it. This section will help you familiarize yourself with beginning Macintosh operations before you start learning how to use ClarisWorks.

If you are an experienced Macintosh user, skip ahead in this chapter to the section called "New Features" (page 19) to find out what is new in ClarisWorks 4.

■ Let's get going

Starting up your computer

Before starting up your Macintosh, make sure all of your other equipment, except the main machine, is turned on. In other words, be sure to turn on things like your printer, scanner, external hard drives, or CD-ROM drives.

Give yourself a few seconds before you rush into turning on your computer, then either press the power key or turn on the switch on the back side of the Macintosh.

✔ **Tip**: *The power key has a triangle that faces left on it. It may be located at the top or right side of the keyboard.*

Macintosh Finder application menu bar

Apple menu   *Main menu items*   *Help and Finder icons*

| | File Edit View Label Special | | ? ▢ |

Once you have the power on, a menu bar appears at the top of your screen. This is the Finder application menu bar. From the Special menu on the Finder application menu bar, you can initialize disks, organize files and folders, delete unneeded items, and shut down your machine.

After your computer is started up, if you place an unformatted disk back into the floppy disk drive, your machine will then try to initialize it. Initializing will erase anything that was on the disk. You must initialize disks the first time you use them.

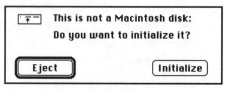

This is not a Macintosh disk:
Do you want to initialize it?

Eject   Initialize

■ Parts of the Macintosh screen

The desktop, or main screen, shows the following items: Apple menu, main menu items, Help menu, Application menu, hard drive icon, trash can, files, application program icons, and file folders.

Parts of the desktop or main screen; the Finder is the current application

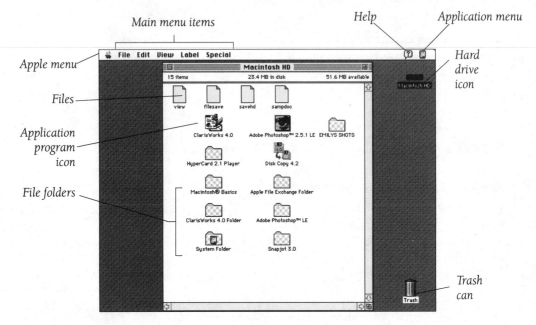

Main menu items

Help

Application menu

Apple menu

Hard drive icon

Files

Application program icon

File folders

Trash can

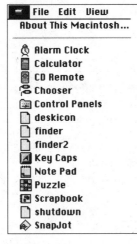

The Apple menu contains all of your desk accessory programs such as an Alarm Clock or the Key Caps pop-up program.

Apple menu

When you click on this icon, a list of all of the miniature programs you have on your machine appears. These programs are also called desk accessories. You might have an Alarm Clock, Calculator, finder, Key Caps, and other useful accessories on the list.

Finder menu items

The menu bar for the Finder application, shown above, has five main items on it: File, Edit, View, Label, and Special. Each of these items helps you manage your disk drives, shut the machine down, or empty unwanted files into the trash. You also have the Apple menu, Help menu, and Application menu. These items help you switch between programs and get help.

Help menu icon

Balloon Help is designed to give you help via a "talking-balloon" pop-up window. If you turn Balloon Help on in this menu, when you move the pointer over an icon or menu item, Balloon Help will tell you what this item does.

To turn on Balloon Help

1. Move the pointer on top of the Help menu, and hold the mouse button down.

2. Let go of the mouse button when you are on top of the Show Balloons menu choice.

Application menu

The Application menu on the far right of the menu bar lets you know which programs are open and lets you quickly switch from one open program to another. Open programs appear at the bottom of the Application pull-down menu. The current active program has a check mark beside it, and its icon appears in the menu bar.

With System 7.0+ (or with System 6.0+ and the MultiFinder installed), you can see which programs have been started and switch between them by following the next few steps.

Using the Application menu

If you want to switch between ClarisWorks and other programs, use the Application menu to see a list of programs that are currently running.

1. Move the pointer to the icon at the top right of the screen, and hold down the mouse button.

2. Drag the cursor down to ClarisWorks 4 or any other program you wish to switch to. The program you choose should appear in a high-lighted bar and have a check mark beside it.

3. Now let go of the mouse button.

Help menu icon

Select Show Balloons and you will see Balloon Help when you pass the pointer over an icon.

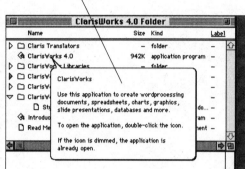

Icon of the active Application

The current application icon appears at the top right of the menu bar. If you click on the icon and hold down the mouse button, you will see a menu.

Desktop icons

The Macintosh hard drive icon, trash icon, and two untitled floppy icons.

The floppy disk will eject when the icon is dragged on top of the trash can. if you shut your machine down, your disk should also eject automatically.

To remove a file, drag its icon on top of the trash can. Next you must be sure to take out the trash by choosing Empty Trash from the Special menu in the menu bar.

Hard drive window: Notice the borders surrounding the window, the scroll bars on the right side, and the name of the window in the top border bar.

Hard disk icon

This icon shows the hard disk (HD). If you double-click on the hard disk icon, you will be able to see what your hard disk drive contains. The list that appears shows both programs and files.

Floppy disk icons

If you have a floppy disk in the floppy disk drive, you will see a picture of a 3 1/2-inch disk. You can double-click on that disk to see the contents.

To remove a floppy disk from the drive

1. Position the mouse cursor on top of the floppy disk icon.
2. Hold the mouse button down and drag the disk on top of the trash can.

To erase a file, a folder full of files, or a disk

1. Click once on the object you want to erase, and hold down the mouse button.
2. Drag the object on top of the trash can.
3. The trash can will appear dark when you have dragged your file to the proper place.
4. Make sure you use the Empty Trash command in the Special menu to actually erase the items, or they'll still be on your disk.

Trash can

The trash can is where you dump all of your unwanted files. You have to remember to take out the trash!

Window

A window is a rectangular area with distinct borders that contains programs, files, or folders. You can have many windows open at the same time. The windows will stack on top of one another.

To move to an open window, you can just click on any part you can see of that window. When you double-click a file folder, you will open a new window listing the contents of that folder.

File folders

File folders are how you organize your hard disk and your floppy disk. You create file folders and place programs and files into them. This is important if you like to stay organized—you can create special areas for your work and your files by topic, by program, or any other way that makes sense to you.

A dark gray file folder indicates the folder is already open. In the top window, you can see the contents of that file folder.

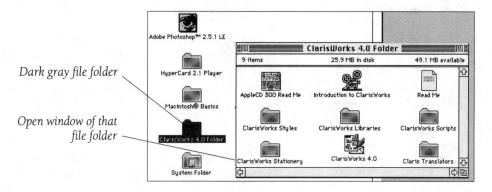

Dark gray file folder

Open window of that file folder

Starting your first program

To start up a program, double-click on the program icon. If the program icon is dark gray, you have already opened the program.

Double-click on the ClarisWorks icon to start the program.

This ClarisWorks icon is dark gray, indicating that the program has already been started up. If you see this, check your Application menu icon to see if the program list shows an additional program open.

✔ **Tip**: *You need to use the proper rhythm and speed for the double-click. Try saying "quickstart" out loud and fairly quickly. Notice the rhythm? The first syllable is quick and the second syllable is a little slower. That is the rhythm you should use. Say "quickstart" while you click and click to the rhythm of the words.*

✔ **Tip**: *Clicking twice on a document will also start a program up! The Macintosh knows to go get the program you need and open the document and the program at the same time.*

Program and Finder menus

You can become confused if you aren't used to System 7.0+. The program menu for your application, like ClarisWorks, appears on the menu bar and replaces the Finder menu you saw when you first started up. If you aren't sure where your program is, or if you have actually started it up, check to see if the menu bar looks different.

Finder menu

| File Edit View Label Special |
| Macintosh HD |
| 11 items   26 MB in disk |
| Adobe Photoshop™ 2.5.1 LE   ClarisWorks 4.0 |

This first picture shows the main startup screen and the system menu.

The second picture shows the screen after ClarisWorks has been started up. Notice that the ClarisWorks icon is dark and the menu items are now different.

ClarisWorks menu

| File Edit View |
| Macintosh HD |
| 11 items   26 MB in disk |
| Adobe Photoshop™ 2.5.1 LE   ClarisWorks 4.0 |

About the conventions in this book

When you should press more than one key, the keys will be designated as follows:

▲ *In text, keys will be separated by hyphens, as in Shift-Command-C.*

▲ *When symbols are used to represent some of the keys, keys will be separated by spaces and then hyphens, as in* ⇧ ⌘ **-C**.

If you can't remember what the menu looked like, click on the Application menu. The Application menu will have a check mark by the active program.

The menu bar on the top of your screen is the menu for the active program. You might still see your hard drive icon, your application window, or other icons on the screen.

The important thing is to understand which menu bar is in front of you.

Leaving your program

Before you turn your Macintosh off, you must quit, or leave, all programs. Make sure you have saved any documents you created before you leave a program.

Quitting a program

Command-Q shuts any program down. The Command key is the key with the ⌘ on it.

1. Hold the ⌘ key down.

2. Tap the Q on the keyboard.

3. Let go of the ⌘ key.

Shutting down your Macintosh

To shut down your Macintosh, you will be using the Special menu, or the sixth item from the left side. Your Macintosh should shut the power off by itself once you have followed the proper steps.

Shutting down the Macintosh using the Special menu

1. On the Finder menu, move the pointer over the Special menu and hold down the mouse button.

2. Choose Shut Down from the Special menu by moving the pointer over the words Shut Down and letting go of the mouse button.

You will see the screen go dark and hear the machine "power itself down," or become silent. If your Macintosh doesn't shut itself off after a minute, turn the power switch off on the back of the machine.

Special	
Clean Up Desktop	
Empty Trash...	
Eject Disk	⌘E
Erase Disk...	
Restart	
Shut Down	

Shut Down

> ✔ **Tip**: *Instructions in this book for selecting commands from a menu will be written like this:*
> *Choose Shut Down from the Special menu.*

■ Getting around in ClarisWorks 4

The opening screen

Once you have started ClarisWorks, you will see an opening screen that lets you choose among word processing, drawing, painting, using a spreadsheet, creating a database, or using communications with your modem. At the bottom of the screen is a checkbox that says Use Assistant or Stationery.

Click on Word Processing in the scrolling list to begin creating a word-processed document

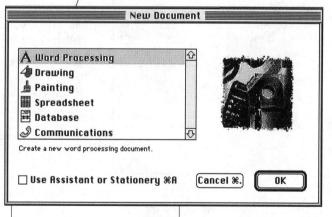

The opening screen of ClarisWorks lets you choose among the six program modes, or you can click on the Use Assistant or Stationery checkbox to access template documents called Assistants.

Begin creating a document in ClarisWorks

1. Click on one of the options such as Word Processing that you see in the scrolling list in the New Document dialog box, or click once in the box labeled Use Assistant or Stationery.
2. Click on one of the Assistants, which are pre-made documents. These automated documents guide you through adding information.

Because all of the program modes such as Word Processing and Database belong to the same program, you will find it is easy to move information from one part of the program to another.

The Word Processing menu with the ruler bar

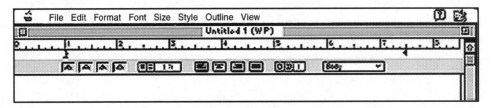

What's on the menu

Each part of the program has its own unique menu. Menu lists pull down from the menu bar. The File menu for the Word Processing program mode is pulled down so you can see the choices in that menu. Each program mode has a different set of menus. In these other program modes, some of the menus have similar commands, while other menus have commands that are unique to that program mode.

Choosing commands from a menu

1. Position the pointer over the menu name, and hold down the mouse button.
2. Move the pointer down the menu until you get to the command you want.
3. When you get to the command you want, let go of the mouse button.

Moving the pointer down the menu creates a highlighted bar. You can tell you are where you want to be when the highlight is on top of the action you want to choose.

Notice the Save command about half way down the File menu. The shortcut key on the right-hand side of the menu is ⌘-S

Shortcut keys use combinations of the Option key or the Command key (⌘) plus an alphabetic letter or number. The Option and Command keys are located next to the space bar on the keyboard. A few commands need the Shift key (⇧) plus the Command key.

Common shortcut keys

Key combination	Symbol	Used for
Command-N	⌘-N	Getting a new file
Command-O	⌘-O	Opening an existing file
Command-W	⌘-W	Closing an active document
Command-S	⌘-S	Saving an active document
Command-P	⌘-P	Printing
Command-Q	⌘-Q	Quitting the program
Command-C	⌘-C	Copying the selected text or picture
Command-X	⌘-X	Cutting the selected text or picture
Command-V	⌘-V	Pasting a copy of the selected text or picture
Command-Z	⌘-Z	Undoing the most recent change
Command-A	⌘-A	Selecting everything on the page
Command-.	⌘-. (period)	Canceling printing, quitting a dialog box

Keyboard shortcuts

If you look at the File menu again in the Word Processing program, you will notice that the commands have symbols and letters on the right-hand side of the pull-down menu.

For example, under the File menu, the Quit command has the key combination ⌘-Q.

✔ Special shortcut key symbols:
⌘ is the Command key
⇧ is the Shift key

✔ **Tip**: *When you use shortcut keys, don't try to push two or three keys down simultaneously. First, hold down the Command key, then hold down the Shift key if you need it. While you are still holding those keys down, quickly tap the appropriate letter of the alphabet. Once you have done that, you can then let go of the Command or Shift key.*

See the chart at the top of this page for a list of the common shortcut keys—keys that are used in almost every Macintosh program, not just in ClarisWorks.

Getting around in ClarisWorks 4

Moving around

You can move around inside of the ClarisWorks document, or any Macintosh document, by any one of three ways.

▲ Click near the text you want to edit or insert, or click once on a picture you want to move or delete.

▲ You can also click on the scroll bars that appear on the right-hand side and horizontally across the bottom of the window. The scroll bars move in larger increments if you click on either side of the scroll box.

▲ The third way of moving around works only if you have an extended keyboard that features keys such as Home, End, Page Down, and Page Up. The chart, "Moving around," shows you a chart of the common key combinations for moving quickly within ClarisWorks.

✔ **Tip:** *To use the scroll bars, make quick, short clicks on the up arrow or down arrow. To move a bigger distance, click in the gray area below the arrow that points up. You will see a box move down the scroll bar area. You can click on either side of the box to move in larger increments.*

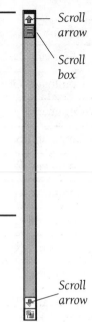

Scroll arrow

Scroll box

Scroll arrow

Moving around

Key combination	Used for
Moving between lines or characters	
Right arrow or left arrow	Right or left one character
Up arrow or down arrow	Up or down one line
Moving between words	
Option-right arrow	Right one word
Option-left arrow	Left one word
Moving from one end of the line to the other	
Command-right arrow	Move to the end of the line
Command-left arrow	Move to the beginning of the line
Moving from paragraph to paragraph	
Option-up arrow	Move to the beginning of the paragraph
Option-down arrow	Move to the end of the paragraph

Switching between ClarisWorks program modes

If you want to switch between parts of ClarisWorks, start a new document by

▲ Choosing New from the File menu, or pressing ⌘-N to start a new document, or

▲ Choosing Open from the File menu, or pressing ⌘-O , to open an existing document in one of the other program modes.

You can start a new document in any of the ClarisWorks modes.

You can switch between program modes and documents by opening the View menu, which lists all of your currently open documents, and clicking on any document listed at the bottom of the View menu.

Word Processing View menu with two open documents listed on the bottom. Document 1 is an untitled Word Processing document (WP) while document 2 is an untitled Database document (DB). Document 2 is the active document. (Note the check mark.)

View
New View
Open Frame
Page View ⇧⌘P
Slide Show...
Show Styles ⇧⌘W
Hide Tools ⇧⌘T
Show Rulers ⇧⌘U
Tile Windows
Stack Windows
Untitled 1 (WP)
✓Untitled 2 (DB)

Switching between documents of any type

Select the document you want to use from the View menu. If you wanted to open a Word Processing document from the View menu and you were currently working in the Database program mode, ClarisWorks will automatically start up the Word Processing program mode for you when the Word Processing document is selected.

Word Processing File menu with the the Save command about halfway down the menu. The shortcut key is ⌘-S.

File	Edit	Format	Font
New...			⌘N
Open...			⌘O
Insert...			
Close			⌘W
Save			⌘S
Save As...			⇧⌘S
Revert			
Document Summary Info			
Shortcuts			▶
Library			▶
Mail			▶
Mail Merge...			⇧⌘M
Page Setup...			
Print...			⌘P
Quit			⌘Q

Saving the document

Before you finish the document you must remember to save it. You will always find the Save command in the File menu.

Saving a document

1. Choose Save from the File menu. You will see "The Save dialog box." This dialog box shows you where your file will be placed or lets you choose a new place to save your file.
2. If you want to save where the pop-up list indicates, type a name in the document name box.
3. Click on the Save button.

✔ **Tip**: *Power outages, a cord accidentally unplugged, shutting down the machine without saving—all of these incidents can accidentally cause you to lose the document, so don't forget to save often while you are working!*

Getting around in ClarisWorks 4

Using the dialog box to name a document

You might not want to save the file to the menu's location. The pop-up list at the top of the screen shows where the file automatically goes and can be used to change the location.

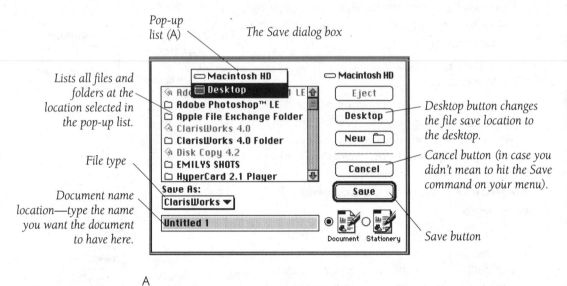

Pop-up list (A)

The Save dialog box

Lists all files and folders at the location selected in the pop-up list.

File type

Document name location—type the name you want the document to have here.

Desktop button changes the file save location to the desktop.

Cancel button (in case you didn't mean to hit the Save command on your menu).

Save button

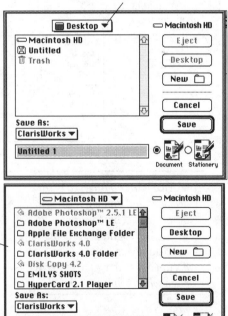

A

B

Changing where the file will be saved

1. Move the pointer on top of the pop-up list (A), and hold the mouse button down.

2. If you want to save your file to another location, such as the desktop, move the pointer to the desktop icon on the pop-up list and then let go.

3. If you want to save your file inside of another folder on your hard drive, double-click on the file folder where you want your file to be saved (B).

4. Choose the file folder you want to save your file in by double-clicking on the name of the folder.

5. Type the file name in the Save As box.

6. Click on the Save button.

■ ClarisWorks Help

Help will give you brief descriptions of how to accomplish your ClarisWorks actions such as mail merge or adding a picture to the library.

ClarisWorks Help text box

Contents   *Index*   *Go Back*

Close box

Keyword box

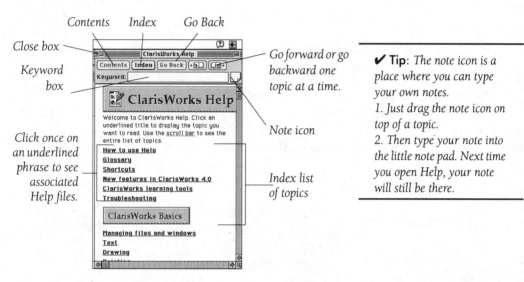

Click once on an underlined phrase to see associated Help files.

Go forward or go backward one topic at a time.

Note icon

Index list of topics

✔ **Tip**: *The note icon is a place where you can type your own notes.*
1. Just drag the note icon on top of a topic.
2. Then type your note into the little note pad. Next time you open Help, your note will still be there.

Using Help

1. Press the Help key, or press ⌘-?.
2. You will see the Help dialog box appear.
3. Type the topic you want to look up in the Keyword box.
4. Press the Return key.

Closing Help

1. Click in the close box.
2. If the Help icon is still active, use the Application menu to switch back to ClarisWorks.
3. Help will close when ClarisWorks is closed.

ClarisWorks Help

Help index

The Help index contains a list of topics that are arranged in alphabetical order. On the left-hand side of the Help Index dialog box, there is a brief list of keywords, while the right side of the screen contains a short description of the topic.

Using the Help index

1. Open Help.
2. Click on the Index button at the top of the Help screen.
3. Scroll down through the list until you find the topic you want, or type the first letter of the topic you want (for example, P for print).
4. To see the topic, click on the Go To Topic button.
5. When you are finished, click on the Done button.

Help Index dialog box

Keyword list

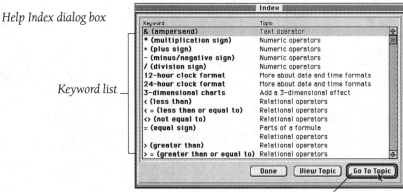

Go To Topic button

ClarisWorks Help menus

The ClarisWorks menu bar for Help is different from the document menu and includes File, Edit, Find, Bookmarks, and View. You will need to remember to use the Application menu to return to ClarisWorks.

Printing a topic

1. Choose your topic using the Index, Keyword, or Contents features.
2. From the File menu, choose Print, or press ⌘-P.
3. Click on the Print button.

You can also choose Print All Topics—but beware—that could take some time and paper!

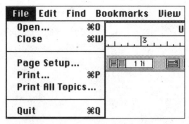

The Help File menu does not have Save on it and is much simpler than your document menu.

(sidebar) ClarisWorks Help

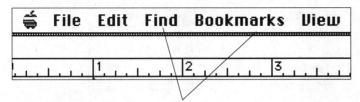

Once you invoke Help, the menu bar will change. You will see Find and Bookmarks menus. Use the Application menu to switch back to the document.

Using the Edit menu while in Help

The Edit menu will help you copy the Help files to a document in ClarisWorks. This is a handy way to build a file or notebook of instructions.

1. Open Help and find the topic you want to copy.
2. Choose Copy Topic Text from the Edit menu.
3. You will see a Copy Topic Text dialog box appear. This dialog box will allow you to edit the text using cut, paste, and copy.
4. When you are finished editing or selecting the text, click on the Copy Selected Text button.
5. Switch back to your ClarisWorks document by using the Application menu.
6. Choose Paste from the Edit menu, or press ⌘-**V**.

Finding a topic using the Find menu

1. Open Help.
2. Choose Global Find from the Find menu, or press ⌘-**F**.
3. You will see a Find dialog box appear. Type a possible keyword in the Find box for your topic.
4. Click on the Find button.
5. If the first topic you find doesn't quite answer your question, you can use Global Find Again, or press ⌘-**G**, to look for the next occurrence of the keyword.

Find	Bookmarks	View
Global Find...		⌘F
Global Find Again		⌘G

Find is a quick and flexible way of finding a topic. You have the option to search for the same word again. This makes it easier to pinpoint the help you need exactly.

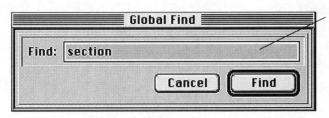

Global Find

Find: section

Cancel   Find

The Global Find dialog box is where you need to type the keyword you are looking for. If the first word you use doesn't work, try using a synonym.

Creating a bookmark with Quick keys

Help Bookmarks in ClarisWorks act just like bookmarks in books do—they are used to save your place. You can have up to 10 Help Bookmarks attached to a single document. You can create Quick keys, which are shortcut keys assigned to the Help Bookmarks command and move you quickly to your Bookmark when you use them.

1. Find the topic you need in Help.
2. Choose Set Bookmark from the Bookmarks menu. Note: You do not need to click in the paragraph or do anything else to set a bookmark at a topic.
3. If you want to attach this Bookmark to a Quick key, choose one of the numbers (from 0 to 9) from the ⌘ Key menu.
4. When you are finished, click on the OK button.

Finding your previous bookmark

1. Open Help.
2. Use your Quick key combination such as ⌘-1. You should immediately be moved to that Help topic.

Editing a bookmark

1. Open Help.
2. Choose Edit Bookmarks from the Bookmarks menu. An Edit Bookmarks dialog box will appear with a list of your topics in the main window.
3. Select the topic you wish to see and use the View Topic button to see the topic.
4. Click on the OK button when you are finished.

Deleting a bookmark

1. Open Help and choose Edit Bookmarks from the Bookmarks menu.
2. Select the topic you wish to delete.
3. Click on the Delete Bookmark button.
4. Click on the OK button to close the Edit Bookmarks dialog box.

This is the Bookmarks menu, with Set Bookmarks and Edit Bookmarks commands. There are no shortcut keys for these actions.

The Set Bookmark dialog box and the Name box

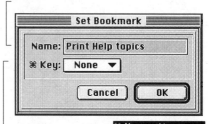

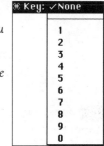

When you click on the ⌘ Key box, you will see a list containing ten numbers. Select one of the numbers to make a Quick key combination with the ⌘ key.

Edit Bookmarks dialog box

Topic list

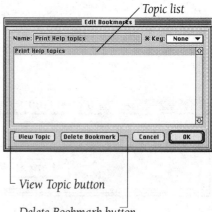

View Topic button

Delete Bookmark button

■ New features

ClarisWorks Assistants

ClarisWorks now contains Assistants that help you make newsletters, envelopes, and home finance documents instantly. These Assistants can be thought of as document templates. When you first start up ClarisWorks, click in the box marked Use Assistant or Stationery. The box will have a check mark in it if it is already selected.

The seven Assistants help you perform a variety of computing tasks without your having to learn

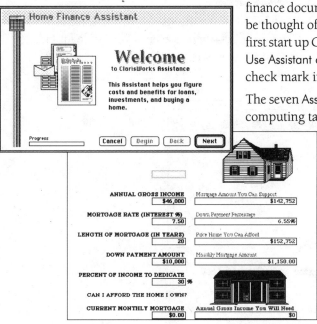

how to set up these types of documents. Three Assistants are new to ClarisWorks 4: certificates, home finance, and mailing labels.

The Assistants guide you through filling in the blanks of a form, step by step. Here is an example of the Home Finance Assistant. You can see all of the parts clearly labeled and a Next button for you to proceed to the next step.

Name & Address List

▲ Helps create a name and address database with formats for personal, business, or student information.

Calendar

▲ Helps create a monthly appointment calendar.

Certificate

▲ Helps create awards, certificates, and diplomas.

Envelope

▲ Helps create and print your envelopes.

Home Finance

▲ Helps answer questions about your net worth, how much mortgage you can afford, and how much an investment will be worth after a designated period of years.

Newsletter

▲ Helps set up a school or business newsletter.

Mailing Labels

▲ Helps quickly create any size mailing label.

Presentation

▲ Helps create overheads, slides, or printed materials for meetings—there is even a "fun" style for kids to use for a classroom presentation.

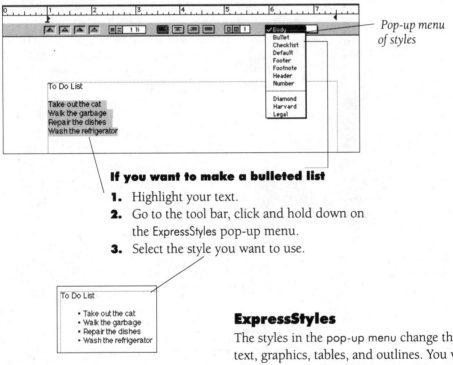

Pop-up menu of styles

If you want to make a bulleted list

1. Highlight your text.
2. Go to the tool bar, click and hold down on the ExpressStyles pop-up menu.
3. Select the style you want to use.

ExpressStyles

The styles in the pop-up menu change the look of text, graphics, tables, and outlines. You will have a variety of "appearances" to chose from, and all of them are already set up for you. For instance, you can use styles from the pop-up menu of styles in Word Processing to format a report. Simply highlight your text and then select the Bullet style from the pop-up menu of styles .

Each part of the program has its own unique style sheets. The Spreadsheet program mode features colorful, classic, or three-dimensional tables. By choosing these styles, you can dress up the document and make it ready to go.

New features

Clip art comes with ClarisWorks 4 and can be found in the Library.

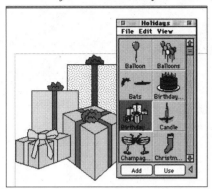

The Database list view makes your mailing list spread the information across the page.

Radio buttons can be clicked on instead of your having to type in the correct information.

The Shortcuts palette gives you button shortcuts for common document operations such as switching from Word Processing to Drawing.

Drag-and-drop libraries

ClarisWorks has added libraries of great clip art you can quickly drag and drop into any document. You'll find "libraries" of pictures featuring world globes, food, education, and holidays.

Use the libraries in the Painting and Drawing program modes, add color and text, and you can create original greeting cards, calendars, and other decorative items.

FastReport, list view, and new field types

FastReport is a tool that lets you search a database quickly and then save that search. You will then be able to use that search any time in the future.

You also have a list view and loads of new field types. Many of these new field types will help you automate your data entry by giving you automatic lists, checkboxes, or radio buttons, instead of just plain text boxes that you have to type into.

General new features

ClarisWorks uses a Shortcuts palette that offers button options so you don't have to access the menus. ClarisWorks also has instant Help that gives you miniature Balloon Help when you hold the mouse over a Shortcuts palette icon. You'll see a description pop up, and you'll no longer have to guess what that cute little paint brush means.

As you go through this book, you'll find even more new features in each section of the program. You'll find out about WorldScript, a language helper, that supports multilingual documents and helps you type in Japanese Kanji or Chinese. You'll also find out how to convert more than one file at a time using automatic drag and drop translating.

So—let's go ClarisWorks!

New features

Beginning Word Processing

■ Word processing basics

When you want to write a letter, address an envelope, or produce an elaborate report that contains drawings, charts, and tables of numbers, you will be doing word processing.

Creating your first document

The first thing you will have to do is obvious.

1. Start the ClarisWorks program by double-clicking on the ClarisWorks icon. You will now see the New Document dialog box.
2. Double-click on Word Processing in the scrolling list.

Once you have entered Word Processing, you can start a new document by choosing New from the File menu or pressing ⌘-N while you are still in a document.

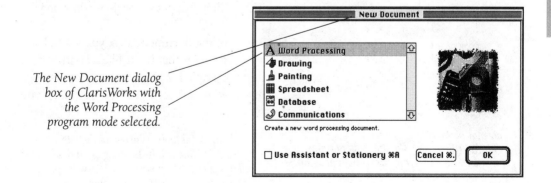

The New Document dialog box of ClarisWorks with the Word Processing program mode selected.

Menus and tool bars

The commands you need to use can be found on the menu bar and menus you see in front of you.

Parts of the Word Processing menu, ruler, and tool bars

Look confusing? All you need are a few tips to properly use the menu and button bars.

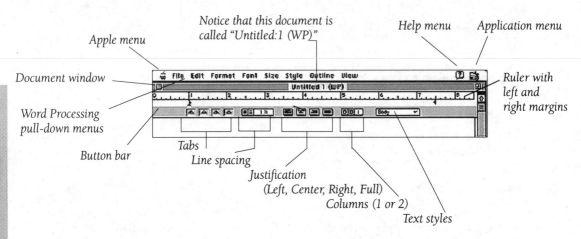

Notice that this document is called "Untitled:1 (WP)"

Help menu

Application menu

Apple menu

Document window

Word Processing pull-down menus

Ruler with left and right margins

Button bar

Tabs

Line spacing

Justification (Left, Center, Right, Full)

Columns (1 or 2)

Text styles

Always remember:

▲ When you want to use a menu or button, the tip of the pointer is the part that must be touching the button or menu item.

▲ Menus require you to hold the mouse button down.

▲ Buttons require you to click the mouse button once to select, or use, that button.

▲ The pointer changes shape depending on what it is on top of.

▲ Inside of the document area, you should see a blinking cursor that looks like a short vertical line. This is called the text indicator or insertion point. If you don't see this blinking cursor, you can't type.

In this example the pointer looks like an I-beam.

The normal pointer looks like a little solid arrow.

Top and side margins appear as light gray lines.

Notice the solid line at the end of the word "type?" This line will be blinking on and off and will indicate where your next letter will appear. The solid line is called the insertion point.

This is the pulsing cursor that means you are ready to type|

■ Word Processing menus

You will see eight menus in the menu bar when you work in the Word Processing program mode. They contain all of the commands you need to create any type of word-processed document.

They include:

▲ The File menu, which contains commands to manage files, such as saving a document or finding a document on the disk.

▲ The Edit menu, which gives you the tools to make changes such as moving text around or eliminating text you don't want.

▲ The Format menu, which gives you commands to change the entire document's margins, indent a paragraph, change spacing between paragraphs, insert page numbers, and create columns.

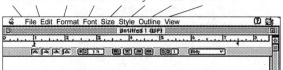

▲ The Font menu, which lets you change the typeface or font of your entire document or just change the typeface or font of a single letter or word in the document.

▲ The Size menu, which gives you choices for the font size.

▲ The Style menu, which lets you choose bold, italic, underline, shadow, outline, or styles, as well as many other special effects for your text.

▲ The Outline menu, which helps you create an organized document.

▲ The View menu, which hides the ruler if you don't want to use it,also lets you see the document as if it is a slide show, and gives you the option to hide the tools.

Using a menu

1. Move the mouse so the tip is just on top of the menu name (for example File).

2. Hold the mouse button down and the menu will drop down. You will see the list of menu items on the left and the shortcut key combinations you could use on the right.

3. Drag the pointer to the command you want to use and release the mouse button.

File	
New...	⌘N
Open...	⌘O
Insert...	
Close	⌘W
Save	⌘S
Save As...	⇧⌘S
Revert	
Document Summary Info	
Shortcuts	▶
Library	▶
Mail	▶
Mail Merge...	⇧⌘M
Page Setup...	
Print...	⌘P
Quit	⌘Q

✔ **Tip:** *See "Common shortcut keys" on page 11 for a list of key combinations that you might want to remember.*

Word Processing menus

Buttons

You will find four types of buttons in ClarisWorks menus: radio buttons, push buttons, lozenge-shaped buttons, and pop-up list buttons. Each type of button is activated or used in a different manner.

ClarisWorks buttons

You will find several types of buttons including:

▲ *Radio buttons: The radio button that has a dark center is the button that has been selected. You select a radio button by clicking in the center of the circle. Selecting one radio button from a group of buttons turns the other buttons in the group off.*

▲ *Push buttons: Examples include the justification and columns buttons from the Word Processing menu bar. When they are selected, push buttons are darker than other buttons.*

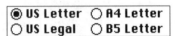

▲ *Lozenge-shaped buttons: They have a darker outline if they are active and appear dimmed if they are not. If a button has a double line around it, you can use that button by pressing the Return key, as well as by clicking on the button with the mouse.*

▲ *Pop-up list buttons: You use these buttons that have small triangles on them, by holding down on the mouse button when the pointer is on top of the button. You will then see a pop-up list.*

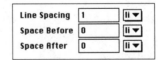

Word Processing menus

■ Document screen

The ClarisWorks basic document screen has several shortcuts on it that are not obvious. These shortcuts will help you:

▲ Close the document window.

▲ Expand a window so it will fit the entire screen.

▲ Zoom in and out on a document.

▲ Open tool bars.

▲ Move to a specific page quickly.

▲ Option-click to show the Preferences dialog box.

▲ Scroll back and forth or up and down in a document.

To use any of these shortcuts, just click once on them.

Using the size box

▲ *Move the pointer on top of the size box and click. The window should expand to the maximum size automatically.*

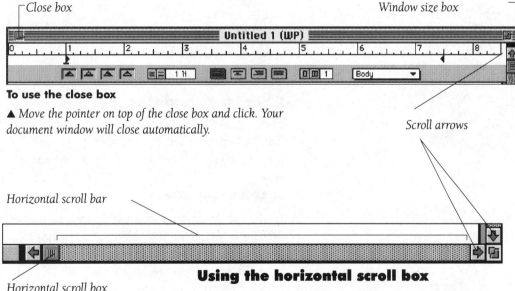

Main Ruler

┌Close box   Window size box

To use the close box

▲ *Move the pointer on top of the close box and click. Your document window will close automatically.*

Scroll arrows

Horizontal scroll bar

Horizontal scroll box

Using the horizontal scroll box

1. Move the pointer on top of the scroll box, and hold the mouse button down firmly.

2. Drag the box to the right or left to see the right or left side of the screen.

Document screen

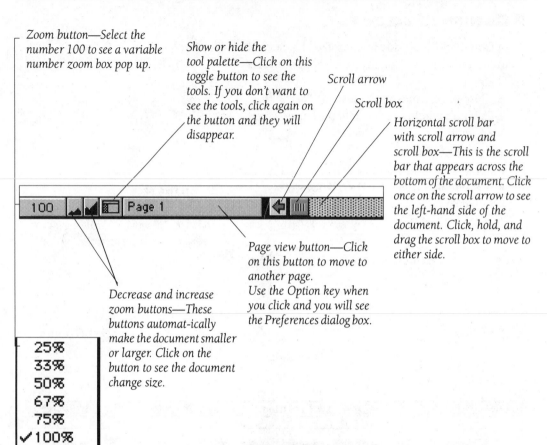

Zoom button—Select the number 100 to see a variable number zoom box pop up.

Show or hide the tool palette—Click on this toggle button to see the tools. If you don't want to see the tools, click again on the button and they will disappear.

Scroll arrow

Scroll box

Horizontal scroll bar with scroll arrow and scroll box—This is the scroll bar that appears across the bottom of the document. Click once on the scroll arrow to see the left-hand side of the document. Click, hold, and drag the scroll box to move to either side.

Page view button—Click on this button to move to another page. Use the Option key when you click and you will see the Preferences dialog box.

Decrease and increase zoom buttons—These buttons automat-ically make the document smaller or larger. Click on the button to see the document change size.

■ Tool bar and Shortcuts palettes

ClarisWorks has two different types of button bars that are options when you are operating in any program mode, the tool bar and Shortcuts palettes.

Tool bar palette

Tool bars are faster ways of switching program modes, drawing objects, coloring objects, and entering text. The tool bar buttons are accessed three ways:

▲ Choosing the Show Tools command from the View menu

▲ Pressing Command-Shift-T (⇧⌘-T)

▲ Selecting the show/hide control button

Using tool bars

Tool bars are universal. They appear the same and operate exactly the same in all program modes. The pull-down menus might change, but the functions of the tool bar do not.

Four main tools

There are four major tools on the tool bar:

▲ The pointer tool—this will help you select or move an object.

▲ The text tool—this tool creates text frames.

▲ The spreadsheet tool—used to create frames within the Spreadsheet mode.

▲ The paint tool—used to create frames within which you can paint or draw.

The rest of the tool bar contains tools for drawing; painting; assigning colors to lines; filling objects with color, pattern, and gradients; and making lines of various thicknesses and with different types of endings, such as arrows.

For more information on the drawing portions of the tool bar, see Chapter 6 on Drawing or Chapter 7 on Painting.

Shortcuts palette

In addition to the regular tool bar, ClarisWorks has a special tool bar called the Shortcuts palette.

This tool bar contains buttons that you can use instead of using the pull-down menus for such actions as getting a new Word Processing or Spreadsheet document, saving or printing a document, or adding in text enhancements such as bold, italic, and underline.

The Shortcuts buttons will change depending on which program mode you are in when you use them.

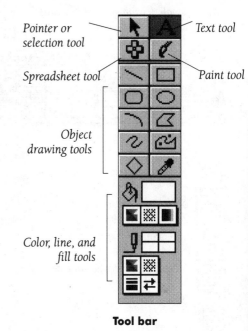

Tool bar

✔ **Tip**: *If you want to find out about Shortcuts palettes for other parts of the program, see the following topics and pages:*

Spreadsheets, page 101
Databases, page 129
Drawing, page 173
Painting, page 190
Communications, page 197

Tool bar and Shortcuts palettes

Using a Shortcuts palette

1. Choose Shortcuts from the File menu.
2. Select the Show Shortcuts option from the Shortcuts submenu. The Shortcuts palette will appear.

Shortcuts palette with general (default) buttons and text-only tools

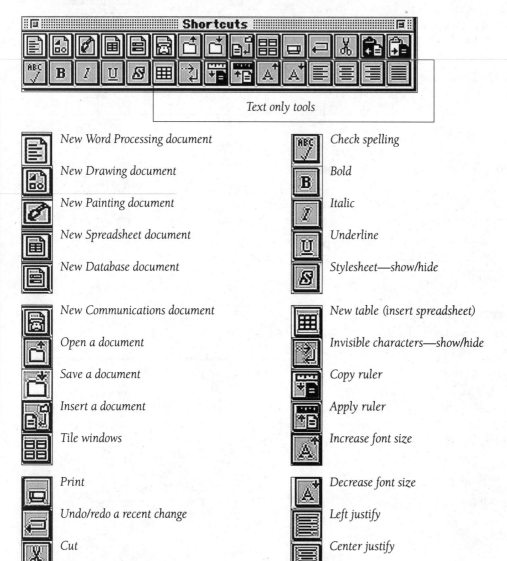

Text only tools

Tool bar and Shortcuts palettes

New Word Processing document

New Drawing document

New Painting document

New Spreadsheet document

New Database document

New Communications document

Open a document

Save a document

Insert a document

Tile windows

Print

Undo/redo a recent change

Cut

Copy to the Clipboard

Paste from the Clipboard

Check spelling

Bold

Italic

Underline

Stylesheet—show/hide

New table (insert spreadsheet)

Invisible characters—show/hide

Copy ruler

Apply ruler

Increase font size

Decrease font size

Left justify

Center justify

Right justify

Full justify

Editing Shortcuts bars

You can change which buttons appear on the
shortcuts bars.

1. Choose Shortcuts from the File menu.
2. Choose Edit Shortcuts from the Shortcuts
   submenu.
3. In the Available shortcuts box, click on any button
   you wish to add. You will see a description of
   that button in the Description box.
4. Click on the Add button to add the button to the
   Shortcuts palette.

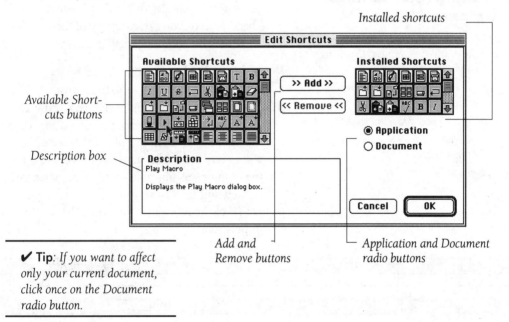

Installed shortcuts

*Available Short-
cuts buttons*

Description box

*Add and
Remove buttons*

*Application and Document
radio buttons*

Tool bar and Shortcuts palettes

✔ **Tip**: *If you want to affect
only your current document,
click once on the Document
radio button.*

Removing a button

Removing a button is almost the same as adding
a button.

1. Choose Shortcuts from the File menu.
2. Choose Edit Shortcuts from the Shortcuts submenu.
3. In the Installed Shortcuts box, click on any button
   you wish to remove.
4. Click on the Remove button to remove that
   button from the Shortcuts palette.

Using Balloon Help: Don't click—just let the pointer rest over the button for a second and then the balloon will appear.

Balloon Help and Shortcuts

Balloon Help can be turned on by selecting Show Balloons from the right of the menu bar. Then any time you need to see what a button does, move the pointer on top of that button and wait a second. A balloon will appear giving you the name of the button and the program mode that it works with, such as WP for Word Processing.

Ruler

The ruler contains icons for the margins or indents, as well as small triangles that indicate where tabs have been placed. You can drag any of these ruler icons to change indention or tab position.

Borrowing ruler settings— margins and tabs

1. *To borrow margins and tab settings, click once in the paragraph that has the correct margins and tabs.*

2. *Choose Copy Ruler from the Format menu, or press ⇧⌘-c.*

3. *Highlight the text you want to change.*

4. *From the Format menu, choose Apply Ruler, or press ⇧⌘-v.*

Dragging ruler icons

1. Highlight the text you want to change.

2. Move the pointer on top of the icon you want to move, hold the mouse button down, and drag the pointer to the left or right. The selected icon will move. If the icon does not move, the tip of the pointer was not right on the icon when you clicked and held the button down.

3. Let go of the mouse button when the icon is in position.

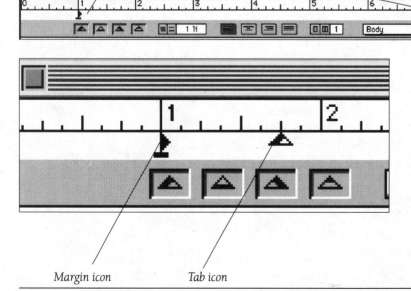

Ruler with margins icons

Margin icon   *Tab icon*

Document Summary information

A Document Summary can be attached to a file and contains notes and information about the file, who wrote it, keywords, and other summary information.

A Document Summary gives you a quick way to find a document by having keywords that the Claris-Works Find function looks through. It's often easier to remember a word or two that you have used in a document than to remember the document's name accurately.

Using Document Summary

1. Choose Document Summary from the File menu. The Document Summary dialog box appears. You will fill in the:
   - ▲ Title
   - ▲ Author
   - ▲ Version of the document
   - ▲ List of keywords
   - ▲ Category of document
   - ▲ Brief description
2. Click inside of the Title box, and type in a title for the document.
3. Press the Tab key to go on to the next item. You will be in the Author box now. Type the information in this box, and continue to use the Tab key to move between Document Summary boxes.
4. When you are finished, click on the OK button.

✔ **Tip**: *You can move between Title, Author, and so on quicker if you press the Tab key after typing in the information.*

Document Summary screen

Keywords are short words or phrases that describe the document, such as "Goldstein" or "Proposal, Brick walkway, New patio, Goldstein."

Tool bar and Shortcuts palettes

■ Setting up a document

Before you begin anything, it helps if you first decide:

▲ The size of paper you want to print on.

▲ The margins you want your paper to have.

▲ The typeface and size you prefer.

▲ Whether or not you want page numbering.

Changing the paper size

Default paper size—You must make sure the paper you want to print on is selected in the program. Fortunately, almost all computer programs think you are going to print on 8 1/2" by 11" paper. This is known as the "default," or automatically chosen size.

1. Choose Page Setup from the File menu. You will see the dialog box labeled something like "LaserWriter Page Setup." The phrase at the top of this box lets you know what printer your computer is set up to use.

2. Pick the Orientation and Paper size you want by clicking either on the orientation icons or clicking in the radio button next to the proper paper size.

Page Setup dialog box—There are four radio buttons for normal paper sizes: Letter, Legal, A4, and B5.

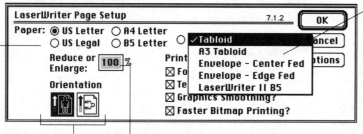

Additional page choices—Five additional choices appear on this pull-down menu. Most printers are not large enough to print Tabloid (11" x 17") size paper. Notice the envelope choices on this menu.

Scaling—You can reduce the printout or enlarge the printout by typing a number smaller or larger than 100% in the Reduce or Enlarge box.

Orientation—You can choose portrait (or tall) orientation and your paper size, for letter size, will be 8 1/2" by 11".

Landscape (or wide) orientation would give you a piece of paper that is 11" by 8 1/2". The printer you use will turn the type sideways— you still put the paper in the printer with the short edge (8 1/2") first.

Changing margins

If you have not changed the margins, the margins
you see are the default margins for the ClarisWorks
document. They show up as light gray lines. Default
margins in ClarisWorks are one inch on all four sides.
You can change the margins, page numbering, where
footnotes appear, and how the document is viewed
by choosing Document from the Format menu.

*The Document
command is in the
Format menu.*

*Document dialog box with the four command areas:
Margins, Page Numbering, Page Display,
and Footnotes*

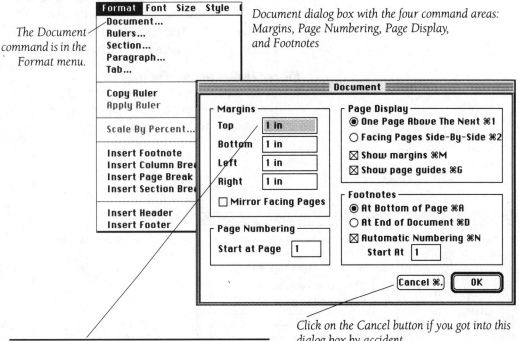

*Click on the Cancel button if you got into this
dialog box by accident.
The OK button saves any changes you make in
this dialog box.*

✔ **Tip 1**: *Notice the Top Margin box has the text
selected? Any time text is selected,
if you just start typing, you will replace anything
that was there before. In this case, if you type the
number "2," the entry "1 in" that is now in this
box will disappear. You don't have to type
"in" for inch. The program understands you
mean inches.*

✔ **Tip 2**: *You don't need to click inside of each
margin box to type in the right number. Once
you have typed in the Top margin you want to
use, press the Tab key and the cursor will move
to the Bottom margin box, and so on.*

✔ **Tip 3**: *Notice that the OK button is surrounded by a double
line? If a button has a double line around it, hitting the Return
key will activate that button. That way you don't have to use
the mouse to click on OK.*

Setting up a document

Mirror Facing Pages

The Mirror Facing Pages checkbox sets up a document that will be both bound in the center and printed on both sides of the paper—like a book. You can also display the pages on the screen as if they are in a book, side by side.

Mirror facing pages margins

1. From the Format menu choose document.
2. Select the Mirror Facing Pages box. The Left and right margins boxes will now say Inside and Outside margins. The Inside margin box is for the binding or center edge of the document.

Mirror facing pages display

3. In the Page Display section of the dialog box, select the Facing Pages Side-by-side radio button, then click on the OK button.

When the Mirror Facing Pages checkbox has an X or check mark in it, the margins are labeled as Inside and Outside instead of left and right.

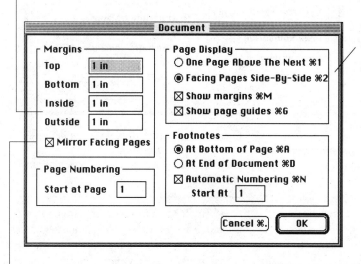

The Facing Pages Side-By-Side radio button is selected.

The Margins section, with the Mirror Facing Pages checkbox selected.

✔ **Tip**: *A normal allowance for the binding edge is 1/4". You'd want to make the binding or inside edge margin 1/4" bigger than the outside margin. If the document is very thick, over 1", make the inside edge margin 3/8" larger than the outside margin.*

Page numbering

Page numbering is inserted into documents by placing a command inside of a header or footer. Headers and footers give you a separate place to type in information that is repeated on every page, such as chapter headings or a company name.

Page numbering—Step one

▲ Choose the Insert Header command from the Format menu, for page numbers on top of the page, or the Insert Footer command from the Format menu for page numbers on the bottom of the page.

```
Format  Font  Size  Style
Document...
Rulers...
Section...
Paragraph...
Tab...

Copy Ruler          ⇧⌘C
Apply Ruler         ⇧⌘U

Scale By Percent...

Insert Footnote     ⇧⌘F
Insert Column Break   ⌘
Insert Page Break    ⇧⌘
Insert Section Break  ⌥⌘

Insert Header
Insert Footer
```

Page numbering—Step two

▲ First make sure you still have a blinking cursor inside of the header or footer. Choose Insert Page # from the Edit menu.

```
Edit  Format  Fon
Can't Undo     ⌘Z

Cut            ⌘X
Copy           ⌘C
Paste          ⌘U
Clear
Select All     ⌘A

Insert Date
Insert Time
Insert Page #...

Writing Tools    ▶
Find/Change      ▶
Publishing       ▶

Preferences...
Show Clipboard
```

Removing page numbers

Change your mind and don't want page numbers? Just remove the header or footer

▲ Choose Remove Header from the Format menu. This choice used to read Insert Header, but because you have a header in the document, it now reads Remove Header.

Setting up a document

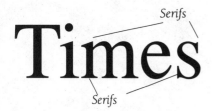

Serifs

Serifs

Times

Times Roman—A serif font

Serifs are tiny feet that extend out beyond the endpoints of the typeface. Times is a very compact, and easy-to-read font, as the serifs force your eye to continually move forward along the page. Other serif fonts include Berkeley Oldstyle, which is the font used for the body text of this book.

Helvetica

Helvetica—A sans serif font

Sans serif fonts resemble block lettering. The word "sans" means "without" in French; thus, sans serif means without serifs. These are simple typefaces that often look best in large sizes. Other sans serif fonts include Futura, which is the font used in the headlines of this book.

■ Changing the font and font styles

There are three aspects of a font that you can change:

▲ The font itself—from Times to Helvetica, for example

▲ The style of the font—from plain to bold, for example

▲ The size of the font

Changing the font

1. Before typing anything in your document, click once and get the insertion point—a blinking line.
2. Pull down the Font menu and select the font you wish to use.

Font

Arial MT Condensed Light
Bodoni MT Ultra Bold
Chicago
Courier
✓Geneva
Gill Sans Condensed Bold
Helvetica
Klang MT
Monaco
New Berolina MT
New York
𝔒𝔩𝔡 𝔈𝔫𝔤𝔩𝔦𝔰𝔥 𝔗𝔢𝔵𝔱 𝔐𝔗
Palatino
Script MT Bold
Σψμβολ
Times

Word Processing Font menu—This pull-down menu lists the fonts and shows you what the fonts look like. The font with the check mark by it is the font that the program is currently using.

Changing the font and font styles

Changing a font style

Font styles are additional enhancements you can add to your text. Options in the Style menu include:

- ▲ Plain Text
- ▲ Bold
- ▲ Italic
- ▲ Underline
- ▲ Double Underline
- ▲ Strike Thru
- ▲ Outline
- ▲ Shadow
- ▲ Condense
- ▲ Extend
- ▲ Superscript
- ▲ Subscript
- ▲ Superior
- ▲ Inferior
- ▲ Text Color

Style	Outline	Vie
✓Plain Text		⌘T
Bold		⌘B
Italic		⌘I
Underline		⌘U
Double Underline		
Strike Thru		
Outline		
Shadow		
Condense		
Extend		
Superscript		
Subscript		
Superior		
Inferior		
Text Color		▶

Style menu—Notice the keyboard shortcuts on the right-hand side.

- ▲ *Plain Text—* ⌘-T
- ▲ *Bold—* ⌘-B
- ▲ *Italic—* ⌘-I
- ▲ *Underline—* ⌘-U

You can use these shortcuts when you:

1. Select your text by highlighting it.

2. .Press down the key combination. For example, for bold text, press ⌘-B.

To change a font style

1. Highlight the text you want to change.
2. Choose the style you want from the Style menu on the ClarisWorks Word Processing menu bar.
3. You may apply more than one font style to text by repeating steps 1 and 2.

Superscript and subscript

Superscript and subscript are font enhancements used most commonly with mathematical formulas such as πr^2 or in chemistry notations such as H_2O.

$$\pi r^2$$

Superscript text is raised, and the type size remains the same as the body type.

Superior and inferior

Superior text is raised, but the type size is much smaller than the regular text size. Inferior text is lowered, and the type size is also much smaller than the normal text size.

Subscript text is lowered, and the type size remains the same as the body type.

This is a sample of ^{Superior} (Superior) and $_{inferior}$ (Inferior) text.

Changing the font and font styles

Text color

Color is fun and livens up a presentation. You need to be careful how you use color.

Text color and overheads

If you are planning colored overheads, be aware that the type of ink many color printers use will not show up as a color when used with the color transparencies used with most overhead projectors. Instead of seeing that awesome yellow and dark green presentation, you could simply see black on the screen.

Some color combinations work better for overheads and slide shows. These include:

▲ Yellow text on a navy blue or dark green background

▲ White text on a black, navy, or dark red background

▲ Cyan (pale blue) text on a black or navy background

In general, you will want to keep your text color white, yellow, or cyan and your background as dark as possible.

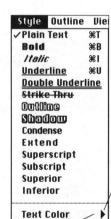

✔ **Tip**: *When you choose a menu command with an arrow next to it, a pop-up box or submenu appears.*

Changing text color

1. Highlight the text you want to change.
2. Choose Text Color from the Style menu. Keep holding the mouse down and you will see a palette with small, colored squares.
3. Move the pointer on top of the color you want to use and let go of the mouse button to select that color from the palette.

Changing the type size

The font size can be found on the Size menu.

1. Highlight the text you wish to change.
2. Choose the size you want to use from the Size menu.
3. If you choose Other, the Font Size dialog box appears. Type in the size you want in the space provided in the Font Size dialog box.
4. Choose the OK button when you are finished.

Text size guidelines

Common text sizes are 10 points, 11 points, and 12 points. A point is 1/72nd of an inch, measured vertically. Here are some samples of different text set in different type sizes. The sample in the left column uses Berkeley Oldstyle; the sample in the right column uses Futura.

Berkeley Oldstyle	Futura
This is 10 points	This is 10 points
This is 11 points	This is 11 points
This is 12 points	This is 12 points

The size that is currently being used has a check mark next to it.

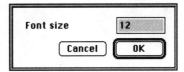

Size	Style	Out
9 Point		
✓10 Point		
12 Point		
14 Point		
18 Point		
24 Point		
36 Point		
48 Point		
72 Point		
Other... ⇧⌘0		

The Other command opens a dialog box where you may type in a different size. A popular and highly readable text size is 11 points. The type size in this box is 12 points.

Font size [12]
Cancel   OK

■ Saving your work

Before you get too far along, you must save the document. Review the section in Chapter 1, called "Saving the document" on page 13.

Save every time you have made a change in the document that is big enough that it would take you some time to redo it. You can't save too often. Saving will not automatically close your document.

Saving a document

1. From the File menu choose Save, or press ⌘-s.
2. If you are saving your document for the first time, the Save dialog box appears. Type a document name in the Save dialog box.
3. Click on the Save button when you are finished.

✔ **Tip**: *The Save command is ⌘-s. You'll use this key combination often so you might want to memorize it.*

Saving your work

■ Closing documents

When you are finished typing, if you don't want to add pictures or statistics to your work, close the document before you begin anything else. Closing it will keep your machine running a little faster.

Closing a document

1. Save your document.
2. Choose Close from the File menu, or press ⌘-**w**.

■ Opening an existing document

If you have saved a document already, closed that document, and are now ready to start working on it again, you must reopen that document.

1. Choose Open from the File menu.
2. Choose the correct disk drive or file folder from the pop-up list at the top of the Open dialog box.
3. If you need to look further down on the list, use the scroll bars or the up and down arrows.

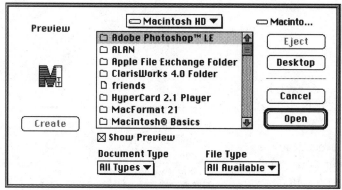

When you choose Open from the File menu, the dialog box that appears lists the documents that you may open. Select the document you want if it appears in the scrolling list, or see a new list by selecting another location in the pop-up list at the top of the list of documents.

To find your file more quickly

▲ Type the first letter of the document name to jump to files that begin with that letter, or

▲ Use the Page Up, Page Down, Home, or End keys to move you through larger sections of the file list.

Opening files created in other programs

ClarisWorks can handle files created in many other programs. You can import plain text, files created in AppleWorks, MacWrite, Microsoft Works, or Microsoft Word and many other word processing, database, and picture files.

Importing a file from another program

1. Choose Open from the File menu.
2. Select the file you want to import.
3. Choose the original file type in the Document Type pop-up list. For example, if the file is a MacWrite II file, click on MacWrite II.

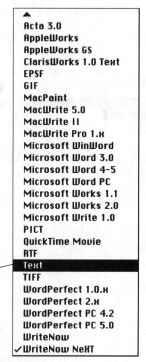

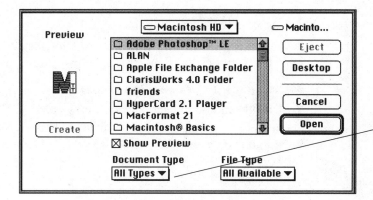

Quick translating using drag and drop

If you are using System 7.0+, you can translate a file from an unknown format to ClarisWorks and start your ClarisWorks program at the same time.

1. At the desktop, select the document you wish to translate.
2. Drag the document on top of the Claris-Works icon.

If ClarisWorks recognizes the original file format, your file will be translated, and ClarisWorks will start up automatically.

Document Type is a way of filtering, or eliminating from view, certain types of documents. For example, if you choose Word Processing, you will see only lists of the word processing documents. Other documents will not be erased, you just won't be able to see their names.

Quick text selection

What you need to select	Mouse or key
Single word	Double-click
Paragraph	Triple-click
Document	Choose Select All from the Edit menu or press ⌘-A

Quick text selection—This chart shows you faster ways to select text. To select a single word, for example, just place the pointer over that word and double-click. To select a paragraph, triple-click anywhere inside of a paragraph.

■ Beginning text editing

To start typing you simply:

1. Click in the document.

2. Begin typing.

What if you make a mistake, want to eliminate a word you have used, or need to insert or add material? You need to select or highlight the part of the text you want to change.

Selecting text

To select one word in the text, use the mouse:

1. Place the I-beam just to the right of the text with the bottom of the I-beam almost even with the bottom of the text.

2. Hold the mouse button down and move to the left.

3. Let go of the mouse button.

You may move the mouse to the left or right, but the first place you click the mouse is the starting point.

Selecting more than one line of text

1. Drag the mouse straight down toward you instead of moving the mouse from left to right.

2. Let go of the mouse button.

Starting point   *Highlighted text*   *I-beam*

"More? You are greedy, my little friends. Ah well, it is sunny, you have nothing better to do, nor do I."

Ending point

Selecting using click-shift-click

This method will select one letter or many pages.

1. Click once where you want your highlight to begin (the starting point).

2. Hold the Shift key down.

3. Click once where you want your highlight to end.

4. Let go of the Shift key and the mouse button.

Deleting text

To erase one character, you use the Delete or the Backspace key. To erase more than one character you need to select or highlight your text. You have three choices about how you delete the text.

▲ After selecting the text, press the Clear, Delete, or Backspace key. This will erase the text but not keep a copy of the text on a special memory Clipboard.

▲ After selecting the text, choose Cut from the Edit menu, or press ⌘-**x**. This will keep a copy of the text on a special memory Clipboard.

▲ After selecting the text, just start typing. The old text will disappear and be replaced by what you are currently typing. No copy will be placed on the special memory clipboard.

Undoing a deletion

Use either the Paste or the Undo command from the Edit menu to recover information you deleted. You can also use the Revert command from the File menu, which will give you the latest saved version instead of the version you currently have on screen.

▲ Without making any changes or moving the text cursor, choose Undo from the Edit menu, or press ⌘-**z** while still in the text screen.

The key labeled Delete or Backspace on your keyboard will erase text that is to the left of your cursor. For example, to erase the "d" in "cad" click just after the "d" and tap the Delete key.

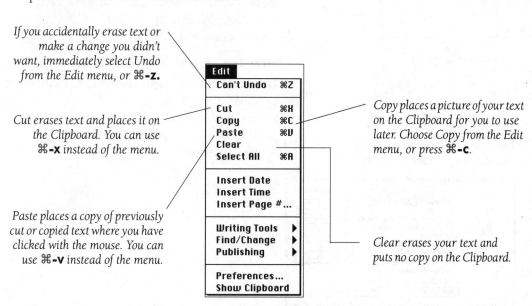

If you accidentally erase text or make a change you didn't want, immediately select Undo from the Edit menu, or ⌘-z.

Cut erases text and places it on the Clipboard. You can use ⌘-x instead of the menu.

Paste places a copy of previously cut or copied text where you have clicked with the mouse. You can use ⌘-v instead of the menu.

Copy places a picture of your text on the Clipboard for you to use later. Choose Copy from the Edit menu, or press ⌘-c.

Clear erases your text and puts no copy on the Clipboard.

Notice Cut, Copy, and Paste on the Edit menu. Each command has a shortcut that is common to all Macintosh programs.

Copying text

To make a copy of your text:

1. Highlight the text you want to copy and choose Copy from the Edit menu, or press ⌘-c.
2. Click where you want the copy to appear.
3. Choose Paste from the Edit menu, or press ⌘-v.

Moving text

1. Select the text you want to move, and hold down the Command and Option keys.
2. Still holding the Command and Option keys down, click in the new location.

Moving using Cut and Paste

1. Select the text you want to move, and choose Cut from the Edit menu, or press ⌘-x.
2. Click where you want the text to appear.
3. Choose Paste from the Edit menu, or press ⌘-v.

Inserting text

1. Click where you want the new text to appear.
2. Start typing.

Old text will be moved to the right to make room for the new text. You can also use the arrow keys (⇐ or ⇒) to move left or right one character at a time until you are where you wish to start typing.

Inserting an entire file at the cursor

1. Choose Insert from the File menu. You will see the Open dialog box.
2. Scroll down until you see the file you want. Double-click on that file, or click on the Insert button.

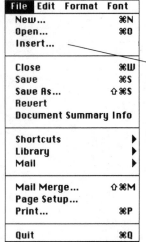

Insert will insert a file right where your pointer is located in your text.

The dialog box that opens when you choose Insert from the File menu.

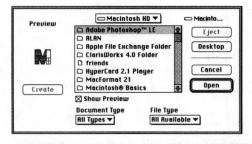

Beginning text editing

matting

ected the default paper size,
you still can make changes
rmatting changes in ClarisWorks

acter

:ument

to how the text is arranged from
n change justification for:
:ument
paragraphs

le line or a paragraph

in a line that ends in a return
a paragraph.
he correct justify button on the
.r.

ire document

ification you want before you
ient, or select the entire
hoosing Select All from the Edit
⌘-A.
stify button you want.

Justification

Basic formatting refers to items such as:

▲ *Centering or justifying a paragraph*

▲ *Indenting just one paragraph*

▲ *Changing the style of a word or phrase so it is underlined or italic*

▲ *Setting up tabs for columns*

▲ *Changing line spacing so your text is single, one and one-half spaced, or double-spaced*

▲ *Inserting the current date or time*

▲ *Using the Thesaurus to help find alternate words*

▲ *Checking spelling in the document*

Justification buttons

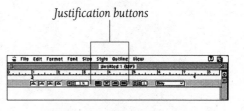

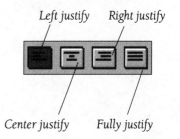

Left justify   *Right justify*

Center justify   *Fully justify*

on	Sample text
	He sat, sunken, blending in with the stone benches in
	He sat blending in with stone benches in the park,
	He sat, sunken, blending in with the stone benches
	He sat, sunken, blending in with the stone benches there.

Basic formatting

Line spacing buttons

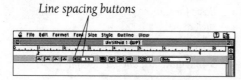

Increase spacing button

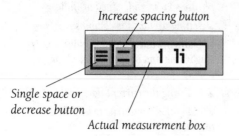

*Single space or
decrease button*

Actual measurement box

Line spacing

The default setting for new documents is single spacing. You can increase spacing by half a line at a time to 1 1/2 lines, 2 lines, 2 1/2 lines, and on up to 10 lines between each text line.

Changing document spacing

1. Before you start typing, or if you have already typed a paragraph, click in an existing paragraph then click on the increase spacing button.

2. Every time you click on the button, the line spacing between the text will increase one-half of a line. For example, to get 2 1/2 lines of space between each text line, click on the increase spacing button three times.

■ Paragraph format

Using the Format menu to change line spacing

Line spacing can be changed using the Paragraph command from the Format menu. The dialog box you then see will let you change line spacing and will also let you make changes to:

▲ Line spacing before a paragraph

▲ Line spacing after a paragraph

▲ Left indent of a paragraph

▲ Right indent of a paragraph

▲ Indention of just the first line of a paragraph

▲ Paragraph justification

▲ Text style, such as applying the Diamond or Bullet styles

Paragraph format

Changing Line Spacing

1. Click inside of the paragraph, select more than one paragraph, or choose Select All from the Edit menu to select the entire document.

2. Choose Paragraph from the Format menu.

3. In the Line Spacing box of the Paragraph dialog box, type the number of blank lines you want to appear between your lines of text.

4. Click on the Apply button.

5. Press the Return key or Click on the OK button.

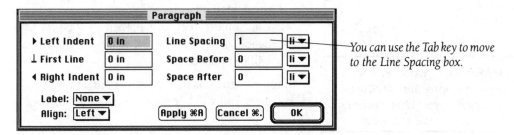

You can use the Tab key to move to the Line Spacing box.

Line Spacing measurement box

The Line Spacing, Space Before, and Space After pop-up lists let you change how you measure the blank space between lines. You have the choice of:

▲ Lines (li)   ▲ Millimeters (mm)

▲ Points (pt)   ▲ Centimeters (cm)

▲ Inches (in)   ▲ Picas (pc)

Here is a section of the Paragraph dialog box. Originally the measurements were set to 1", but now the measurements appear in points for the Line Spacing box, millimeters for the Space Before box, and picas for the Space After box.

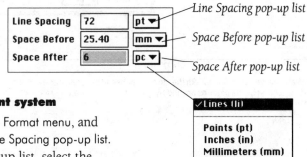

Line Spacing pop-up list

Space Before pop-up list

Space After pop-up list

Changing your measurement system

1. Choose Paragraph from the Format menu, and move the pointer to the Line Spacing pop-up list.

2. From the line spacing pop-up list, select the desired measurement system.

3. Select the desired measurement system in the pop-up lists for the Space Before and the Space After.

4. Press the Return key or click on the OK button in the Paragraph dialog box when you are finished.

Paragraph format

Paragraph format

Space Before and Space After a paragraph

Instead of hitting the return key many times for extra spaces between paragraphs, you can use the Space Before and Space After options.

Space Before

1. Click anywhere in the paragraph, then choose Paragraph from the Format menu.

2. Hit the Tab key until you are in the box that says Space Before. Type how many blank lines you want to appear before the beginning of the paragraph.

3. Click on the Apply button, then click on the OK button, or click on the OK button and the format will be applied.

If the paragraph is the first paragraph at the top of the page, you will not see any blank lines before it.

✔ **Warning:** *If you use both Space Before and Space After on all of the paragraphs, you will have twice as much space as you may want.*

Space Before

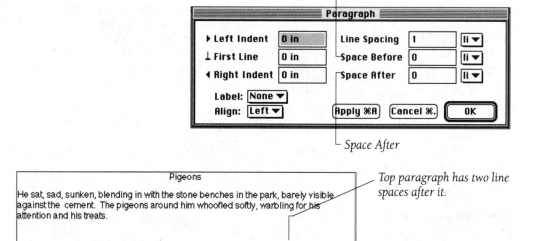

Space After

Top paragraph has two line spaces after it.

Second paragraph has two line spaces before it and two line spaces after it.

Indenting a paragraph

You can change the margins of a single paragraph by using the Left Indent and Right Indent options in the Paragraph dialog box.

First line indent

Instead of hitting the Tab key, you can use the First Line indent option to indent a paragraph.

Indenting the first line of a paragraph

1. Click anywhere in the paragraph, select several paragraphs, or choose Select All from the Edit menu to select your entire document.

2. Choose Paragraph from the Format menu and tap the Tab key until you are in the First Line indent box.

3. Type in the number of inches (in tenths) that you want for a paragraph indention.

4. Click on the OK button or press the Return key.

Typical first line indents
You used to be told to indent five spaces when we used typewriters. We can't indent in spaces anymore. The usual text paragraph is indented .25, .33 or, .5 of an inch—whichever looks better to you.

Paragraph format

*First Line indent—
This paragraph is
indented .5".*

> Pigeons
>
> He sat, sad, sunken, blending in with the stone benches in the park, barely visible against the cement. The pigeons around him whoofled softly, warbling for his attention and his treats.

*The First Line indent
option will indent
only the first line of a
paragraph. You can use
this choice instead of using
the Tab key to indent
a paragraph.*

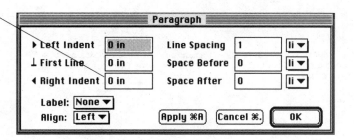

Left and right indents

Using a combination of left and right indents changes both sides of a paragraph and is used in papers where three or more lines of a quotation are cited.

Creating a left indent and right indent

1. Click anywhere inside of the paragraph, select several paragraphs, or choose Select All from the Edit menu to select your entire document.
2. Choose Paragraph from the Format menu.
3. In the Left Indent box, type in how many inches or tenths of an inch you want the paragraph to be indented from the left.
4. Press the Tab key until you are in the Right Indent box.
5. In the Right Indent box, type in how many inches or tenths of an inch you want the paragraph to be indented from the right.
6. Click on the OK button or press the Return key.

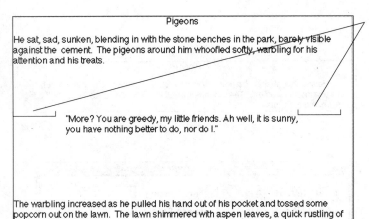

Pigeons

He sat, sad, sunken, blending in with the stone benches in the park, barely visible against the cement. The pigeons around him whoofled softly, warbling for his attention and his treats.

"More? You are greedy, my little friends. Ah well, it is sunny, you have nothing better to do, nor do I."

The warbling increased as he pulled his hand out of his pocket and tossed some popcorn out on the lawn. The lawn shimmered with aspen leaves, a quick rustling of wind, then silence again.

This paragraph has been indented 1 inch from the left margin and 1 inch from the right margin.

Hanging indents

Hanging indents are characterized by the paragraph being indented from the left margin only and the first line of the paragraph not being indented at all. The first line "hangs" out—that's how this style got the name "hanging indent."

Creating a hanging indent

1. Click anywhere in the paragraph, then choose the Paragraph command from the Format menu.
2. In the Left Indent box, type in the number for your left indent. The sample is indented .5".
3. Hit the tab key to move the insertion point to the First Line indent box.
4. In the First Line indent box, type a hyphen (-) followed by the same number you typed in the Left Indent box.
5. Click on the OK button when you are finished.

The First Line indent measurement is the same as the Left Indent measurement, but is typed as a negative number.

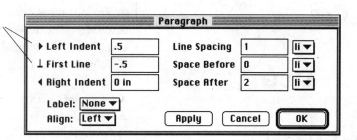

Paragraph format

Hanging indent
The top line is "out-dented" or hanging out .5" while the rest of the paragraph is indented .5."

Berglin, S. (1994). Visual QuickStart Guide: Word 6 for Windows. Berkeley, CA: Peachpit Press.

Brown, C. A. (1995). Visual QuickStart Guide: ClarisWorks for Macintosh. Berkeley, CA: Peachpit Press.

Tolman, J'ann. (1994). Visual QuickStart Guide: FrameMaker 4 for Windows. Berkeley, CA: Peachpit Press

Weinmann, E., & Lourekas, P. (1994). Visual QuickStart Guide: Photoshop for Windows. Berkeley, CA: Peachpit Press.

First Line indent expressed as -.5"

1/2"

Left Indent line—expressed as .5"

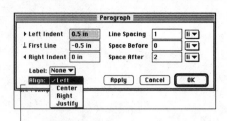

Align pop-up list—Notice the active or current alignment has a check mark beside it.

Aligning text using the Format menu

You can use the button bar buttons to align text, as shown in "Justification" on page 47. You can also change the alignment or justification with the Paragraph command in the Format menu.

Aligning a paragraph

1. Click in any paragraph and choose Paragraph from the Format menu.
2. Choose the alignment you want to use from the Align pop-up list in the lower-left corner of the dialog box.
3. Click on the OK button.

■ Setting tabs

Tabs must be set when you need to type columns of words or numbers. Tabs can be set from the button bar or using the Tabs choice in the Format menu.

There are four types of tabs:

▲ Left tab—The tab is on the left-hand side of the text. This is the normal tab.

▲ Right tab—The tab is on the right-hand side of the text.

▲ Center tab—Text is centered on the tab stop.

▲ Decimal tab—Periods or decimal periods line up with the tab.

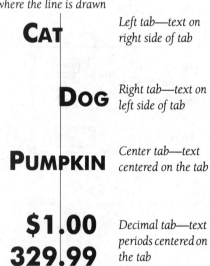

Text tab sample—All tabs are set where the line is drawn

CAT — *Left tab—text on right side of tab*

DOG — *Right tab—text on left side of tab*

PUMPKIN — *Center tab—text centered on the tab*

$1.00
329.99 — *Decimal tab—text periods centered on the tab*

Setting tabs using the Format menu

To create tabs using the Format menu:

1. Click in the paragraph or select the text needing tabs.

2. Choose Tab from the Format menu.

3. On the Alignment section of the Tab dialog box, select the radio button next to the tab type you wish to use.

4. Look at the ruler in the document menu and decide where you want this tab.

5. In the Position box, type the measurement you choose from the ruler.

6. Click on the Apply button, then click on the OK button, or press the Return key.

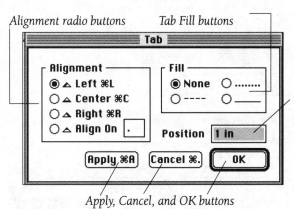

Alignment radio buttons   *Tab Fill buttons*

Tab Position box—
Position is 1 inch from
the margin, not the edge
of the paper.

Apply, Cancel, and OK buttons

Setting tabs from the ruler

Creating tabs from the document ruler is a more visual process than creating tabs using the Format menu. The principle advantage is that you can see your text and adjust the tabs in such a manner that they work best.

Creating tabs from the ruler

1. Click in the paragraph, or select the text that needs tabs.

2. Drag the tab icon you want to the desired ruler position.

✔ **Tip:** *If you are not sure where your tabs should be, type the columnar text, pressing the tab key only once between each item. Then select your entire paragraph and set the tabs. While the text is still selected you can move the tabs around until the appearance of the text is pleasing.*

Setting tabs

Moving tabs with selected text

If your text is still selected, you can move the tabs:

1. Drag the tab to the left or right on the ruler.

2. Watch your text and when the text looks the way you want it to appear, let go of the mouse button.

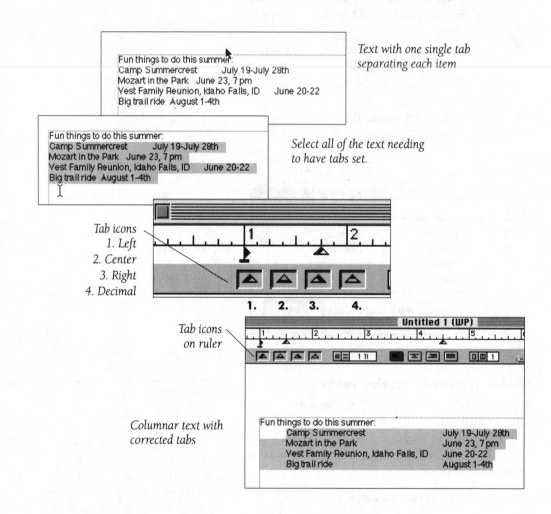

Fun things to do this summer:
Camp Summercrest   July 19-July 28th
Mozart in the Park   June 23, 7 pm
Vest Family Reunion, Idaho Falls, ID   June 20-22
Big trail ride August 1-4th

Text with one single tab separating each item

Fun things to do this summer:
Camp Summercrest   July 19-July 28th
Mozart in the Park   June 23, 7 pm
Vest Family Reunion, Idaho Falls, ID   June 20-22
Big trail ride August 1-4th

Select all of the text needing to have tabs set.

Tab icons
1. Left
2. Center
3. Right
4. Decimal

1.   2.   3.   4.

Tab icons on ruler

Untitled 1 (WP)

Columnar text with corrected tabs

Fun things to do this summer:
    Camp Summercrest   July 19-July 28th
    Mozart in the Park   June 23, 7 pm
    Vest Family Reunion, Idaho Falls, ID   June 20-22
    Big trail ride   August 1-4th

Filled tabs

Filled tabs are tabs that are filled from the left to the right with dots or dashes.

Creating filled tabs

1. Highlight the text needing tabs, then choose Tab from the Format menu.
2. In the Alignment options, select the radio button next to the tab type you want to use.
3. Decide where you want this tab to appear by looking at the ruler; in the Position box, type the measurement you need from the ruler.
4. In the Fill box, select the radio button that has the type of fill style you want to use.
5. Click on the Apply button, then click on the OK button, or press the Return key.

■ Find and change

Find and change help you make quick text changes to an entire document or to any section of selected text. You can:

▲ Find a partial word, whole word, or paragraph
▲ Refind the same text
▲ Find text and change it at the same time
▲ Select text in the document, then find anything that matches the text you have selected
▲ Look for your text in just lowercase, all upper-case, or title case (initial words capitalized)

Finding a word

1. Choose Find from the Edit menu, or press ⌘-F.
2. Type the word you want to find in the Find box, and click on the Find Next button.
3. To refind a word, click on the Find Next button. You can click on the Find Next button as many times as you want to.
4. Click on the close box when you are finished.

Table of Contents

These right tabs are filled with dot leaders.

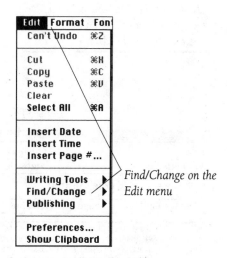

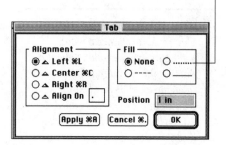

Find/Change on the Edit menu

Find/Change submenu—Notice the shortcut keys on the right-hand side of the menu.

Find and change

Refinding a word from the document

1. After returning to the document you can choose Find/Change from the Edit menu.
2. Then choose Find Again, or press ⌘-E.

Find/Change text

You can substitute one word for another quickly using Find/Change text. When you ask ClarisWorks to change a word, you have a choice of changing any word by "case" or just changing any word. When there is a check mark in the Case sensitive box, ClarisWorks will check to see how the word is capitalized.

Changing text

1. Choose Find from the Edit menu, or press ⌘-F.
2. Type the word you want to find in the Find box.
3. Press the Tab key to move the insertion point to the Change box then type the word you want to change to in this box.
4. Click on the Change button, or click on the Change, Find button to find that same word again, or click on the Change All button to change all of the words in the document without being asked about each word.
5. Click on the close box when you are finished.

✔ **Warning**: *When you use Change All to change a word, make sure you are talking about a whole word or you may be changing an embedded word. A good example of an embedded word is the word "embedded" itself. It contains the word "bed" in the center. If you ask ClarisWorks to change "bed" to "couch," your word "embedded" would then become "encouchded."*

Find and change

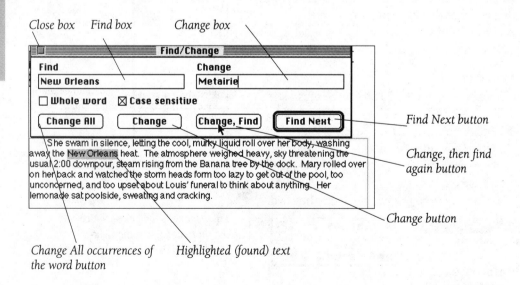

Close box   Find box   Change box

Find Next button

Change, then find again button

Change button

Change All occurrences of the word button   Highlighted (found) text

Limiting your search

You can limit the area Find/Change will work with by selecting text before you use the Find/Change command to start the search.

1. Select the text area you wish to search in and choose Find from the Edit menu, or press ⌘-**F**.

2. Type the word you want to find in the Find box.

3. Click the Find Next button or one of the change option buttons. ClarisWorks will search only within the selected area.

4. Select the close box when you are finished.

Finding special characters and automatic text

Finding special characters and automatic text is almost the same as typing a word in the Find box and looking for that word. You can look for several types of special characters and automatic text including:

▲ Automatic dates   ▲ Paragraphs

▲ Automatic time   ▲ Soft return

▲ Page numbers   ▲ End of columns

▲ Tab key   ▲ End of pages

Use the steps in "Finding a word" on page 57 to find a special character.

Special characters and automatic text

Special character or automatic text	Character to type in
Automatic date	\d
Automatic time	\h
Page numbers	\#
Tab key	\t or ⌘-**TAB***
Paragraph (Return key)	\p or ⌘-**RETURN**
Soft return (Shift-Return)	\n or ⌘-⇧-**RETURN**
End of column	\c or ⌘-**ENTER**
End of page	\c or ⌘-**ENTER**

In the Find box, when you use commands that are expressed in this table as \p or ⌘-Return, if you choose to use ⌘-Return, do not type the preceding "\" character, but just hold down the ⌘ key and tap the key indicated.

Find and change

Writing tools

■ **Writing tools**

Writing Tools is found in the Edit menu and contains tools designed to help you finish the document. You'll find:

▲ Thesaurus

▲ Hyphenation

▲ Word Count

▲ Spelling

▲ A place to add in a new specialized dictionary such as a legal dictionary

▲ The ability to edit your own dictionary, hyphenation dictionary, or thesaurus

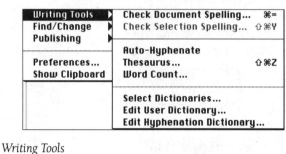

Writing Tools

List of Writing Tools available including spelling, Thesaurus, and Word Count

Using Writing Tools

1. Choose Writing Tools from the Edit menu. You will see a submenu pop out from the side.

2. Still holding the mouse button down, move the pointer to the right into the Writing Tools menu and choose the item you want.

Thesaurus

The Thesaurus helps you find alternative words.
You can use the Thesaurus by either:

▲ Selecting a word, or

▲ After accessing the Thesaurus dialog box,
typing a word directly into the Thesaurus
Find box.

Using the Thesaurus

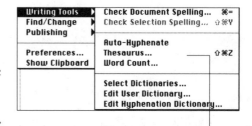

1. Choose Thesaurus from the Writing Tools
submenu in the Edit menu, or press ⇧⌘**-z**. A
dialog box appears with the selected word in the
Find box.

2. Click on the Lookup button or press the
Return key. A list of alternate words appears in the
Word Finder/Thesaurus box.

3. Click in the close box when you are finished.

Looking up a word without selecting text

If you just want to look up an alternate word , you
don't need to select any text. Just follow the same
steps from the previous paragraph. The only
additional instruction you need to know is to:

1. Type the word you want to look up in the
Find box, then click on the Lookup button or press
the Return key.

2. If you want to look up any of the choices,
click in that word.

3. Click Lookup and you will see a new list.

4. Click in the close box when you are finished.

*Choose Thesaurus from the Writing
Tools submenu in the Edit menu, or
press ⇧⌘-z .*

Writing tools

*Word Finder Thesaurus dialog box—
Notice the alternate selections in this dialog
box. To use one of these selections you may
either select the word you want using the
mouse, or you may use the arrow keys to
move around.*

*Find box—The word
"general" was selected
in the text before
opening the Thesaurus
dialog box.*

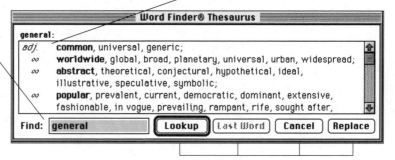

*The Lookup button, Last or Next Word
button, Cancel button, and Replace button*

Using an alternate word to replace a selected word

1. In the Word Finder Thesaurus dialog box, select the word you wish to use.
2. Click on the Replace button to place the word in your text and close the Thesaurus dialog box.
3. Click on the Cancel button if you don't want to use any of the words.
4. Click in the close box when you are finished.

Hyphenation

Hyphenation is either on or off, and when hyphenation is on you won't have to worry about using it—it takes care of itself automatically.

Turning on hyphenation

▲ Choose Auto-Hyphenate from the Writing Tools submenu in the Edit menu.

The next time you check Auto-Hyphenate on the Writing tools submenu in the Edit menu, a check mark will appear by Auto-Hyphenate and your text will automatically hyphenate.

Hyphenating a portion of a document

You can only hyphenate an entire document in ClarisWorks. Even if you select a section of text before turning hyphenation on, ClarisWorks will still hyphenate the entire document.

✔ **Tip**: *Your text will look more professional if you use hyphenation with full justification—but turn hyphenation off with left, right, or centered text.*

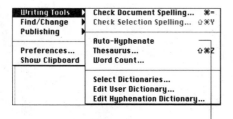

Choose the Auto-Hyphenate command from the Writing Tools submenu in the Edit menu.

Word Count

Writers often have to write to an exact word count, and ClarisWorks will help you do just that. The Word Count feature found in the Writing Tools submenu in the Edit menu tells you:

▲ How many characters are in the document

▲ How many total words the document has

▲ How many lines of text, not counting blank lines, are in the document

▲ How many paragraphs are in the document

▲ How many pages are in the document

▲ How many sections are in the document

You can also count those same characteristics in any selected section, as well as counting the characteristics of an entire document.

Using Word Count

1. Choose Word Count from the Writing Tools submenu in the Edit menu.

2. The Word Count dialog box appears and shows you how many characters, words, lines, paragraphs, pages, and sections are in your document.

3. Click on the OK button when you are done viewing this information.

Counting a portion of a document

1. Select the section of text you wish to count, and choose Word Count from the Writing Tools submenu in the Edit menu.

2. In the Word Count dialog box, click in the Count Selection box or use ⌘-**c**.

3. The statistics will now show just for the selected section of text.

4. Click on the OK button when you are done viewing this information.

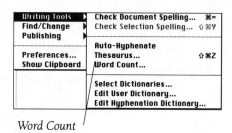

Word Count

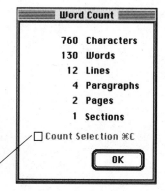

Notice the "Count Selection" checkbox in the Word Count dialog box. When this box has a check mark in it, ClarisWorks will count just selected text and ignore the rest of the document.

Writing tools

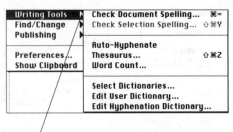

Choose Check Document Spelling from the Writing Tools submenu in the Edit menu, or press ⌘-=.

Checking Spelling

Check Document Spelling corrects most spelling and typing errors—however, the Spelling Check options can't correct words that are correctly spelled but used incorrectly, for example, using the word "there" instead of the possessive pronoun "their."

Using the spelling checking feature

1. To check the spelling in an entire document, click once anywhere in the document and press ⌘-= (Command-equal) or choose Check Document Spelling from the Writing Tools submenu in the Edit menu.

2. To check the spelling in a portion of a document, select the text you want to check, then press ⇧⌘-Y. The Spelling dialog box will appear. Claris Works will stop when it finds a word that is
   ▲ Spelled incorrectly, or
   ▲ A word the spelling checker doesn't know.

3. To change the word, click on one of the word choice options.

4. To add the word to the user's spelling dictionary, click on the Learn button.

5. To ignore a word without changing it and without adding it to the spelling dictionary, select the Skip button.

6. Click on the Done button when you are finished.

Current word is highlighted in the text.

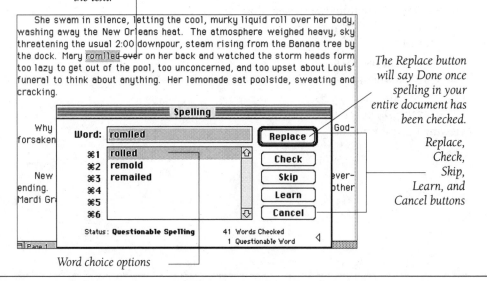

The Replace button will say Done once spelling in your entire document has been checked.

Replace, Check, Skip, Learn, and Cancel buttons

Word choice options

Writing tools

■ Printing

Printing using ClarisWorks is simple. You need to make sure of only three things:

▲ That the Chooser is set to the correct printer

▲ That ClarisWorks understands what kind of paper and what orientation the paper is that you are using

▲ That the Print Options and Print dialog boxes are filled out correctly

Chooser

The Chooser is used to select the printer you want to use or to connect you to a network.

1. Choose the Chooser from the Apple menu.
2. In the left-hand side of the dialog box that appears, select the printer you want to use. You may have to choose a printer port or AppleTalk in the right-hand section of the dialog box.

Page setup

Each printer has its own unique Page Setup dialog box. Additional information for some printers can be found in a second dialog box called the Print Options dialog box that opens when you check the Options button on the Page Setup menu.

The Print Options dialog box includes:

▲ How many copies you want to print

▲ How much of the document you want to print: all, a page, or a few pages

▲ Whether the paper is manual feed or not

▲ Different options depending on the printer, such as print quality

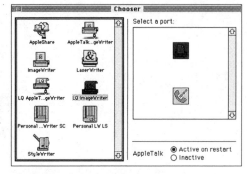

The Chooser dialog box—on the left-hand side are the printers. The right-hand side of the Chooser dialog box shows you your current settings for AppleTalk or printer port connections.

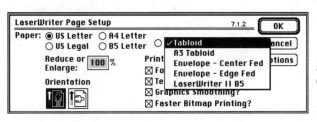

LaserWriter Page Setup dialog box with Orientation icons and Paper pop-up list.

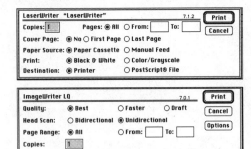

*ImageWriter and LaserWriter Print
dialog boxes*

Basic printing

1. Choose Print from the File menu.

2. In the Print dialog box, change the number of copies you want and make any other changes you need to make.

3. Click on the Print button.

Printing one page

1. Choose Print from the File menu.

2. Click once inside of the From box and type the page number you wish to start printing.

3. Press the Tab key. This action will move you to the To box.

4. Type the last page number you wish to print.

5. Click on the Print button or press the Return key.

If you want to print one page the page number in the From box and the page number in the To box will be exactly the same number.

Advanced Word Processing

■ What's in this chapter

Now that you have learned some basics of Claris-Works Word Processing mode, you'll need some additional tools. First, you will find a couple of quick tricks like:

▲ Inserting a date without having to look up the date and type it out

▲ Adding more than one file together

▲ Using ClarisWorks libraries of clip art

You'll also learn about document automation tools such as style sheets, outlines, sections, and macros.

Mail merge, which requires a combination of Database and Word Processing, can be found in "Mail merge" on page 213.

■ Entering date and time text automatically

Your computer always knows what day, date, and time it is. This piece of knowledge is part of the operating system and can be used by ClarisWorks to your advantage.

Inserting the date or time

1. Open a word-processed document you have previously created, or create a new one.
2. Choose Insert Date from the Edit menu.
3. To insert the time, choose Insert Time from the Edit menu.

Edit	
Can't Undo	⌘Z
Cut	⌘H
Copy	⌘C
Paste	⌘U
Clear	
Select All	⌘A
Insert Date	
Insert Time	
Insert Page #...	
Writing Tools	▶
Find/Change	▶
Publishing	▶
Preferences...	
Show Clipboard	

Date, Time, and Preferences menu choices— These choices are used to insert text automatically or change the format of the automatic text.

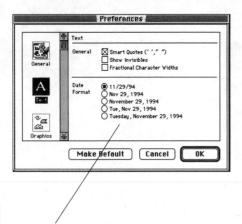

Date Preferences formats

Changing the date appearance

If you don't like the way the date looks in your text, you can change the appearance using the Preferences command from the Edit menu.

1. Choose Preferences from the Edit menu.
2. Select the Text icon in the Preferences dialog box.
3. Choose the date appearance you want to use.
4. Click on the OK button.

■ Inserting a file

If you need to put two or more files together, you can easily do this by using the Insert command from the File menu.

1. Click where you want the second file to appear. Make sure you are on a blank line, and if you are not on a blank line, press the Return key.

✔ **Tip:** *Once in a while you might want that second file to be part of an existing paragraph.*
If that's true, you won't want to press Return, just press the space bar after your last sentence.

The Insert command in the File menu

2. Choose Insert from the File menu. You will see the Insert file dialog box, which is almost the same as the Open dialog box.
3. Change file folders, disk drives, or other locations until you can see the file you need to add.
4. Select that file and click on the Insert button, or double-click on the file.

✔ **Tip:** *Double-clicking works whenever you want to do two things: choose something or fill in a blank—and then press the OK, Insert, or Open buttons (or any button that completes an action). The second mouse click actually presses the OK button for you.*

Inserting a file

■ Formatting characters

Formatting characters are commands that are generated by your using the space bar, tab key, soft return or line break command (Shift-Return), or pressing the Return key.

Show/Hide invisibles

1. Choose Preferences from the Edit menu.
2. Select the Text icon in the Preferences dialog box.
3. Select the checkbox by the Show Invisibles menu choice.
4. Click on the OK button.

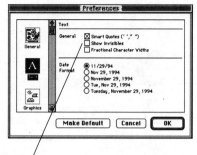

Show Invisibles Checkbox

■ Footnotes and endnotes

If you've ever done a school or academic paper, you're well acquainted with footnotes and endnotes. Footnotes appear at the bottom of the page, while endnotes appear as a group at the end of the document.

Creating a footnote

1. Click at the end of the sentence where you want your footnote to appear. Don't worry about footnote numbering, as the program will take care of this automatically.
2. Choose Insert Footnote from the bottom of the Format menu, or press ⇧⌘-F. The mouse cursor will now be blinking at the bottom of the page.
3. Type your footnote.
4. When you are finished, click back up in the text just after the footnote number, and continue typing your text.

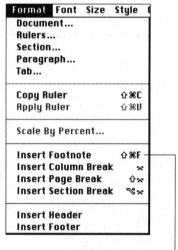

Insert Footnote in the Format menu

Before your footnotes start, the program will automatically draw any lines you need at the bottom of the page to separate your footnotes from your main text. When you insert a footnote, the footnote number will automatically appear below that line and the cursor will appear to the right of the number. All you need to do is to start typing your footnote.

Formatting characters

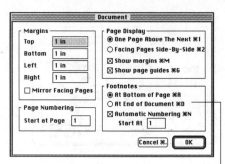

Automatic Numbering and
At End of Document
radio buttons

Special character Mark with box—Cut and paste between your character program (such as PopChar) to this box.

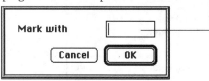

✔ **Tip**: *If you want to use the section mark §, single dagger †, or double dagger ‡, you must cut and paste these symbols from a program like ASCII Chart (a Desk Accessory) or PopChar, which will give you a list of available symbols.*

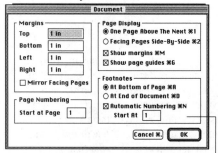

Start At box

Creating an endnote

1. Before typing an endnote, choose Document from the Format menu.

2. In the Document dialog box, select the At End of Document radio button in the Footnotes options box.

Changing footnotes to endnotes

Use the same steps you did above, clicking on the proper Footnotes radio button.

Special characters or symbols for footnotes

1. Click where you want the footnote to appear and choose Document from the Format menu.

2. In the Footnotes section of the dialog box, check to see if the Automatic Numbering checkbox has an X in it. If it does not, click in the checkbox.

3. Click on the OK button.

4. Choose Insert Footnote from the Format menu. The Mark with dialog box will appear.

5. In the Mark with dialog box, type the special character you want to use as the footnote marker.

6. Click on the OK button.

Restarting footnote numbering

1. Make a new section prior to the place where you want footnotes to start renumbering, for example, at the start of a new chapter. See "Sections" on page 88 for instructions on making a new section.

2. Before typing your first footnote, where you want the footnotes to start renumbering—as in starting a new chapter—click in the text where you want the first footnote in the new series.

3. Choose Document from the Format menu.

4. Make sure the Automatic Numbering check box has a check mark in it, then click in the Start At box. Type in the starting number you want for your footnotes.

5. Click on the OK button.

6. Now insert your footnotes by choosing Insert Footnote from the Format menu, or ⇧⌘-**F** as you normally would.

Footnotes and endnotes

Removing footnotes and endnotes

1. In your text, select the footnote number.

2. Press the Delete or Clear button on the keyboard. The footnote number and the attached footnote or endnote will disappear.

■ Libraries

Libraries are collections of clip art provided for your use by ClarisWorks. The clip art can be used in any part of ClarisWorks, including Word Processing. You can use the library art

▲ To create a letterhead with a logo

▲ As graphic bullets for an overhead

▲ For flyer or brochure illustration

Using libraries

Opening a library

1. Choose Library from the File menu, then drag the pointer to the right and choose Open from the Library submenu. You will see a dialog box that lists the libraries.

2. Scroll through this dialog box until you see the name of the library you want to use.

3. Select the name of the library, for example, Foods.

4. Click on the Open button. You will see the library dialog box open with a picture of the first piece of clip art on the top and a list of items below.

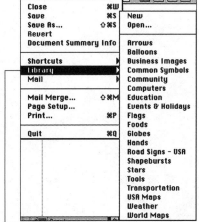

ClarisWorks libraries pop out to the right on a submenu. To use them, make sure you move the mouse directly to the right, then move the mouse up and down the Library submenu.

ClarisWorks comes with an extensive selection of clip art called libraries, including:

▲ Arrows	▲ Events & Holidays	▲ Shapebursts
▲ Balloons		▲ Stars
▲ Business Images	▲ Flags	▲ Tools
▲ Common Symbols	▲ Foods	▲ Transportation
▲ Community	▲ Globes	▲ USA Maps
▲ Computers	▲ Hands	▲ Weather
▲ Education	▲ Road Signs—USA	▲ World Maps

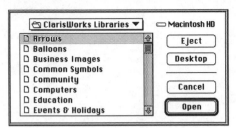

Open dialog box for the
ClarisWorks libraries

Changing the library view

1. Choose By Object from the View menu in the library's window to see pictures of all items rather than a list, or choose By Name to see a list of all items rather than seeing pictures.

2. Choose Alphabetize to alphabetize the list of pictures.

3. Choose View Options to change the size of the pictures.

4. In the Palette Size section of the View Options dialog box, increase or decrease the number of rows to make the pictures smaller or larger.

5. Click on the OK button when you are finished.

View menu—The By Object and By Name commands will change the way you can view pictures. View Options will help you change the picture size in the library's window.

By Name—The Library default view is to give you a list of picture names. To see what a picture looks like, you must click once on the name and select it. The picture will then appear at the top of the menu.

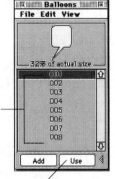

Use button

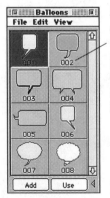

By Object—When you click on By Object in the View menu, you will see the actual pictures instead of just the names. The names will appear just below each picture.

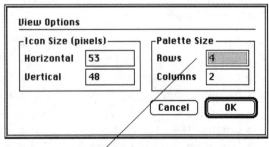

View Options—The quickest way to see larger pictures is to increase the rows in the Palette Size section of the View Options dialog box.

Libraries

Using a picture

1. Click in the document where you would like the picture to appear, then choose Open from the Library submenu in the File menu.

2. Select the library of clip art you want to use and click on the Open button.

3. In the library's View menu, click on the picture you want to use.

4. Click on the Use button at the bottom of the library window.

Leaving the library

▲ In the library's window, choose close from the File menu, or click in the close box in the upper right-hand corner of the library dialog box.

Using the Edit menu in the library's window

The Edit menu gives you access to six different tools that can be used to manipulate the drawings in the library's window.

▲ Cut   ▲ Delete

▲ Copy   ▲ Duplicate

▲ Paste   ▲ Select All

Using Copy

If you want to make a copy of any library picture so you can use it more than once in the document:

1. Open the library you want to use and click once on the picture you want to use.

2. Choose Copy from the Edit menu.

3. In your document, click where you want your picture to appear.

4. Choose Paste from the Edit menu, or press ⌘-v to paste your copy directly into your document.

Using Select All

▲ Open the library you want to use and choose Select All from the Edit menu. You can now paste all of the pictures into your document at the same time.

Eliminating pictures from a library

1. Open the library you want to use, and click once on the picture you want to delete.

2. Choose Cut or Delete from the Edit menu.

The close box—click on this box to close the library.

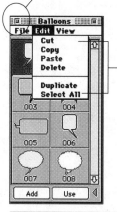

Many of the tools that are in the library's Edit menu are tools you will find in the main Word Processing program.

✔ **Tip**: *Don't close the library if you want to use more pictures. You can drag and drop one or more pictures by clicking on the picture you want to use. Then hold down in the mouse button and drag the picture and the mouse over into the document.*

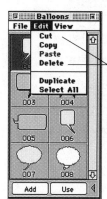

Cut vs. Delete—Cut eliminates the picture from the library window but leaves a copy of the picture on your Clipboard. You can Paste anything that has been cut. If you choose Delete, however, the picture is eliminated from the library and you will not be able to paste it anywhere.

Libraries

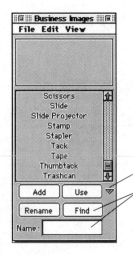

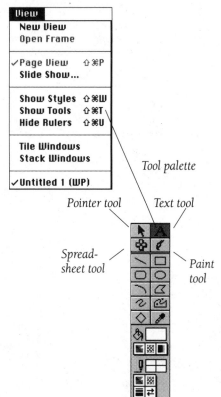

Tool palette

Pointer tool   *Text tool*

Spread-sheet tool   *Paint tool*

Finding a picture in the library

1. Click in the triangle found in the lower-right corner of the library window. A dialog box will appear at the bottom of the library window.

2. In the Name text box, type the picture's name.

3. Click on the Find button.

4. When you are finished, click in the close button to close the library.

To find a file:

1. Select the library's find triangle.

2. Type the name of the picture in the Name box.

3. Click on the Find button.

Inline vs. free graphics

Inline graphics are graphics that act like text and are in a line with text. They cannot be moved around freely. An example would be when you want to use pictures as bullets instead of the bullet symbol.

Creating an inline graphic

1. Using the mouse, click in the text where you wish the graphic to appear.

2. Open the library and click on a graphic. The graphic will appear in that line of text as though it were a special character.

Creating a freestanding graphic

Freestanding graphics are in graphics frames and can be moved around freely.

1. Choose Show Tools from the View menu, or press ⇧⌘-T.

2. Select the pointer tool on the tool palette.

3. Open the library you want to use and click on the picture you want to use.

4. Click the Use button. The picture will be surrounded by four dots, one on each corner. This is the cue that the picture is a freestanding graphic and can be moved anywhere.

5. Click on the close box to close the library.

Moving a graphic

1. Choose Show Tools from the View menu, or press ⇧⌘-T.

2. Select the pointer tool on the tool palette, then click on the picture you want to move.

3. Position the cursor in the center of the picture and drag it left, right, up, or down until it is in the proper position.

Reshaping a file

The picture below is shown using three different shapes. To change the shape of a file:

1. Using the pointer tool from the tool palette, move the pointer on top of one of the handles (the lower right is the easiest to use).

2. Drag that handle in to shorten the file from right to left, or up to short the file from top to bottom. To keep the file in proportion, drag at a 45 degree angle from the bottom left-hand corner to the upper right-hand corner.

Pointer tool—The pointer tool is a selection tool. In any program mode, clicking on the pointer tool, then clicking on an object, graphic, or frame, will select that item. You can then:

▲ Click in the center of your object and move it.

▲ Click on one of the corner points and resize the object.

▲ Press the Delete or Clear key, or choose Cut from the Edit menu, and erase the object.

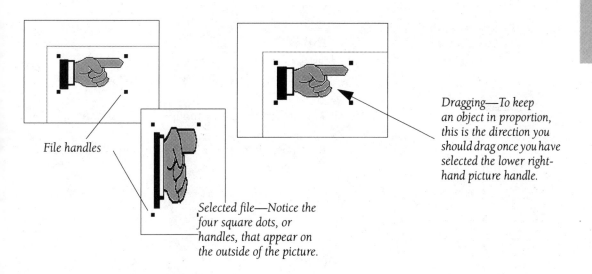

File handles

Selected file—Notice the four square dots, or handles, that appear on the outside of the picture.

Dragging—To keep an object in proportion, this is the direction you should drag once you have selected the lower right-hand picture handle.

Libraries

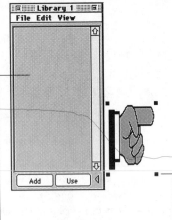

*New Library palette
Notice that the palette is
empty and the object to
be added to the palette is
selected (see the little
square handles).*

Creating a library

If you have a collection of pictures you have created in Painting or Drawing program modes, or if you would like to build your own library of clip art from any source, you can create a custom library.

1. Choose Library from the File menu.
2. Choose New from the Library submenu. You will see an empty library window. The name of the library window is Library 1. Libraries are numbered sequentially.
3. In the document, click once on the picture you wish to add to the library and then click on the Add button.
4. Add all of the pictures you wish and when you are finished choose Save from the File menu.
5. In the Save dialog box, give the library a unique name, then click on the Save button.
6. Close the library by choosing Close from the File menu or clicking in the close box.

■ Styles

Styles are collections of font, indent, and special character information. Each individual preset collection has been given a name, such as Checklist for a style that will give you checkboxes in front of each paragraph of text.

Ruler bar

*Ruler bar pop-up
menu of styles*

Styles are available on the ruler bar and can be accessed by holding down on the ruler bar style button with your pointer.

1. Click in the paragraph in which you want to apply a style.
2. Choose a style in the styles pop-up menu in the ruler bar.

Using Label to format text

The Label pop-up list in the Paragraph dialog box supplies you a shortcut for formatting text. Predefined styles include special characters like check marks or check boxes, numbered paragraphs, diamonds, and bullets, and letter and legal styles.

Using the Paragraph dialog box to access preset styles

1. Click in the paragraph you want to change (or select several paragraphs or the entire document) and choose Paragraph from the Format menu.
2. Choose the style you want from the pop-up list.
3. Click on the Apply button.

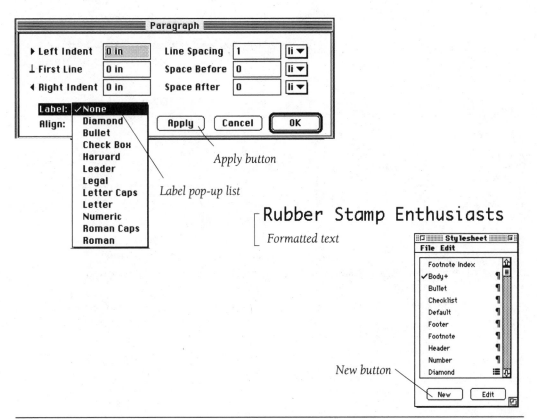

Apply button

Label pop-up list

Formatted text

New button

Defining styles

You can capture information about:

▲ Line spacing

▲ Space before or after paragraphs

▲ Font name, style, and size

▲ Justification (left, right, center, full)

Style type radio buttons

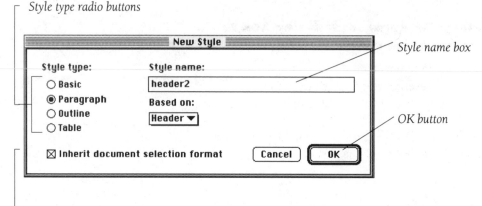

Style name box

OK button

Inherit document selection format check box

Capturing this information is called creating a style. You can create your own style from text you have already formatted or start from scratch.

Creating Styles from preexisting text

To define a style when you have already formatted your text:

Expanded Edit Style dialog box

Edit menu

New button   Done button   Properties list

1. Make sure your paragraph text looks exactly the way you want it to look then click inside of that paragraph.

2. Choose Show Styles from the View menu, or press ⇧ ⌘-W.

3. Click on the New button at the bottom of the Edit Styles dialog box. In the New Style dialog box, type a name inside of the box labeled Style name.

4. Click in the Inherit document selection format checkbox at the bottom of this menu.

5. Select the Paragraph radio button in the Style type list.

6. Click on the OK button or press the Return key.

Style type

There are four style types you can choose from:

▲ Basic—a body text style that would apply to the entire document.

▲ Paragraph—a text style that would apply to an entire paragraph.

▲ Outline—a text style that would apply to an outline document.

▲ Table—a text style that works with tables or imported spreadsheets.

Style editing cursor

Editing a style

You can change any attributes of a style such as the font, size, or paragraph indentions. To do this you need to use the Show Styles from the File menu.

1. Choose Show styles from the File menu. You will now see the Stylesheet dialog box.

2. Select the style you wish to change and click on the Edit button.

3. The Properties box on the right-hand side of the Edit Styles box will show the characteristics and base styles of the style you wish to edit. Your cursor will now be a capital S, the style editing cursor.

4. Make your changes using the Word Processing pull-down menus like Format, Font, Size, and Style.

5. When you have finished all of your changes, click on the Done button.

Your changes will not be saved until you save the document—so don't forget to save immediately.

The Edit menu at the top of the Edit Style box is the menu you use to change the properties, or characteristics, of the style you select from the left hand box.

The Edit Style dialog box shows you a list of yur styles on the left hand side. When you click on a style name on the left, you will see the properties, or characteristics, of the style listed in the right hand properties box.

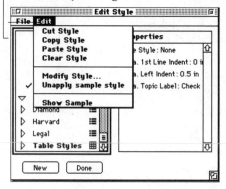

The Copy Style command from the Edit menu in the Edit Style dialog box

Using Based on—This sample contains three styles. The very top style, called Header 1, was used to create Header 2 and Header 3.

Original style ⌐

Header 1

Header 2
Header 3

This is where the body text be-gins...

Style differences
Headers 1, 2, and 3 all use the same type style and size. Headers 2 and 3 change the indention or add italics to the original Header 1 style.

Borrowing style attributes: Creating a new style using Based on

The Based on pop-up list will let you borrow a style that has already been created and add your own characteristics to that style. For example, you could borrow the Header style and create two related styles, Header 1 and Header 2.

One advantage is that these three styles then become linked. If you make a font change, for example, in Header, the fonts in Header 1 and Header 2 will automatically change.

Creating a new style using Based on

1. Choose Show Styles from the File menu. You will see the Stylesheet dialog box.
2. Click once on the style you wish to copy, then click on the New button. You will now see the New Style dialog box.
3. Choose the proper Style type (Basic, Paragraph, Outline, or Table) and type a name for the style in the Style name box.
4. Choose the style that has the attributes or characteristics that you want to borrow in the Based on pop-up list.
5. Click on the OK button. You will now have the capital S style editing cursor.
6. Make the changes you need to the style using the Format, Font, Size, and Style menus.
7. When you have finished all of your changes, click on the Done button.
8. Don't forget to save the document.

Deleting a style

The Edit Style dialog box has a small menu that consists of File and Edit. Use the Edit menu to delete a style.

1. Choose Show Style from the File menu.

2. Click once on the style you wish to remove in the Stylesheet dialog box, then click once on the Edit button.

3. Choose Cut style from the Edit menu in the Edit Style dialog box, then click on the Done button.

4. Be sure to save the document.

Copying styles to another document

Styles are copied from document to document by using an export and import function.

Exporting styles

1. Choose Show Styles from the File menu.

2. Choose Export Styles from the File menu. You will now see a dialog box labeled Select styles to export.

3. Select the checkbox for each one of the checked styles you want to export, or click on the Check All button if you want to export all styles. If you make a mistake and click on too many styles you didn't mean to select, use the Check None button to erase the check marks.

4. When you are finished, click on the OK button.

5. You will see the ClarisWorks Styles file folder in a Save dialog box. Give the style collection a name by typing a name in the Save as box.

6. Click on the Save button.

Cut Style

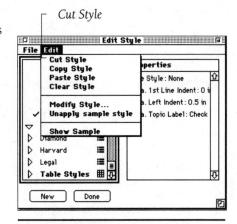

✔ **Warning:***Using Cut Style from the Edit menu will not cut a style that is used or has been applied to text in the current document.*

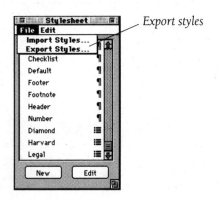

Export styles

Export styles box—
Use the checkboxes to
select the styles you
need to export.

Check None button

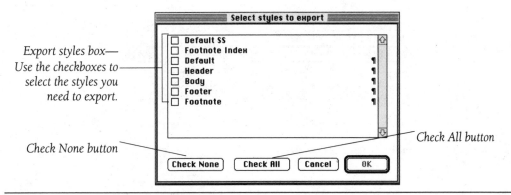

Check All button

Styles

Import styles—Select the check boxes for the styles you wish to import.

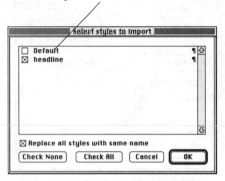

✔ **Tip**: *If you don't want to keep any of your existing styles in addition to the styles you are importing, make sure you cut all of the existing styles before you start importing them.*

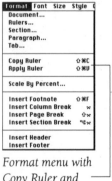

Format menu with Copy Ruler and Apply Ruler commands

Importing styles

If you want to use a collection of styles, you must first import them into the document.

1. Choose Show Styles from the File menu.
2. Choose Import Styles from the File menu in the Stylesheet dialog box that appears. You will now see the ClarisWorks Styles folder.
3. Click once on the style collection you wish to import, then click on the Open button. You now see a Select styles to import dialog box.
4. If you want to use all of the styles click on the Check All button.
5. Click on the OK button when you are finished. Your Stylesheet dialog box will now list both your existing styles and your new styles.

■ Copying rulers

You can copy ruler bars—and the tabs and margins that are associated with the ruler bars—and use the copies to transfer these characteristics to a new file.

Copying a ruler bar

1. Click inside of a paragraph that is formatted the way you want.
2. Choose Copy Ruler from the Format menu, or press ⇧⌘-c.
3. Move to the paragraph you want to format and click anywhere inside of that paragraph.
4. Choose Apply Ruler from the Format menu, or press ⇧⌘-v.

Left Margin   Tabs   Right Margin

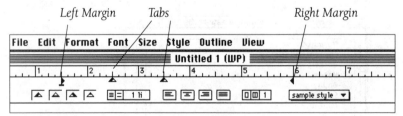

This is a typical ruler bar with margins and tabs set up for a table. Copying this ruler bar will help keep table formats consistent throughout the document.

Copying rulers

■ Outlines

Outlines are thought organizers. They help you divide information into an outline form by creating topics and subtopics.

This outline form can later be collapsed to show you just the major points while temporarily hiding the minor ones, or the it can be edited by moving topics around to different sections of the outline.

Creating an outline

1. In the pop-up list of styles, click on one of three outline styles you can use:
   ▲ Diamond
   ▲ Harvard
   ▲ Legal
2. Choose New Topic from the Outline menu, and type the information for your first major point.
3. Press the Return key, and continue typing each of your major points.
4. Every time you press the Return key, a new topic number is created.

There are three styles used with outlines. Make sure you select one of them before you begin making an outline. Later on, if you want to use a different outline style, just highlight all of your text and select the new style.

Body
Bullet
Checklist
Default
Footer
Footnote
Header
Number
Diamond
✓Harvard
Legal

Business Plan-Visualize Stamps

I. Start-Up Phase
   A. Licenses
   B. Advertising
   C. Initial inventory
       1. Rubberstampmadness
       2. Vive Las Vegas
   D. Personnel

Harvard style

◆ Start-Up Phase
   ◇ Licenses
   ◇ Advertising
   ◆ Initial inventory
       ◇ Rubberstampmadness
       ◇ Vive Las Vegas
   ◇ Personnel

1. Start-Up Phase
   1.1. Licenses
   1.2. Advertising
   1.3. Initial inventory
       1.3.1. Rubberstampmadness
       1.3.2. Vive Las Vegas
   1.4. Personnel

Diamond style

Legal style

Outlines

First topic—New Topic starts your outline. New Topic Left starts a topic indented one level from the previous topic, while New Topic Right "out-dents" a topic one level.

```
┌─────────────────────────┐
│ Outline  View           │
├─────────────────────────┤
│ New Topic               │
│ New Topic Left      ⌘L  │
│ New Topic Right     ⌘R  │
├─────────────────────────┤
│ Move Left          ⇧⌘L  │
│ Move Right         ⇧⌘R  │
│ Move Above              │
│ Move Below              │
├─────────────────────────┤
│ Collapse                │
│ Expand                  │
│ Expand To...            │
│ Raise Topic             │
└─────────────────────────┘
```

Making subtopics

1. After typing a major topic, press the Return key.

2. Choose New Topic Right from the Outline menu, or press ⌘-**R**.

3. Your cursor will indent. Begin typing this subtopic and the subtopic numeral or alphabetic section character will appear.

Sample Outline

Level 1 heading—This heading is the furthest left (toward the left-hand margin).

Level 2 heading—This heading is indented one tab stop to the right.

Level 3 heading—This heading is indented two tab stops to the right.

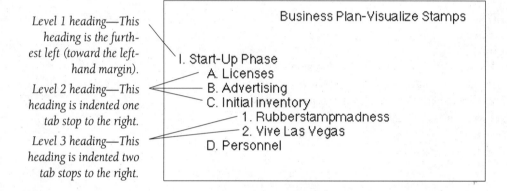

Returning to the main topic level

1. After typing a subtopic, press the Return key.

2. Choose New Topic Left from the Outline menu, or press ⌘-**L**. The cursor will move to the left.

3. Begin typing this subtopic and the subtopic numeral or alphabetic section character will appear.

Subtopics—A topic is "left" or "right" relative to the topic in the line just before it.

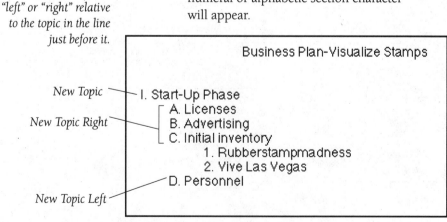

Changing topics to subtopics and vice versa

1. Click in the topic you want to change, and choose Move Left from the Outline menu, or press ⇧⌘-L if you want to move the topic out one level.

2. Choose Move Right from the Outline menu, or press ⇧⌘-R if you want to move the topic in one level.

Rearranging topics

1. Click in the topic you wish to move, and choose Move Above from the Outline menu to jump the topic over the topic just above it.

2. Choose Move Below from the Outline menu below to jump the topic under the topic just below it.

Raising the level of a topic

If you have made something a subtopic and you want it to be a major topic:

▲ Click in the topic, and choose Raise Topic from the Outline menu. Your subtopic should now be raised one level.

Outline	View
New Topic	
New Topic Left	⌘L
New Topic Right	⌘R
Move Left	⇧⌘L
Move Right	⇧⌘R
Move Above	
Move Below	
Collapse	
Expand	
Expand To...	
Raise Topic	

Changing topic levels—Use the Move Left or Move Right commands to change the level of topic indention.

Notice the position of topic D, Personnel.

In this sample, topic D, Personnel, has been moved to the right and is now topic 3.

Topic D, Personnel, has been moved above one level and now appears above the topic Initial Inventory.

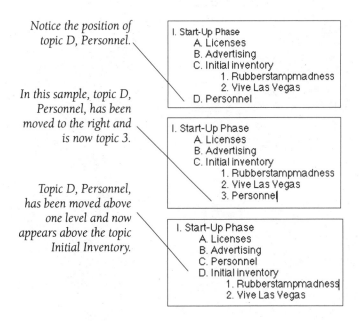

```
I. Start-Up Phase
    A. Licenses
    B. Advertising
    C. Initial inventory
        1. Rubberstampmadness
        2. Vive Las Vegas
    D. Personnel
```

```
I. Start-Up Phase
    A. Licenses
    B. Advertising
    C. Initial inventory
        1. Rubberstampmadness
        2. Vive Las Vegas
        3. Personnel
```

```
I. Start-Up Phase
    A. Licenses
    B. Advertising
    C. Personnel
    D. Initial inventory
        1. Rubberstampmadness
        2. Vive Las Vegas
```

Outlines

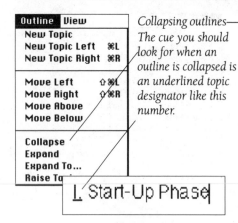

Collapsing outlines— The cue you should look for when an outline is collapsed is an underlined topic designator like this number.

L Start-Up Phase

Use the Expand command to see subtopics that were previously collapsed. You can either select an entire outline, or click in one topic and expand just that topic.

Collapsing topics

If you want to see just the major points of your outline:

1. Highlight your entire outline, then choose Collapse from the Outline menu. Your outline will now show only the major points.

2. Any major topics that have subtopics will have the alphabetic or numeric designation underlined as a cue that there is further information.

Expanding topics

To see your minor points again you must expand the outline.

1. Either click inside of the major topic needing to be expanded or select your entire outline if you wish to expand the entire outline.

2. Choose Expand from the Outline menu. Your outline should show all subtopics.

Outlines

Limiting expansion

If your topic has more than one subtopic indention level, you can limit the rate of expansion.

1. Click inside of the major topic you wish to expand or select your outline, then choose Expand To from the Outline menu. You will see the Expand To dialog box.

2. In the Expand to box, type the number of levels you wish to see.

▲ 1 level represents just the major topics.

▲ 2 levels represents the major topic plus the first level of subtopics, and so on.

3. Click on the OK button.

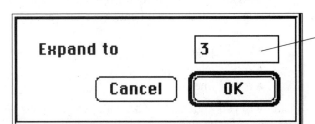

Type in how many levels you want to expand to here.

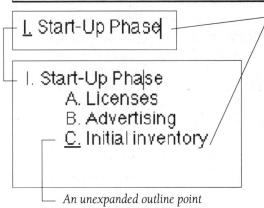

Originally Start-Up Phase and all of the accompanying subtopics were completely collapsed. Start-Up Phase was then expanded to 2 levels. Notice that C, Initial Inventory, is still collapsed. This is a partial expansion.

An unexpanded outline point

Outlines

Use the Insert Page Break command from the Format menu to end a page manually.

■ Page breaks

You might want to force a page to stop, for instance, to make sure that a chart appears on a page by itself.

1. Click at the end of the paragraph or sentence where you want the page to stop and press the Return key so that you are on a new blank line.

2. Choose Insert Page Break from the Format menu, or press ⇧-Enter from the numeric keypad. Your cursor should now move down to a new page.

Page breaks are related to section breaks, but do not affect formatting or page numbering in quite the same way.

■ Sections

Sections are ways of controlling different formats for varying parts of the document. A section can begin on either:

▲ A new page

▲ A new left or right page

▲ A new line

To help you understand a section, here are a few common examples:

▲ A newspaper, where the masthead runs across the entire top of the page, but the rest of the newspaper is in two columns.

▲ A book like this one, where the right pages and left pages have different headers.

▲ A report, where only one page of the report must be in multiple columns.

The Section command should be used right here.

You will need to start a new section when you want to have some text running all of the way across the page and the rest of the text in multiple columns.

Friars News

Blessing of the Animals

Today one of the most interesting Franciscan's in the city of Saint Francis—Father Lotito—will bless the animals at the Tenderloin Center block.

Starting a new section

1. Choose Section from the Format menu.

2. Choose one of the four choices in the Start Section pop-up list.

▲ New Line

▲ New Page

▲ New Left Page

▲ New Right Page

Changing page numbers for a section

1. In the Section dialog box, click on the Restart Page Number radio button.

2. In the Page Number box to the right of the radio button, click and type in the page number you want the section to begin with.

3. Click on the OK button when you are done.

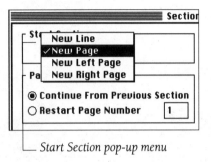

Start Section pop-up menu

Section dialog box

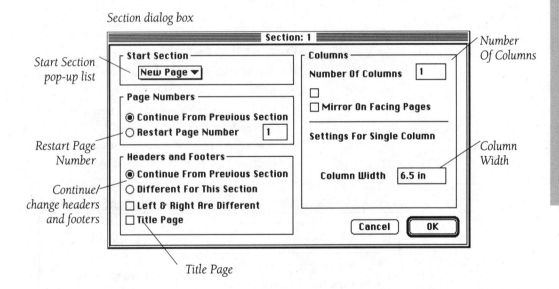

Start Section pop-up list

Restart Page Number

Continue/ change headers and footers

Title Page

Number Of Columns

Column Width

Sections

Changing headers and footers in a section

1. Choose Section from the Format menu.

2. In the Section dialog box, click on the Different For This Section radio button and click on the OK button.

3. In the document, choose Insert Header from the Format menu, then type the information for the right-hand page (odd-numbered or recto pages).

4. When you begin to type on page 2, choose Insert Header from the Format menu.

5. Type the information for the left-hand page (even-numbered or verso pages).

Sections sample

Header

Section 1 with masthead

Section 2 with 3 columns

Creating title pages

If you want the first page to have no headers or footers:

1. Click in the first page of your text and choose Section from the Format menu.

2. Select the Title Page checkbox in the Headers and Footers section of the Section dialog box.

3. Click on the OK button.

Click once in the Title Page checkbox to eliminate any headers or footers on the first page of your document.

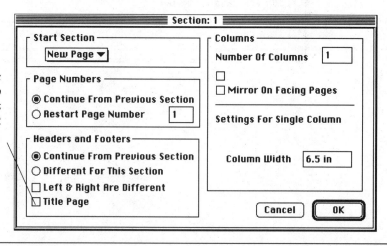

Sections

■ Columns

Columns are used for newsletters, press releases, and other text matter where you want the text to flow down the left-hand column and continue on in the right-hand column—so don't confuse this type of column with the type of column you create using tabs. This type of column is called a newspaper column.

Creating more than one column

▲ In the ruler bar, click on the increase columns button. Each time you click you will increase the number of columns by one. You can have up to nine columns on a page.

If you want to create a newspaper-type layout with some text running across the entire page, you will have to create a new section first.

Using the Section dialog box

1. Choose Section from the Format menu.
2. In the Number of Columns box, type the number of columns you want.
3. Click on the OK button.

Changing column width and gutters

Column width refers to how wide you want each column to be. Gutters are the small blank areas between columns. Make sure the total width of the columns plus the Space Between the columns (gutters) adds up to no more than the space between your two margins.

1. Choose Section from the Format menu.
2. In the Settings For All Columns area, click inside of the Column Width box and type in how wide you want the columns to be.
3. Click in the Space Between box and type in how wide you want the gutter to be.
4. Click on the OK button.

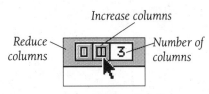

Increase columns

Reduce columns

Number of columns

Column button from the main ruler bar.

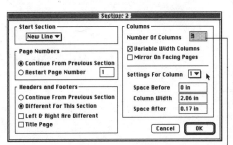

Type the number of columns needed for this section of your document.

✔ **Tip**: *The default, or standard gutter space between columns is .167" or .25." Professionally laid-out newspapers, flyers, and brochures need at least 50% empty space—and that includes the gutters.*

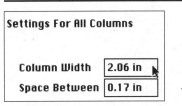

Settings For All Columns

Column Width	2.06 in
Space Between	0.17 in

Creating columns with a masthead on the first page

1. Type your headline text and press the Return key.
2. Choose Insert Section Break from the Format menu. A section break will appear in your document.
3. Choose Section from the Format menu.
4. In the Section dialog box, select the Start Section pop-up list and change the start of this section to New Line.
5. Change the number of columns in the box on the right-hand side of the page to the number of columns you want. Just type the number there.
6. Make any changes you want to the Column Width and Space Between boxes.
7. Click on the OK button when you are finished.

Columns

Friars News I

Blessing of the Animals

Today one of the most interesting Franciscan's in the city of Saint Francis—Father Lotito—will bless the animals at the Tenderloin Center block.

This newsletter has three columns in the second section.

Making variable-width columns

Variable-width columns means that if you have two columns on a page, each column has its own width.

1. Choose Section from the Format menu, and in the Number of Columns box, type in how many columns you want.

2. Click in the Variable Width Columns checkbox. The Settings For Column pop-up list now will list each of your columns.

3. In the Space Before box, type in how much space you will want to the left side of your first column. You probably will want 0 inches because the first column usually starts at the left-hand margin.

4. In the Column Width box, type how wide you want the first column to be.

5. In the Space After box, type in how wide you would like the gutter to be between columns one and two.

6. Choose the next column in the pop-up list. In this column, leave the Space Before box alone. The setting you see is the same as the setting you typed in the Space After box for the first column. This is the width of your gutter.

7. Click in the Column Width box, and type in how wide you would like this column to be. The computer will calculate how much space is left over on your page. The result will appear in the Space After box.

8. Click on the OK button when you are finished.

Mirror on facing pages

If you want your columns to appear as mirror images on the left and right pages:

1. Choose Section from the Format menu.

2. Click in the Mirror on Facing Pages box in the Section dialog box.

3. Click on the OK button when you are finished.

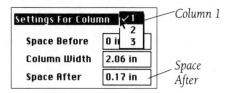

Variable-width columns—Each column width is set separately, with the Space Before equaling the Space After of the previous column.

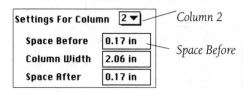

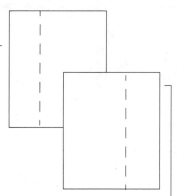

Mirrored pages—This left page (even- numbered page) has a narrow column on the left- hand side, while the right column is quite wide.

Mirrored pages, cont.—This right page (odd numbered page) has a narrow column on the right- hand side, while the left column is quite wide.

Columns

■ Macros

Macros work like tape recorders. You turn on the macro recording, and the macro makes a copy of absolutely everything you do.

You could be typing text, filling in dialog boxes, or making menu choices. The macro will record every action you take—even your mistakes. Since macros are super-fast, you don't need to worry about changing the macro when you make typing or menu choice mistakes as long as you continue on and correct your error.

When you are done with your task, you turn the recorder off. Later on, when you want to repeat the same thing, you just play back your macro.

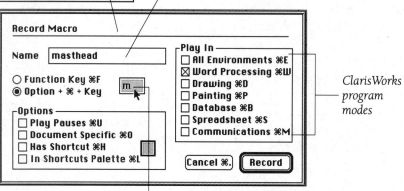

Macro Name box

ClarisWorks program modes

The Option key box is where you designate a shortcut key—an alphabetic key that will work with the Option and Command keys.

Creating a macro

1. Choose Record Macro from the Shortcuts submenu in the File menu, or press ⇧⌘-J. The Record Macro dialog box will appear.
2. Type a name for the macro in the Name box.
3. Choose a shortcut key for running the macro the easy way by clicking on the Function Key radio button and designate which function key you want to run the macro, or click in the Option+⌘+ key box next to the radio button and type in a letter. That way the Option + ⌘ + your letter will start the macro.
4. Click on the Record button.
5. When you are finished recording your macro choose Stop Recording on the Shortcuts submenu in the File menu.

Playing your macro

There are three ways to play your macro:

▲ Using Play Macro from the Shortcuts submenu on the File menu

▲ Using the shortcut key you assigned

▲ Using a button you can create and play from the Shortcuts palette

Using the menu to play a macro

Use the File menu to play a macro.

1. Choose Play macro from the Shortcuts submenu on the File menu. You will see the Play Macro dialog box.

2. Using the scroll arrows on the side, move down until you see your macro name and select it.

3. Click on the Play button.

Using the shortcut key to play a macro

When you created your macro, hopefully you gave it a key combination like Option+⌘+H, or some other letter. If you want to play your macro:

1. Hold down the Option key. While holding down the Option key, hold down the ⌘ key.

2. Now tap the letter you assigned to the macro.

Play macro

Play button

Macro buttons usually appear as the last buttons on the Shortcuts palette. There are two macro buttons on this palette. One has an arrow pointing to the right. The second macro has the initials CAB on it.

Using the shortcuts palette

If you have a macro that is already assigned to the Shortcuts palette, here is how you use it.

1. Open the Shortcuts palette by choosing Show Shortcuts from the Shortcuts submenu in the File menu, or pressing ⇧⌘-x.

2. You should recognize the button on the Shortcuts palette. It will probably be a button on the third row. Click on that button to play the macro.

✔ **Tip**: *Check out the section called "Has Shortcuts and In Shortcuts Palette" on page 98 to find out how to create a button on the Shortcuts palette.*

Macros

Changing a macro

If you don't like the shortcut key you assigned your macro, would like it available in other programs, or would like to limit the macro's availability, you can edit the macro. Editing a macro will also let you create a button that will appear in the Shortcuts palette.

Editing a macro

1. Choose Edit Macro from the Shortcuts submenu in the File Menu. The Edit Macro dialog box will appear.

2. Select your macro from the Macro pop-up list.

3. Make your changes to:
- ▲ Macro name
- ▲ Shortcut key box
- ▲ Macro options
- ▲ Play In environments

4. Click on the Done button when you are finished.

Edit Macros dialog box

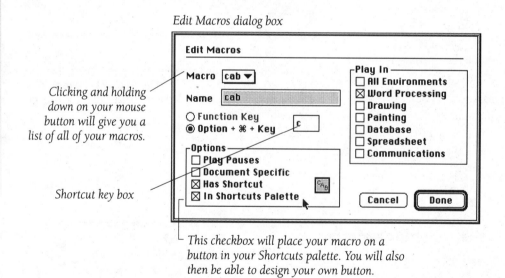

Clicking and holding down on your mouse button will give you a list of all of your macros.

Shortcut key box

This checkbox will place your macro on a button in your Shortcuts palette. You will also then be able to design your own button.

Macro availability

The Play In section in the Edit Macro dialog box gives a list of the program modes in which the macro works. The list will assign your macro to:

▲ All Environments   ▲ Painting

▲ Word Processing   ▲ Database

▲ Drawing   ▲ Spreadsheet

▲ Communications

Options

The Edit Macro dialog box has four options to assist you in playing back your macro:

▲ Play Pauses

▲ Document Specific

▲ Has Shortcut (button)

▲ In Shortcuts Palette

Play Pauses

Play Pauses plays the macro back slowly, step by step, so you can see the action as it happens. Your macro will play back much more slowly this way, but you will also be able to tell where you made a mistake when you recorded the macro.

Turn this option on by clicking in the checkbox, then play your macro. Later, turn the option off by removing the check mark in the checkbox. Your macro will then run at the normal speed.

Play Pauses check box

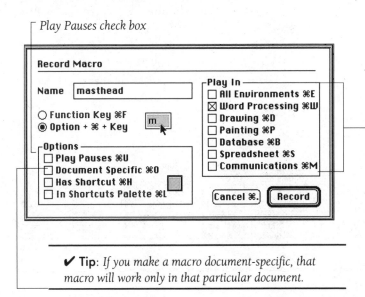

✔ **Tip**: *If you want to make a macro work in all environments, you must be sure that the actions you take while recording that macro will work in spreadsheets, for instance, as well as in painting.*

✔ **Tip**: *If you make a macro document-specific, that macro will work only in that particular document.*

Macros

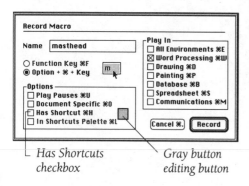

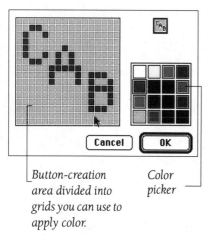

L Has Shortcuts
  checkbox

Gray button
editing button

Button-creation
area divided into
grids you can use to
apply color.

Color
picker

For more information on the regular
Shortcuts palette buttons and how to
change them, see "Tool bar and
Shortcuts palettes" on page 28.

Here is an example of
the button created
above from the edit
button dialog box.

Has Shortcuts and In Shortcuts Palette

You can create your own unique button for your macro. This button will show up on the Shortcuts palette if you click in the In Shortcuts Palette box. You can assign a macro you have previously created to a button using these steps, or you can assign a macro to a button on your Shortcuts palette while you are first recording the macro.

Creating your own button design

1. Choose Record Macro if you have not yet created your macro, or Edit macro if you have already created your macro, from the Shortcuts submenu in the File menu.

2. In the Record Macro dialog box or the Edit macro dialog box, click in the Has Shortcuts checkbox and select the little gray button. You will now see the edit button icon dialog box.

3. Using the color palette on the right, you can create designs by first clicking on the color you want to use.

4. Now click in the gray grid. You will see the color appear in the grid square you clicked on. Don't like that color? Just click in that grid square again and the color will disappear.

5. Continue editing and when you like the look of your new macro button, click on the OK button.

6. Click on the Done button in the Edit Macros dialog box.

7. Open the Shortcuts palette by choosing Show Shortcuts from the Shortcuts submenu in the File menu, or by pressing ⇧⌘-x.

8. Use your new macro button by clicking on it.

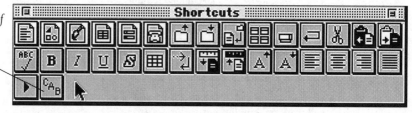

Deleting a macro

Every now and then you might want to get rid of a macro—and this is very simple in ClarisWorks.

To delete a macro you no longer want, make sure that if the macro is specific to a document, you are in that document. If that macro is specific to one of the program modes like Drawing or Painting program mode, make sure you are in that mode.

Just remember, once the macro has been deleted, you cannot play it or recover it, so be very sure you really want to get rid of any macro.

Erasing or deleting a macro

1. Choose Delete Macro from the Shortcuts submenu in the File menu. You now should see the Delete Macro dialog box, which resembles the Play Macro dialog box.

2. Select the name of the macro you want to delete in the scrolling list.

3. Click on the Delete button.

4. Click on the Done button.

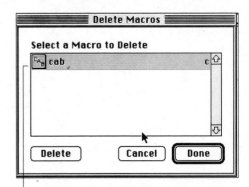

Your macro will appear by name and by button. When you want to delete it, just click on the Delete button. One warning though: if you have deleted the macro, you will not be able to get it back.

Macros

Spreadsheets

■ Beginning spreadsheets

Spreadsheets are designed for projects that involve columns and rows of numbers, such as creating budgets, analyzing "what-if" scenarios, and figuring out loan and mortgage costs.

You can also keep track of such information as names and addresses, but it is easier to work with that type of information in the Database portion of ClarisWorks.

Spreadsheet terminology

Spreadsheets consist of columns, rows, and cells, and also have a menu similar to Word Processing.

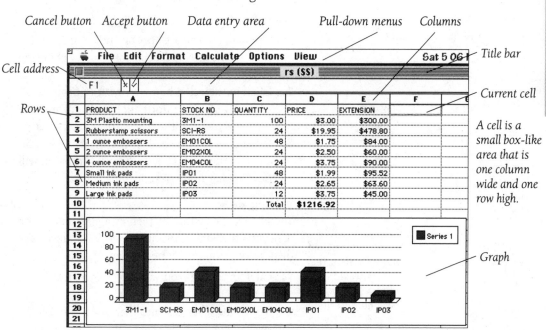

Cancel button   Accept button   Data entry area   Pull-down menus   Columns

Cell address

Rows

Title bar

Current cell

A cell is a small box-like area that is one column wide and one row high.

Graph

## Chapter 4

Columns are lettered as follows:

A B C...X Y Z...AA AB AC...AH

The data entry area contains the text that will go in the cell.

A2	× ✓	3M Plastic mounting

	A	B
1	PRODUCT	STOCK NO
2	3M Plastic mounting	3M1-1
3	Rubberstamp scissors	SCI-RS

The active cell is surrounded by a slightly heavier or colored line.

✔ **Tip**: *You can enter information that is actually longer than the cell is wide. For example, here is an entry in cell A1. You can see that it seems to extend across several cells. If text had been entered in cell A2, any text extending out over cell B1 and further to the right would be hidden.*

Accept button   Data entry area

A2	× ✓	

	A	B	C
1	Entries can extend across cells		
2			
3			
4			
5			

This text was all entered in cell A1.

If text were entered in cell B1, the text in cell A1 would display only to the beginning of cell B1.

Spreadsheet characteristics

When you start a spreadsheet, you start a document with only one page—a very large page. Spreadsheets are divided into rows and columns. The first column in the document is column A and the first row is row 1. Columns available for use by default are columns A through AH, and rows 1 through 500.

Entering data

In spreadsheets, text is normally left-justified and numbers are right-justified. Numbers are entered without any dollar or percent signs, and without trailing decimal places that end in "0."

Entering data

Type of data	Actual data	What you enter
Currency	$3.95	3.95
Currency	$3.00	3
Currency	-$3.00	-3
Numbers	123,456	123456
Formulas	add cells A1 and A2	=sum(A1+A2)

Entering data

1. Open a new spreadsheet by choosing Spreadsheet from the New Document list or by choosing New from the File menu.
2. Click in the cell where you wish to begin and start typing. Your information will appear in the data entry area at the top of the spreadsheet.
3. When you are finished, press the Return key, or click on the accept button. Your information will now appear in the actual spreadsheet.

Editing data

You change data either by reentering the data in the data entry area or by editing individual characters of the text or numbers in the data entry area.

1. Click in the cell you want to change, then click in the data entry area.
2. Make your changes, and then press the Return key, or click on the Accept button.

Erasing cell contents

1. Click in the cell you want to erase.
2. Choose Cut from the Edit menu, or press ⌘-x.

Moving around

To move around quickly, use the Go To command.

1. Choose the Go To Cell command from the Options menu, or press ⌘-G.
2. Type the column and row, or cell address, in the Go To Cell At Address box.
3. Press the Return key or click on the OK button.

Note: Remember that cells have an address that consists of the column letter (for example C) and the row (for example 113). In that instance, the cell address would be C113—with no spaces between the column and row designators.

■ Resizing columns and rows

Changing column widths

Text and numbers should be able to fit within one column width. Often what is typed is too wide to fit in the default width. You can resize columns easily.

1. Move the pointer to the the right-hand line of the column you wish to change. When your pointer is exactly on top of the right-hand line, your pointer will appear as a double-headed arrow.
2. Drag the double-headed arrow to the right or left to widen or narrow the column. You will see a ghost line of how wide or narrow your column will be while you are dragging.
3. When the column looks like the width is correct, let go of the mouse.

If you see pound signs (#), it means the column needs to be widened in order to display all of the data.

The Go To Cell dialog box

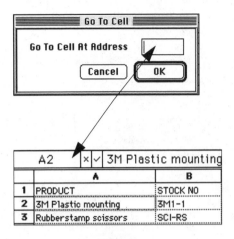

Position the pointer at the top of the document just to the right of the column you want to change. When the pointer is in the correct position, you will see this unique pointer.

B ↔	C
STOCK NO	QUANTITY
3M1-1	100
SCI-RS	24
EM01COL	48
EM02XOL	24
EM04COL	24

Notice the faint line that indicates where the new column margin will be and the existing line, which does not really move until the mouse button is released.

Amou	On Account/Paid
###	$100.00
###	$100.00
###	$100.00
###	$0.00
###	$300.00

Row 2 has been deepened to accommodate extra text. The text will not automatically wrap to fill this cell. For instructions on how to create a text-wrap within a cell, see "Creating text wrap within a cell" on page 105.

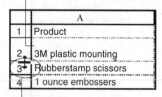

When you resize a row or column, you will see a double-sided pointer. If you continue dragging up for rows, or to the left for columns, the row or column will become hidden from view.

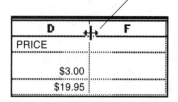

In this example, row 5 appears to be missing because it has been hidden from view. The example below has a hidden column E with the pointer positioned to uncover column E.

D		F
PRICE		
$3.00		
$19.95		

Resizing rows

You can make a row deeper in much the same way you resize a column.

1. Move the pointer to the line indicating the bottom of the row you wish to change. When your pointer is exactly on top of that line, you will see a double-headed arrow.

2. Drag the double-headed arrow up to shorten the row or down to make the row deeper. You will see a ghosted line showing how deep your row will be.

3. When the row is the correct depth, let go of the mouse button.

Hiding columns and rows

If you drag to the left far enough when resizing a column, or up enough when resizing a row, the column or row will be hidden.

To bring back a hidden column or row:

1. Move the pointer to the column or row divider where that column or row appears to be missing.

2. Drag to the right to unhide a column or drag down to unhide a row.

3. Let go of the mouse when the column or row is the correct size.

Resizing columns and rows

Creating text wrap within a cell

1. Make sure you have clicked once in the cell that contains the text you want to wrap. Make the row deep enough to accommodate the text you wish to wrap using the steps on the previous page in Resizing rows.

2. Choose Alignment from the Format menu.

3. Choose Wrap from the Alignment submenu. Your text will now be wrapped in the column, but you may need to make that row deeper to accommodate everything.

Cell A2 has a large amount of text in it. You can see this text in the data entry area. The cell is deeper than the other rows, but not deep enough to see all of the text in the spreadsheet itself.

| A2 | ×✓ | 3M Plastic mounting which is really fantastic, super-sticky mounting material |

	A	B	C	D	F	G	H	
1	PRODUCT	STOCK NO		QUANTITY	EXTENSION			
2	3M Plastic mounting which is	3M1-1		100	$300.00			
3	Rubber stamp scissors	SCI-RS		24	$479.80			

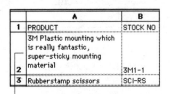

	A	B
1	PRODUCT	STOCK NO
2	3M Plastic mounting which is really fantastic, super-sticky mounting material	3M1-1
3	Rubber stamp scissors	SCI-RS

This is cell A2 after the wrap was corrected and the cell was made deep enough for all of the text.

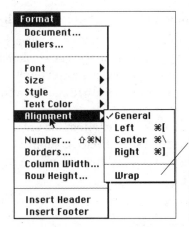

The Wrap command from the Alignment submenu in the Format menu will make your text wrap in the selected cell. General alignment means just let the text align the way it naturally should—in the case of numbers, the text will align on the right-hand side of the cell, while text will align on the left-hand side of the cell.

Spreadsheet ranges

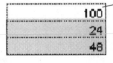

Type of range	Example
Single cell	A1
Row	A1..AH1
Column	A1..A500
Block of cells	A1..C5

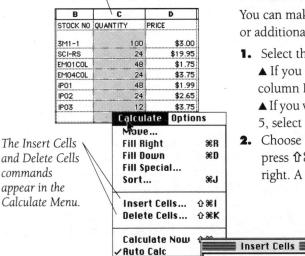

The first cell you select has a heavy border around it. The other cells will be highlighted.

✔ **Tip**: *This column has been selected the easy way—click once in the area where the column alphabetic designator appears and the entire column will be selected.*

The Insert Cells and Delete Cells commands appear in the Calculate Menu.

■ Selecting ranges

Before you begin adding columns or rows or changing information, you must know how to select areas on the spreadsheet.

Selecting an area is called selecting a range. Ranges are used to:

▲ Block and highlight information in order to change the font, font size, or font color; add borders and add fills; or make other appearance changes.

▲ Create addition formulas that add up a range of information, such as adding all of the information between and including cells A1 to A15.

1. To select a range, begin by placing the pointer in the upper left-hand corner of the area. You will see a heavy border around that cell.

2. Drag to the left for more columns and down to include more rows.

3. Let go of the mouse when you reach the last cell in the range you want to select.

■ Adding columns and rows

You can make more individual cells, new columns, or additional rows. The procedure is the same.

1. Select the cells you wish to move.

▲ If you wish to make a new column where column B is now, select column B.

▲ If you wish to add a row in between rows 4 and 5, select row 5.

2. Choose Insert Cells from the Calculate menu, or press ⇧⌘-I. A selected column will move to the right. A selected row will move down.

Use Shift Cells Down to create a new row.
Use Shift Cells Right to create a new column.

■ Moving columns and rows

When you move columns or rows, make sure you don't try to move them on top of existing ones. Moving does not automatically shift cells over and create a new row—it overwrites information—so be very careful.

1. Select the column or row you wish to move, and choose Move from the Calculate menu. The Move dialog box will appear.

2. Type the first cell at the top of a column or at the right of a row where you want the new data to be moved.

3. Click on the OK button.

Copying information

You can make copies of single cells, entire rows, entire columns, or ranges of information.

To copy information

1. Select the cell, row, column, or block you wish to copy.

2. Drag to the left and down until all of the cells are selected.

3. Choose Copy from the Edit menu, or press ⌘-**c**.

4. Click in the first cell where you want the copy to appear.

5. Choose Paste from the Edit menu, or press ⌘-**v**.

If you want to move column C to column F, in the Move Selected Cell(s) To box, type F1.

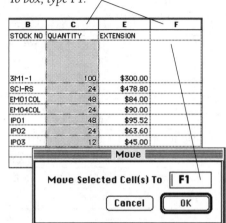

✔ **Tip**: *To select an entire range, click in the upper left-hand cell, (for example cell A1), hold the Shift key down, and click in the lower right-hand cell, (for example cell C5).*

✔ **Tip**: *You can copy formulas and the formulas will automatically create the correct cell references without your having to edit each individual formula.*

This spreadsheet has cells A1..C5 selected as a range. Start with the mouse in cell A1, then drag over to cell C1 and down to cell C5.

	A	B	C	E
1	PRODUCT	STOCK NO	QUANTITY	EXTENSION
2	3M Plastic mounting which is really fantastic, super-sticky mounting material			
	3M1-1		100	$300.00
3	Rubber stamp scissors	SCI-RS	24	$478.80
4	1 ounce embossers	EM01COL	48	$84.00
5	2 ounce embossers	EM02XOL	24	$60.00
6	4 ounce embossers	EM04COL	24	$90.00
7	Small ink pads	IP01	48	$95.52
8	Medium ink pads	IP02	24	$63.66

Step 1—Click here in the upper left-hand corner of the range.

Step 2—Hold the Shift key down and click here in the lower right-hand corner of the range.

Types of fill data

Type of fill	Example
Number	1, 2, 3, 4
Time	8:00 am, 9:00 am
Date	January 1, January 2, January 3
Day	Monday, Tuesday, Wednesday, Thursday
Month	January, February, March, April, May
Quarter	Qtr 1, Qtr 2, Qtr 3
Pattern of your choice	

Filling cells with data automatically

You can fill cells with sequential information by using a fill command. This works kind of like Copy, but increases the information on each subsequent cell.

For example, you can fill cells with times such as 8:00 am, 9:00 am, 10:00 am, and so on. Or you can use textual information such as Monday, Tuesday, Wednesday, etc. You won't have to type any of this information in; the fill command will type it for you.

Creating fill data

1. Select the range of cells you want to automatically fill with information.

2. Choose Fill Special from the Calculate menu.

3. Click on the radio button for the type of fill you want to use.

4. Press the Return key or click on the OK button.

The Fill Special dialog box has seven radio buttons that give you fill choices such as Date, Day, and Month.

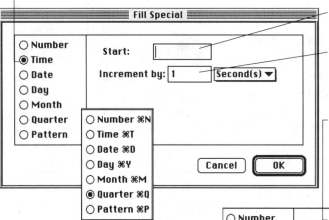

The Start box is where you type the value for the first cell.

The Increment by box is where you type how much each fill entry is to be increased in subsequent cells.

The Start by box turns into a pop-up menu when you select Month from the Fill Special dialog box. To make a selection in that menu, scroll to your choice and release the mouse. ˙

Some radio button choices give you additional choices to make. For the Month radio button, you must choose a style for the months: Full, Abbreviate, or Initial.

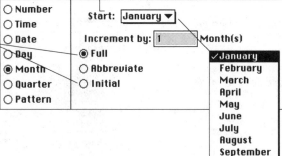

Fill Down and Fill special

These two commands are most closely related to the Copy command. They copy information from part of the spreadsheet and fill a selected area with that information.

Filling down

1. Select the cell that has the information you wish to copy and continue highlighting the range of cells you want to have filled with this information.

2. Choose Fill Down from the Calculate menu.

Filling with a pattern

1. Highlight the cell or range of cells you want to have automatically filled with information.

2. Choose Fill Special from the Calculate menu.

3. Click on the Pattern radio button.

4. In the Pattern box, type the data you want to have repeated in each of your highlighted cells.

5. Click on the OK button.

The example on the left was filled using Fill Special. The example above was filled using Fill Down.

■ Formatting the spreadsheet

You can change the text font and the number appearance, add borders or fills to cells, and copy formatting commands to other areas of the spreadsheet.

Formatting the document

Formatting a document lets you change margins and change the size of the spreadsheet itself. Remember that the default size of the spreadsheet is 40 columns and 500 rows—but you can make your spreadsheet much larger.

1. Choose Document from the Format menu. The Document dialog box will appear.

2. In the Size box, type in how many columns and rows you want.

3. Click on the OK button.

The Document dialog box allows you to change margins, number of columns, and number of rows.

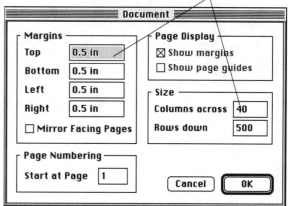

Formatting the spreadsheet

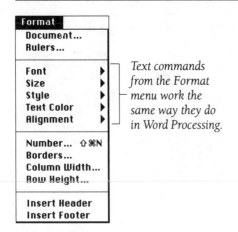

Text commands from the Format menu work the same way they do in Word Processing.

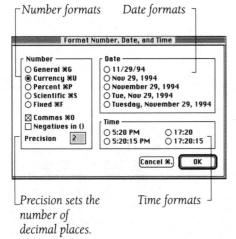

Row 1 needed to be deeper once the text size was increased.

Number formats   Date formats

Precision sets the number of decimal places.

Time formats

Formatting text

The Format menu contains all of the controls for text and justification. The controls include:

▲ Font
▲ Size of the font
▲ Style, such as bold, underline, or outline
▲ Text Color
▲ Alignment

Changing text formatting

1. Select the cells that have text you want to change.
2. Select one of the following options from the Format menu.

▲ Font
▲ Size
▲ Style
▲ Text Color
▲ Alignment

3. Choose the options you wish to use in the submenu that appears. Check and make sure that your columns are wide enough and your rows are deep enough to accommodate any font changes.

Formatting numbers

The appearance of numbers is set by the Format menu, which adds such characteristics as dollar signs, commas, and decimal places.

1. Select the cell, column, row, or range of cells that you want to change.
2. Choose Number from the Format menu, or press ⇧⌘-N.
3. Click on the radio button of your choice from the Number, Date, and Time sections in the Format Number, Date, and Time dialog box.
4. If you have selected Number, type how many decimal points you need in the Precision box.
5. Click on the OK button when you are finished.

Formatting the spreadsheet

Setting a default font

The default font is the font that the spreadsheet uses automatically. You can always change fonts by using the Format menu, but you can also change the default font for the spreadsheet.

1. Choose Default Font from the Options menu.

2. Select the font you want to use from the Font scrolling list in the Default Font dialog box.

3. Type in the size you want to use in the Size box.

4. Click on the OK button.

Options
Make Chart...   ⌘M
Lock Cells   ⌘H
Unlock Cells   ⇧⌘H
Add Page Break
Remove Page Break
Remove All Breaks
Lock Title Position
Set Print Range...
Default Font...
Display...
Go To Cell...   ⌘G

The Default Font command on the Options menu is where you change the default font for the entire spreadsheet.

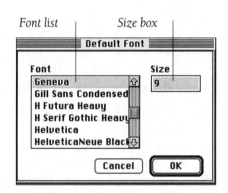

Font list   Size box

The Copy Format and Paste Format commands will transfer cell attributes.

Copying formats from cell to cell

Once you have a cell looking the way you want it to look, you can copy the attributes, such as font, font size, number format, date or time formats, and alignment.

Copy Format   ⇧⌘C
Paste Format   ⇧⌘V
Paste Special...
Paste Function...

1. Click in the cell that has formats you want to use.

2. Choose Copy Format from the Edit menu, or press ⇧⌘-c.

3. Select the cell or range of cells that you want to use the format in.

4. Choose Paste Format from the Edit menu, or press ⇧⌘-v.

Formatting the spreadsheet

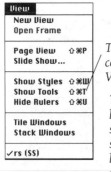

The Show Tools command in the View menu

The show/hide tools button resembles a small sketch of the spreadsheet with a tool bar area at the left-hand side of the bottom bar.

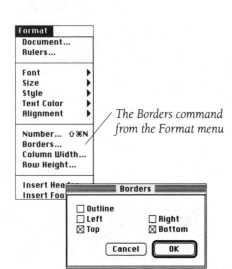

The Borders command from the Format menu

The Borders dialog box

■ Adding borders

You can add borders to an individual cell, range of cells, or the entire spreadsheet. Before you add borders, make sure you can see the tool bar on the left-hand side of the spreadsheet.

Showing the tool bar

▲ Choose Show Tools from the View menu, or press ⇧⌘-T; or click on the show/hide tools button at the bottom of the ClarisWorks screen.

Tools do not automatically appear when you are in the Spreadsheet mode. You must either choose to view them from the View menu, or choose them from the show/hide tools button at the bottom of the screen.

Creating a border

1. Select the cell, row, column, or range that you wish to give borders.
2. Choose Borders from the Format menu. A Borders dialog box then appears.
3. Click on one of the five following choices:
   ▲ Outline—outlines your selection including the top, bottom, left, and right part of the selection.
   ▲ Left or Right —places a border on the left or right part of the selection.
   ▲ Top or Bottom—places a border on the top or bottom line of the selection.
4. Click on the OK button when you are finished.
5. In the tool box, choose the pen color palette and click on a color.

Note: You cannot change the thickness of the border. It appears as a slightly heavier line, but the solid pattern of the line and the thickness of the line will always appear the same.

Removing a border

1. Select the area that has the border, and choose Borders from the Format menu.
2. Click in any of the checkboxes that contain a check mark.
3. Click on the OK button when you are finished.

Adding color and patterns

1. Highlight the area of the spreadsheet you with to fill with a color or pattern.
2. Choose the color or pattern from the fill color or fill pattern tool box.

■ Changing the screen appearance

Spreadsheets can appear with any of the following elements:

▲ Grid lines—the dotted or solid lines that show the borders of cells, rows, and columns

▲ Column and row headings—the alphabetic and numeric designators that tell you which column and row you are in

▲ Formula results or the actual formulas

▲ Circular references—solid dots in a cell indicating your formula is incorrect

Changing screen options

1. Choose Display from the Options menu. You will see a Display dialog box.
2. Click on the checkboxes that contain display options you wish to use.
3. Click on the OK button when you are finished.

The color and fill pattern tools will work with spreadsheets, but the gradation tool will not.

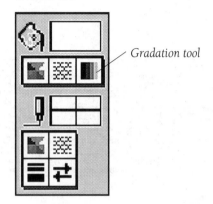

Gradation tool

✔ **Tip**: *To keep a record of your spreadsheet formulas, click on the checkbox labeled Formulas. When you print out the spreadsheet, print one copy with the formulas exposed and another copy with the checkbox deselected so you can see the results of the formulas.*

Display

☒ Cell grid	☒ Column headings
☐ Solid lines	☒ Row headings
☐ Formulas	☒ Mark circular refs

[Cancel] [OK]

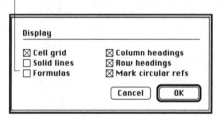

The top box shows the normal spreadsheet with formula results. The bottom box shows the spreadsheet with the Formulas option checked in the Display dialog box.

| 100 | $3.00 | $300.00 |
| 24 | $19.95 | $478.80 |

| 100 | $3.00 | =SUM(C2*D2) |
| 24 | $19.95 | =SUM(C3*D3) |

▪ **Shortcuts**

Just like the other ClarisWorks modes, Spreadsheets has its own Shortcuts palette that includes both the standard shortcut buttons and the special spreadsheet shortcut buttons.

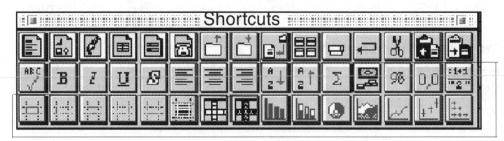

The Shortcuts palette contains some shortcuts that work with all program modes. These shortcuts are on the top row of the palette, and the first eight tools on the second row. The balance of the tools work only with spreadsheets.

 Sort ascending

 Sort descending

 Auto sum—adds up a column

 Currency format

 Percent format

 Comma format

 Show/hide formulas

 Outline border

 Left border

 Top border

 Right border

 Bottom border

 Align wrap

 Insert cells

 Delete cells

 Bar chart

 Stacked bar chart

 Pie chart

 Area chart

 Line chart

 Hi-low chart

 Pictogram chart

■ Math

You can use simple algebraic formulas or more complicated functional formulas to perform math in spreadsheets.

Entering simple formulas

Simple formulas use the designator "=" just before the formula itself.

This is a simple formula typed in the data entry area at the top of the spreadsheet.

1. To enter a simple formula, first decide which cells contain the information you need to perform math, then click in the cell where you want the results to appear.
2. Click in the data entry area at the top of the spreadsheet where the formula is entered.
3. Type an equal (=) sign and then type the formula. Refer to the examples in the table called Simple formulas at the bottom of this page.
4. Press the Return key or click on the Accept button which appears as a check mark just to the left of the data entry area.

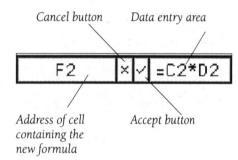

Cancel button   *Data entry area*

Address of cell containing the new formula   *Accept button*

Simple formulas

Example	How it is typed	Mathematical operator	What it means
Multiply two cells together. For example: cells C2 and C3	=C2*C3	Asterisk or *	Multiply
Add one or more cells together. For example: add cells C2, C3, and C4	=C2+C3+C4	Plus sign or +	Addition
Subtract two cells. For example: C3 subtracted from cell C2	=C2-C3	Subtraction or - (hyphen)	Subtraction
Divide two cells. For example, C2 divided by C3	=C2/C3	Division or / (back slash)	Division
Multiply real numbers by cells. For example: cell C2 by .085 (the California sales tax expressed in decimals)	=C2*.085	You can use both cell references and real numbers in simple and functional formulas. This is a common example that shows multiplying a cell containing information (C2) times the figure for the state sales tax (.085 or 8 1/2%).	

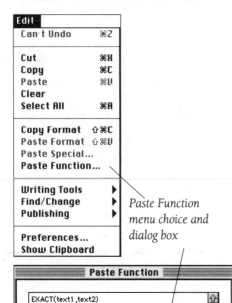

Paste Function menu choice and dialog box

✔ **Tip**: *To move to a functional formula more quickly, as soon as the dialog box appears, type the first letter of the name of the formula. For example, for the functional formula SUM, type an "s." This will move you to all formulas that start with an "s."*

Data entry area containing the Sum formula with range

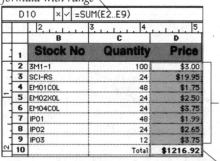

Selected range

Cell containing the formula and results

■ Functional formulas

Functional formulas are formulas that are already made up for you to use. The categories of functional formulas include:

▲ Business/financial   ▲ Numeric/algebraic

▲ Date and time   ▲ Statistical

▲ Informational   ▲ Text

▲ Logical   ▲ Trigonometric

Entering a functional formula: SUM

SUM is a general formula that can be used to rapidly add up a column of information or can work with more complex algebraic expressions.

1. Choose Paste Function from the Edit menu. You will see a Paste Function dialog box.
2. Scroll down the list in the Paste Function dialog box until you see SUM(number1,number2,...) and click on the SUM formula.
3. Click on the OK button, or double-click on the SUM formula. The SUM formula now appears in the data entry area.
4. To add up a column or a range in your spreadsheet, highlight the range of numbers you want to add together. These numbers appear inside of the SUM formula along with some information you will not need.
5. To erase the unnecessary information, select the comma after your numbers and the phrase "number2,..." and tap the Clear key.
6. Press the Return key or click on the Accept button to the left of the data entry area. The answer for your formula will appear in the cell that contains the formula.

Some examples of formulas that will work with the Sum functional formula include:

=SUM(C2*C3)/2

=SUM((C2+C3)*(D2+D3))

Notice how parentheses are used to set off or separate the various elements of the math itself. Operations in the innermost set of parentheses are performed first.

Functional formulas

Following are two examples of types of functional formulas. These models should help you understand how to fill in the blanks as required for various types of formulas.

Entering a functional formula: IF

IF is a logical functional formula that is entered a little differently than the Sum formula. IF is made up of logical statements—the formula looks at a cell, then evaluates that cell on a set of conditions. Depending on the results, IF can print text or numbers that express whether or not the conditions were true.

1. Click in the cell where you want the results of the formula to be displayed.
2. Choose Paste Function from the Edit menu.
3. Scroll down the list in the Paste Function dialog box until you see IF (logical, true-value, false-value) and double-click on that formula.
4. In the data entry area at the top of the spreadsheet, the logical portion of the formula is selected. Type in the address of the cell you want to be evaluated and the conditions. In the sample to the right, I examined cell E2 to see if it was greater than zero.
5. Select the true-value portion of the formula and type what you want to have displayed if, in this case, the number is greater than zero. You can display either text or numbers.
6. Select the false-value portion of the formula and type in what you want to have displayed if the logical condition is false.
7. Press the Return key or click on the Accept button when you are finished.

This is the Help screen's explanation of IF. The Format section tells you how the formula is supposed to be typed in the data entry area. The term logical refers to the area of the spreadsheet you want to evaluate. The terms true value and false value refer to the answers you want to appear once the cell is evaluated.

> Determines whether a value or logical expression is zero (FALSE) or nonzero (TRUE) and returns the value in true-value or false-value.
>
> **Format**: IF (logical, true-value, false-value)

This use of the IF function looks at cell E2 and decides if this cell is greater than zero.

| F2 | ✕ ✓ | =IF(E2>0,"DUE","PAID") |

The first item after the comma is the answer for the true-value. Since it is text, you need to enclose the text in double-quotes. The second item is the answer for the false value. Notice that the entire contents of the formula are enclosed in parentheses and no spaces are typed between parts of the formula.

	A	B	C	D	E	F
1	Customer	Invoice No	Amount	On Account/Paid	Balance due	
2	Glen Cohn	4317	$125.00	$100.00	$25.00	DUE
3	Martha Molinez	4318	$127.60	$100.00	$27.60	DUE
4	Janna White	4319	$100.00	$100.00	$0.00	PAID
5	Ted Burkhardt	4320	$35.00	$0.00	$35.00	DUE
6	Glenda Leeson	4321	$289.93	$300.00	-$10.07	PAID

E	F
Balance due	
$25.00	DUE
$27.60	DUE
$0.00	PAID
$35.00	DUE
-$10.07	CREDIT

=IF(E6>0,"DUE",IF(E6<0,"CREDIT"," "))

I got a little fancy here. Here we need to look at three conditions, so the false value portion of the formula becomes yet another IF formula.

Compare the values in column E to understand what the IF formula is actually evaluating. The results of the evaluation are in column F.

Functional formulas

Calculates payments given the interest rate, number of periods, preset value, future value, and type of payment.

Format: PMT (rate,nper,pv{, fv}{, type})

For a complete list and additional information on functional formulas, see Appendix A, Functional Formulas, on page 227.

Using the payment formula

Payment is a convenient business and financial formula that figures out how much payments will be on a given amount of money. To use this formula you need to know:

▲ The interest rate per year

▲ The number of payments per year and number of years for the loan

▲ The amount of money involved

The interest rate is 9%, so in the rate area, to convert that interest rate to a monthly rate, 9% is divided by 12. If the payments are going to be monthly, the interest must be a monthly interest rate, not a yearly rate.

The loan amount is $15,000 and appears last.

C9   × ✓ =PMT(0.09/12,3*12,15000)

-$477.00

Here is the answer: $477.00. One peculiarity of this formula is that the answer comes out as a negative number.

The payments are going to be monthly for three years. In the period area, the number of months is multiplied by the number of years. You could also just enter the number 36.

Entering the PMT formula

1. Click in the cell where you want the answer to appear.

2. Choose Paste Function from the Edit menu.

3. Select the PMT function from the Paste Function dialog box.

4. The first part of the formula, rate, requires you to enter the interest rate divided by 12 if you want to figure out monthly payments. Enter the interest rate divided by 12 in this area by selecting rate and typing the correct number.

5. The second part of the formula, nper, or number of periods, requires you to enter the number of monthly payments in this area by selecting nper and typing the correct number.

6. The third part of the formula, pv, or present value is where you enter the total amount of money by selecting pv and typing in the correct number.

7. Press the Return key when finished or click on the Accept button. The answer appears in the cell you clicked in step 1.

✔ **Tip**: *There are four possible error messages you can receive if you type a formula incorrectly. They are #VALUE!, #DIV/0!, #REF!, and bold dots that indicate the formula is a circular reference or the formula contains an improper cell reference to itself. If this happens, go back and check the cells and ranges used in the formula.*

● $ 35.00 ● ● DUE ●

These bold dots indicate something is wrong with the formulas that are in these two cells.

Functional formulas

Using help with functional formulas

Help will give you the details on all functional formulas and also will give you a list of the categories and formulas that appear in each category.

Using help with formulas

1. Hold down the ⌘ (Command) key and tap the question mark.
2. In the Keyword box of the ClarisWorks Help dialog box, type the word functions. You will see a list of topics.
3. In the ClarisWorks Help list, double-click on the word Functions. You will see a list of categories.
4. Double-click on any of the categories to see the list of formulas for that category.
5. Double-click on the formula you need information about.
6. To leave Help, click in the close box.

Help Keyword box

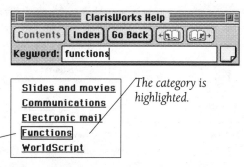

The category is highlighted.

Functional formulas

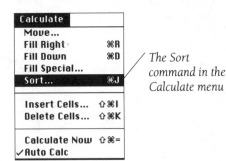

The Sort command in the Calculate menu

■ Sorting the spreadsheet

If you want to reorganize the rows or columns of data in your spreadsheet, you sort the information. You can sort vertically or rearrange rows, or sort horizontally, which rearranges the columns from left to right using sort.

Sort requires you to select a cell that you want to sort by, and this cell is called the first sort order key. You can also sort by additional cells. For example, if you wanted to rearrange your information so that it was in order by state, then within the states, in order by the name of the city you would need two keys, one for the state and one for the city.

The column labeled Invoice No., or column B, has been chosen as the column to sort on. This means the rows are going to be arranged in invoice number order.

Don't include the column headings or they will be included in the sort. Rearranging the rows of the spreadsheet is called a vertical sort.

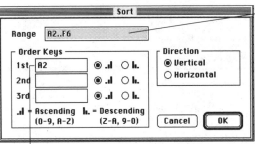

Customer	Invoice No	Amount	On Account/Paid	Balance due	
Glenda Leeson	4321	$289.93	$300.00	-$10.07	CREDIT
Glen Cohn	4317	$125.00	$100.00	$25.00	DUE
Martha Molinez	4318	$127.60	$100.00	$27.60	DUE
Ted Burkhardt	4320	$35.00	$0.00	$35.00	DUE
Janna White	4319	$100.00	$100.00	$0.00	paid

In order to rearrange the spreadsheet correctly, the Range box must include all of the cells in the spreadsheet except for the column headings.

Sort

Range A2..F6

Order Keys
1st A2   ⦿ .ıl ○ lı.   Direction
2nd   ⦿ .ıl ○ lı.   ⦿ Vertical
3rd   ⦿ .ıl ○ lı.   ○ Horizontal

.ıl = Ascending   lı. = Descending
(0-9, A-Z)   (Z-A, 9-0)   [Cancel] [OK]

The first sort order key should show only one cell in the column you want to sort by.

Creating a sort by row

1. Click in the the column that contains the information you wish to sort by.
2. Choose Sort from the Calculate menu, or press **⌘-J**.
3. Type the Range for the entire spreadsheet in the Sort dialog box—but do not include any column headings in that range.
4. In the Order Keys, type the address of a single cell in the column you want to sort by.
5. Click on the Ascending or Descending radio buttons to change the sort order.
6. Make sure the Direction radio button is set to Vertical. Horizontal will move the columns from left to right. Vertical sorts out the rows.
7. Click on the OK button when you are finished.

Sorting the spreadsheet

■ Charts and graphs

You can display the spreadsheet information in a variety of charts and graphs including:

- ▲ Bar
- ▲ Area
- ▲ Line
- ▲ Scatter
- ▲ Pie
- ▲ Pictogram

- ▲ Stacked bar
- ▲ Stacked area
- ▲ X-Y line
- ▲ X-Y scatter
- ▲ Hi-low
- ▲ Stacked pictogram

You also have a variety of options available with each chart form including:

- ▲ Adding color to the chart
- ▲ Making a chart horizontal
- ▲ Creating a shadow contrast
- ▲ Three-dimensional charts

Creating a simple bar chart

1. Select the range of the spreadsheet that contains the information you want to have charted.
2. Choose Make Chart from the Options menu, or press ⌘-M.
3. Click on the picture of the bar chart in the Chart Options dialog box.
4. To turn the bars horizontally, select the checkbox labeled Horizontal at the bottom of the Chart Options dialog box.
5. Click on the OK button when you are finished.

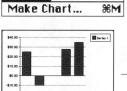

Use the Make Chart command to create graphics based on the spreadsheet data.

Charts and graphs

Axes—lets you label the X axis, or the bottom of the chart, and the Y axis, or the side of the chart.

Series—refers to the columns of numbers that contain the data.

Labels—gives you a way of labeling each individual bar in the chart.

General—sets general preferences such as row data or column data.

Choose your chart style from the Gallery options.

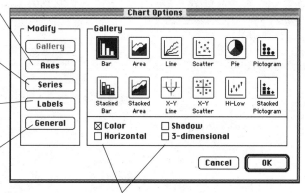

Choose enhancements such as color or three-dimensions from the checkboxes.

Enhancing your chart

You can set enhancements in the Chart Options dialog box before you click on the OK button, or you can double-click on the chart to make changes.

Some of the options work best with series of data. A series can be two or more columns of information. Each column is considered one series. A series can also be two or more rows of information, with each row being a separate series of data.

There are the checkbox options of the Chart Options dialog box. Add any of these enhancements to your chart simply by clicking in the checkbox you wish to use.

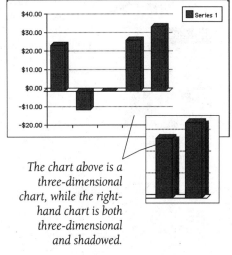

The chart above is a three-dimensional chart, while the right-hand chart is both three-dimensional and shadowed.

Making changes

1. Double-click anywhere inside of an already created chart and the Chart Options dialog box appears.
2. Select the Chart Options that you want to use such as checkbox options, or the Axes, Series, Labels, and General buttons.
3. To change the chart type, simply click on the chart of your choice in the Chart Options dialog box.

Using the checkbox options

1. Color—click in the Color checkbox to change the bars of your bar chart or slices of your pie chart to color. There will be one color for each series of data.
2. Shadow—click in the Shadow checkbox to place a small shadow beside and behind the bars or behind the circles of a pie chart. This option looks best with three-dimensional charts.
3. Horizontal—Click on the Horizontal checkbox to turn the chart horizontally so bars will be extending across the page.
4. 3-dimensional—Click in the 3-dimensional checkbox to change bars and pie charts so they display in three-dimensions.

Charts and graphs

Working with Axes options

Axes options include creating titles for the X axis (bottom of the chart) or Y axis (side of the chart), adding a grid, and changing the steps of the Y axis data. To work with Axes options:

1. Double-click in an already created chart.
2. Click on the Axes button to see the Axis section of the Chart Options dialog box.
3. Select any of the changes you wish to make.
4. Click on the OK button when you are finished.

✔ **Tip**: *You can move to the Axes, Series, or Labels menus by double-clicking directly on the area you want to change. For example, if you want to change the Axes options, click directly on some of the Y axis data.*

Click on the X or Y axis radio buttons then type a title in the Axis label box.

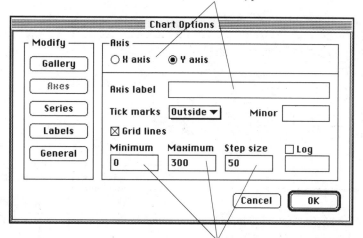

Minimum and Maximum set the range of numbers for the X axis. Step size sets the increments in which the data will be displayed.

Maximum number

Step—or data—increment, which is 50 in this example.

Maximum number

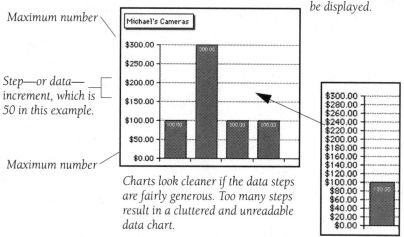

Charts look cleaner if the data steps are fairly generous. Too many steps result in a cluttered and unreadable data chart.

Charts and graphs

Working with Series options

Series options include the option of labeling the bars with the actual figures from the spreadsheets. You can position the labels anywhere on the bars themselves or within a pie chart slice.

1. Double-click on an already created chart.
2. Click on the Series button to see the Series section of the Chart Options dialog box, and click on any of the changes you wish to make.
3. Click on the OK button when you are finished.

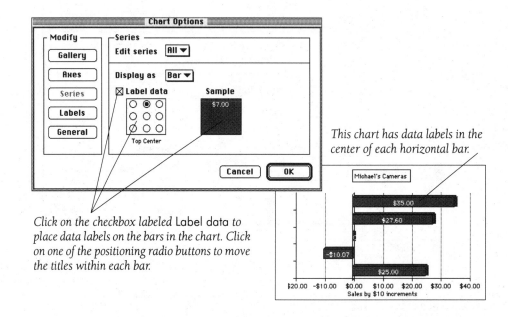

This chart has data labels in the center of each horizontal bar.

Click on the checkbox labeled Label data *to place data labels on the bars in the chart. Click on one of the positioning radio buttons to move the titles within each bar.*

Charts and graphs

Working with Labels options

The Labels button in the Chart Options dialog box
presents options such as titles of the chart and titles
of the series legend. Use these to set the options and
position any labels you wish to use.

1. Double-click on an already created chart.

2. Click on the Labels button to see the Labels
section of the Chart Options dialog
box, and click on any of the changes you wish
to make.

3. Click on the OK button when you are finished.

*Type a title for the entire chart in the Title box.
Use the Horizontal and Shadow checkboxes for
additional enhancements.*

A shadow title

*Use the positioning buttons
to move the title and legend
around on the chart.*

*The Legend options are exactly the
same as the Title options.*

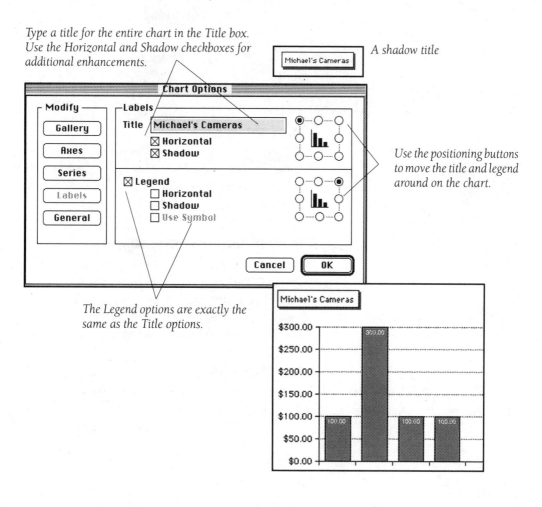

Charts and graphs

Options

Make Chart...	⌘M
Lock Cells	⌘H
Unlock Cells	⇧⌘H
Add Page Break	
Remove Page Break	
Remove All Breaks	
Lock Title Position	
Set Print Range...	
Default Font...	
Display...	
Go To Cell...	⌘G

The Lock Title Position command is in the Options menu.

■ Locking titles

If you are creating an exceptionally long or wide spreadsheet that cannot be displayed entirely on the screen, you can lock the row and column titles so you will at least see the headings and row labels.

Creating locking titles

1. Highlight the column titles or row titles you wish to lock into position.
2. Choose Lock Title Position from the Options menu. You can now scroll back and forth or up and down and you will always see your titles.

	A	B	C	D	E	F
1	Customer	Invoice No	Amount	On Account	Balance due	
2	Glen Cohn	4317	$125.00	$100.00	$25.00	DUE
3	Glenda Leeson	4321	$289.93	$300.00	-$10.07	CREDIT
4	Janna White	4319	$100.00	$100.00	$0.00	PAID
5	Martha Molinez	4318	$127.60	$100.00	$27.60	DUE
6	Ted Burkhardt	4320	$35.00	$0.00	$35.00	DUE

	A	B
1	Customer	Invoice No
32	Glen Cohn	4317
33	Glenda Leeson	4321
34	Janna White	4319
35	Martha Molinez	4318
36	Ted Burkhardt	4320

Unlocking titles

To unlock the titles, simply follow the instructions above. Instead of saying Lock Title Position, your menu will read Unlock Title Position.

■ Preventing changes

You can prevent changes to your work by locking the cells. You might want to do this to part of a spreadsheet if you have set up a spreadsheet that does calculations and you have an inexperienced employee doing data entry in that spreadsheet.

Locking a cell

1. Select the cells that you want to be sure aren't accidentally changed.
2. Choose Lock Cells from the Options menu, or press ⌘-s.

Unlocking cells

1. Select the cells that you want unlock.
2. Choose Unlock Cells from the Options menu, or press ⇧⌘-H.

■ Printing

If you want to print a spreadsheet, you can't just issue a Print command—you will have to select the area of the spreadsheet you want to print first. Remember that spreadsheets can be very long and wide—even longer and wider than the computer paper.

Creating page breaks

Spreadsheets are set up to print on 8 1/2" by 11" paper. You can add manual page breaks if you want to separate some information out.

1. Select the row where you want the page break to occur.

2. Choose Add Page Break from the Options menu. You can also set page breaks to occur by selecting a column. This will limit the width of the final printed page.

A page break appears as a slightly heavier dashed line. This page break was created by selecting the row containing the data for Martha Molinez.

8	Glenda Leeson	4321	$289.93
9	Janna White	4319	$100.00
10	Martha Molinez	4318	$127.60
11	Ted Burkhardt	4320	$35.00
12	Glen Cohn	4317	$125.00

Add Page Break
Remove Page Break
Remove All Breaks

✔ **Tip**: *Remember that the quick way to highlight a row or a column is to click in the row number or column letter designation area.*

Removing page breaks

1. Select the row or column that has the page break in it.

2. Choose the Remove Page Break command from the Options menu.

Removing all page breaks

▲ Choose the Remove All Breaks command from the Options menu.

Printing

Printing a spreadsheet

Before you print, you might want to set a few options that will make the results look better.

The Print Range dialog box contains two buttons. The Print All Cells With Data is the default setting and will print everything in the spreadsheet.

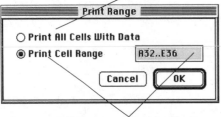

The Print Cell Range works with cells you have manually selected and prints only those cells.

1. Lock the titles so the titles of the rows and columns will print on every page. To see how to lock titles, refer to "Creating locking titles" on page 126.

2. If you do not want to print absolutely every cell that has information in it, select the data you do wish to print.

3. Choose Print Range from the Options menu. The Print Cell Range radio button should be selected and the information in the Print Cell Range box will show you what area of your spreadsheet you selected.

4. Click on the OK button.

Sending the spreadsheet to the printer

1. Choose Print selection from the File menu, or press ⌘-P.

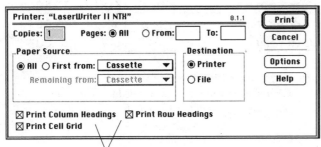

Use these three checkboxes to set various options for the final printout.

2. Click on any of the following checkboxes you wish to use when you print:
   ▲ Print Column Headings—this refers to the alphabetic designators at the top of the columns that name the column.
   ▲ Print Row Headings—this refers to the numeric designators at the left of the rows that name each row.
   ▲ Print Cell Grid—this will print the dotted outlines for the cells.

3. Click on the Print button when you have selected all of the options you wish to use.

Databases

■ What is a database?

You can think of a database as an organized collection of information like you might find in an address book. The collection itself is called a database, while information on an individual is called a record.

Each person in the address book is one record and each record has its own place for the name, address, city, state, zipcode, and telephone numbers. These individual places within a record are called fields.

■ Database fundamentals

There are three functional parts of any database that you must understand in order to construct a working database:

▲ Fields and field types
▲ Printed and on-screen reports
▲ Database actions such as sort and find

The entire entry is called a record. All of the entries are called a database.

In this simple example, each child on a little league team has an entry exactly like this. The entry for one child is a record. The individual pieces of information about that child (Parent's name, Little League Position, etc.) are fields. The entire collection of information is a database.

Los Altos Little League Roster

Parent's name	Wesley & JoAnna Logan
Child's name	Mark
Emergency phone number	415 123-1234
Little League Position	Shortstop
Street address	3131 El Camino Real
City	Palo Alto
Zip	97303

Individual fields in this sample are surrounded by a box.

Field types

Before you create your first database, you must understand something about field types, as the very first task you will have to accomplish is to set up fields and assign them a type.

There are thirteen basic field types:

▲ Text   ▲ Radio button
▲ Number   ▲ Check box
▲ Date   ▲ Serial number
▲ Time   ▲ Value list
▲ Name   ▲ Record information
▲ Pop-up   ▲ Calculations
                        ▲ Summary

Field types

Field type	Definition	
Text	Text is any number, character, or special symbol that does not require any math to be performed on it.	John Jones 415 777-7777 97501
Number	Number fields accept any type of numerical data and you can format them in any style, such as percent.	$43.95 627,000 .34 34%
Date	This field is used to enter the date in any date format you desire.	November 12, 1952 4/1/96
Time	Date fields and Time fields can be used to calculate spans of time, as in figuring out how many hours an employee worked from the time she arrived to the time she left.	23:10 11:10 10 pm :30
Name	Name fields are also text fields, but are designed to simplify sorting by coding entries so that data entered in this field will always sort by the last name instead of the first piece of text.	John M. Marshall J. D. Salinger
Pop-up	This field lets you create a list of items to choose from and places them on a pop-up menu.	

Field types, continued

Field type	Definition	
Radio button	Radio button fields are used to list options that you may select only one at a time. Selecting one radio button turns the others in a group off.	shipping ⊙ Federal express ○ UPS ○ Pickup ○ US mail ○ DHL ○ Other
Checkbox	Checkbox fields are used to indicate whether something is true or not, such as whether or not a box is checked for customers that want to be placed on a mailing list.	☐ Mailing list?
Serial number	Serial numbers are entered for each record starting with your initial value.	Record 1 1001 Record 2 1002
Value list	Value list creates a list of items which are displayed as a scrolling list that you can choose from when that field is displayed on the screen.	Regular price Regular price Sale Item Credit Item Special Offer
Record information	Record Information records when the individual data record was created by dating and time-stamping the record.	Date of entry 7/5/95
Calculation	Calculation fields use simple algebraic calculations or complex formulas that are the same as those in the Spreadsheet portion of ClarisWorks.	See illustration below.

Calculation field

This sample shows two numeric fields, Qty and Unit Price, followed by a Calculation field labeled Total Due. Total Due is a multiplication of the quantity times the unit price.

Summary	Summary fields are used to total calculation fields.	See illustration above.

Reports

Reports are the form in which databases are printed and displayed on the screen. In "Creating a report" on page 157, you will learn to create your own report.

The database screen

The database screen has several menus that help you access important functions such as sorting the database, copying information, creating reports, and editing and deleting data.

You also have a Rolodex that allows you to move from record to record and a record count box that will tell you how many total records are contained in your database.

The Database menu bar is similar to the Word Processing menu bar. File, Edit, and Format pop-up menus contain many of the same items.

Main database screen with a simple database

Pull-down menus

Rolodex

Current record

Total number of records
Sort indicator

Layout tool and Search tools
(Left to right)

Sort tool and
Report tools (Left to right)

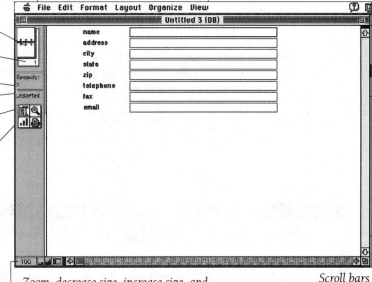

A note about total number of records

If two numbers appear, the first number will be the number of visible records. The second number will be in parentheses and will be the total number of records in the database.

Zoom, decrease size, increase size, and show/hide tools button

Scroll bars

Tool palette button detail

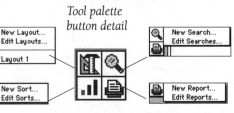

Database views

There are four basic views used when you want to look at database information:

▲ Browse

▲ Find

▲ Layout

▲ List

These views can be found on the Layout menu.

Layout	Organize	View
✓Browse		⇧⌘B
Find		⇧⌘F
Layout		⇧⌘L
List		⇧⌘I
Define Fields...		⇧⌘D
Insert Field...		
Insert Part...		
Tab Order...		
✓Show Multiple		
New Layout...		
Edit Layouts...		
✓Layout 1		

Notice the four views and the shortcut keys. These views are the main way you look at data or create reports for the screen or for printing.

Rolodex helps you move through your records

Browse shows the fields as they appear in the on-screen default layout—the first field on line one, the second field on line two, and so on.

Find helps you search for a record or a set of records.

Notice that the tools are different in this view and that there is now a Find button.

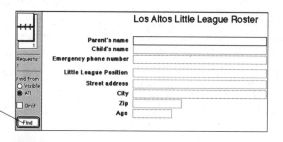

Layout helps you design on-screen forms that can be used for data entry or for printing or viewing reports.

In this view, you no longer see the information, you see where the fields are positioned

List places all of your fields in rows and columns as though they had been entered in a spread-sheet instead of a database.

Now the information is spread across the screen. You can see more entries this way.

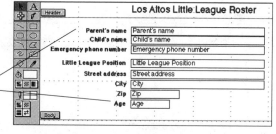

■ Creating a database

From the opening screen of ClarisWorks, you must select the Database program mode. You will then see the Define Database Fields dialog box.

When you create the database, make sure you know what fields and field types you are going to use, although you can go back later and add more fields or change field types.

Using the Define Database Fields dialog box

Field Type	✓Text
Delete	Number
	Date
it will hold from	Time
	Name
	Popup Menu
	Radio Buttons
	Check Box
	Serial Number
	Value List
	Record Info
	Calculation
	Summary

These are the field types listed in the Field Type pop-up menu in the Define Database Fields dialog box. The active field type has a check mark by it. If you change field types, you will receive a warning if your field contains data. If you proceed, your data could be erased.

1. Choose New from the File menu, and then click once on the Database dialog box choice.
2. In the Field Name box, type a short name for the field you want to create.
3. Choose the Field Type pop-up menu. You will see the list of ClarisWorks fields appear.
4. Scroll down through the list and select the type of field you want to use.
5. Click on the Create button.
6. Repeat steps 2 through 5 until you have created every field you need for the database.
7. When you are finished click on the Done button.

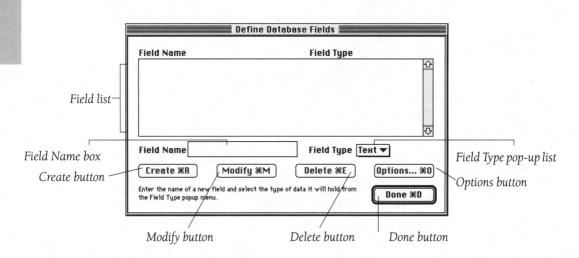

Field list — Field Name box — Create button — Modify button — Delete button — Done button — Field Type pop-up list — Options button

Entering data

When you finish setting up the database fields, you will be ready to enter data.

Entering data into your first record

1. Start typing in the first field.

2. When you are done typing in the first field, press the Tab key, or use the mouse to click in the next field.

3. When you want to start a new record, choose New Record from the Edit menu, or press ⌘-**R**.

4. When you are finished entering records, choose Save from the File menu, and give your database a name.

Entering compound names in name fields

Name fields naturally sort on the last word in the field. For example, if you have entered John Q. Public, the database will sort on the word Public.

Some names need to be sorted differently; for example, the last name Van Damm should be sorted under V for Van. When you enter this type of data into name fields, you must enter it a little differently:

▲ To enter a name like Van Damm, instead of using a regular space between the words Van and Damm, press the Option key and the space bar at the same time. This will glue the two words together.

▲ To force the database to sort by the first word in the record, type the symbol @ just before you type the name. For example: @Toybox Toys and Games will sort under T for Toybox but print as Toybox Toys and Games.

▲ To enter a Tab key in a field, use ⌘-**TAB**.

Edit	Format	Layout
Can't Undo		⌘Z
Cut		⌘H
Copy		⌘C
Paste		⌘U
Clear		
Select All		⌘A
New Record		⌘R
Duplicate Record		⌘D
Delete Record		
Copy Summaries		
Writing Tools		▶
Find/Change		▶
Publishing		▶
Preferences...		
Show Clipboard		

The New Record command in the Edit menu creates a new record.

✔ **Warning:** *Be sure you don't select the New Record twice, or you will have a blank record in your database. This could result in a false record count.*

For a complete list of special characters, see the table "Special database characters," below.

Special database characters

Character	Mouse or Key
Tab	⌘-**TAB**
Current date	⌘-**HYPHEN** (*In date field*)
Current time	⌘-**HYPHEN** (*In time field*)
Keep two words together in a name field	**OPTION-SPACE BAR**
Force a word to sort first in the name field	@

Creating a database

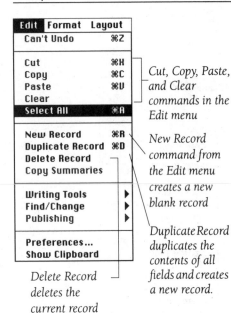

Cut, Copy, Paste, and Clear commands in the Edit menu

New Record command from the Edit menu creates a new blank record

Duplicate Record duplicates the contents of all fields and creates a new record.

Delete Record deletes the current record on the screen

✔ **Tip**: *If you accidentally cut information inside of a field, select Undo Cut from the Edit menu, or press ⌘-z. The Undo/Redo command is a toggle and will work only immediately after you've done an action. If you've done anything else in the meantime, Undo/Redo will not work.*

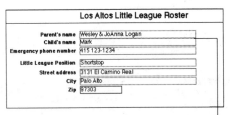

Triple-click inside of any field before you Edit, Cut, Copy, or Paste.

Adding a new record

Once you have entered information for the first record, you must add a new record for the next set of information.

▲ Choose New Record from the Edit menu, or press ⌘-R.

Duplicating information

▲ If you want to copy some information from the previous record, you can use Duplicate Record from the Edit menu, or press ⌘-D.

▲ If you have duplicated a record, just triple-click in any field you want to change and start typing.

Editing field information

▲ Triple-click inside of the field you want to change. Type the new information and it will replace the selected information, or

▲ Double-click inside of any single word in a field to select just that word.

▲ Type the new information and it will replace the selected word.

Using Edit, Cut, Copy and Paste

If you want to copy information from any field:

1. Triple-click inside of the field you want to copy.

2. Choose Copy from the Edit menu, or press ⌘-c.

3. Create a new record and click inside of the field into which you want to paste the information you just copied.

4. Choose Paste from the Edit menu, or press ⌘-v.

Creating a database

Deleting a record

If you need to delete a complete record, not just change information in a field:

1. Click anywhere inside the record you want to delete.

2. Choose the Delete Record from the Edit menu.

The record will disappear and you will not be able to recover it, so make sure you really mean to delete it.

Editing field types from the Layout menu

If you need additional fields:

1. Choose Define fields from the Layout menu, or press ⇧⌘-**D**. You will see the Define Database Fields dialog box.

2. Add any fields you need, using steps 2 through 5 in "Using the Define Database Fields dialog box" on page 134.

Changing field types

1. To change a field type, in the Define Database Fields dialog box, select the Field Name you want to change.

2. Scroll down the Field Type pop-up menu until you see the field type you want to use.

3. Click on the Modify button. You will see a Warning dialog box warning you that anything in the field you are modifying will be permanently erased.

4. If you are certain you want the change to take effect, click on the OK button.

5. Click on the Done button when you are finished.

Deleting more than one record

You can even delete a complete group of records, for example, all members who have not paid their dues since last year, but you must first use Find. To understand more about Find and how to delete a group of records, see "Finding data" on page 152.

Layout	Organize	View
✓Browse		⇧⌘B
Find		⇧⌘F
Layout		⇧⌘L
List		⇧⌘I
Define Fields...		⇧⌘D
Insert Field...		
Insert Part...		
Tab Order...		
✓Show Multiple		
New Layout...		
Edit Layouts...		
✓Layout 1		

Define Fields command in the Layout menu is used to access the Define Database Fields dialog box.

Creating a database

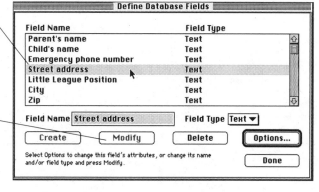

When you select the field name in the Define Database Fields dialog box, the field name will be highlighted. Then you can change the name or the field type.

Use the Modify button to save any changes you make.

Define Database Fields

Field Name	Field Type
Parent's name	Text
Child's name	Text
Emergency phone number	Text
Street address	Text
Little League Position	Text
City	Text
Zip	Text

Field Name [Street address]   Field Type [Text ▼]

[Create]   [Modify]   [Delete]   [Options...]

Select Options to change this field's attributes, or change its name and/or field type and press Modify.

[Done]

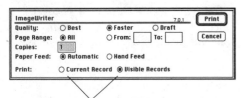

Notice the two new radio buttons: Current Record and Visible Records. The Current Record radio button will print just the single record that is on the screen. Visible Records will print all of the records that appear in the Record count box.

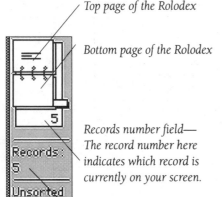

Top page of the Rolodex

Bottom page of the Rolodex

Records number field— The record number here indicates which record is currently on your screen.

Records count box—The number here reflects how many total entries are in your database.

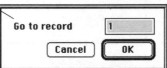

Go to record dialog box

Printing your database

You can print the entire database, one record, or a group of selected records. To learn how to select a group of records, see "Finding data" on page 152.

To print the entire database:

1. Make sure all of the records are visible by checking the Records count box that appears below the Rolodex.

2. Choose Print from the File menu.

3. You have two new radio buttons in the Print dialog box: Current Record and Visible Records. To print just the current record on the screen, select the Current Record radio button.

4. Click on Print.

Printing all records

Follow steps 1 through 3, clicking on the Visible Records radio button. When you select the records using the Find function, you will want to print all visible records.

Moving around

You can move between records in four ways:

Using the Rolodex

▲ Select the top page of the Rolodex to move backward one record.

▲ Select the bottom page of the Rolodex to move forward one record.

Using the record number field

1. Click in the record number field.

2. Type the record number you wish to move to.

Using the Go To Record command

1. Choose Go To Record from the Organize menu, or press ⌘-G.

2. In the Go to record dialog box, type the number of the record you want to move to.

3. Click on the OK button or press Return.

Creating a database

Using movement keys on the keyboard

See the chart below, "Database movement keys", for
a complete list and instructions.

Database movement keys

Where you need to go	Mouse or key
Forward one record	Tab
Forward one record	Select bottom Rolodex page
Forward one record	⌘-**RETURN**
Backward one record	Shift-Tab
Backward one record	Select top Rolodex page
Backward one record	⇧⌘-**RETURN**
Jump or Go To	Select Rolodex number and type the record number
Jump or Go To	⌘-**G**

■ Using options

Options in field definitions let you set up a field so
that it will:

▲ Contain unique information

▲ Force an entry to be made so a field cannot be
left blank

▲ Automatically fill in any text you designate

▲ Automatically fill in the current date, time,
name of creator, date and/or time last modified,
and name of person modifying the information

▲ Set a numerical range for numbers that are to
be entered

▲ Automatically enter the user's name

▲ Give a list of information to choose from when
entering data

▲ Use complex functional formulas such as
statistics, financial formulas, and mathematical
and logical functions

Options button —

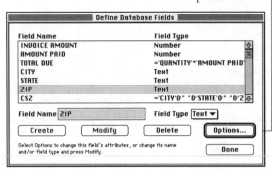

Text field options: Notice the checkboxes labeled *Cannot Be Empty* and *Must Be Unique.*

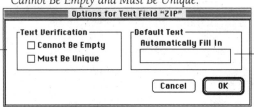

The Default Text section is the place you type in text you want to have automatically entered into a field.

Creating field options

These steps use the Text and Name field types but are the same steps used to create options attached to any field type. The option choices will vary from field type to field type.

1. Choose Define Fields from the Layout menu, or press ⇧⌘-**D**.

2. In the Define Database Fields dialog box, create the field including the name and field type.

3. Click on the Options button in the Define Database Fields dialog box.

4. If you want to make sure this field is always filled out, select the Cannot Be Empty checkbox.

5. If you want to make sure no other record contains the same information as any other record, select the Must Be Unique checkbox.

6. If you want the database to always fill the field in with some specific text, type the text in the Automatically Fill In box in the Default Text section.

Note: Default text will appear automatically but can always be replaced by manually entered text.

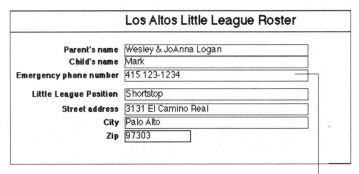

Unique information—When you set up a mailing list, it is a good idea to have one field that must be unique, so people aren't entered twice by accident. One good field to use for this is often the Telephone number field.

Options with number fields

The options that are available with this field are the same as with the text fields, but in addition, you can specify a range of numbers that must be entered. Numbers entered outside of this range will not be accepted.

Creating ranges

1. Click on the Options button in the Define Database Fields dialog box.
2. Choose Define Fields from the Layout menu, or press ⇧⌘-**D**, and click once on the box labeled Must Be In Range.
3. In the From box, type the lowest acceptable number of the range.
4. In the To box, type the highest acceptable number in the range.
5. Click on the OK button when you are finished.

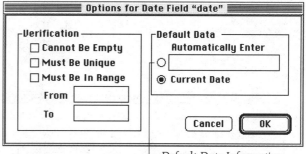

Options with date and time fields

Date and time fields give you the choice of typing in a date or time, or ClarisWorks can automatically insert the date or time into these fields.

Creating Date and time data

1. Choose the Define Fields command from the Layout menu, or press ⇧⌘-**D**.
2. Click on the Options button in the Define Database Fields dialog box .
3. Select the Current Date radio button if you want the current date to always be entered into a new record.
4. Type a date in the Automatically Enter box, if you want a special date to always be entered into a new record.
5. Click on the OK button when you are finished.

Default Date Information

Record Information options box
Select radio button for the choice that
you want to use.

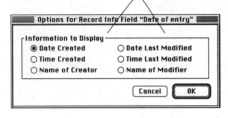

A note about value lists

You may need to expand the size of your
field in your report form in order to see
all of the checkboxes or radio buttons.
See "Creating a report" on page 157 for
how to alter field sizes on screen.

A note about record info fields

Record information fields have options that are related to the date and time fields. For automatic entry of this information, select the radio button of your choice.

Pop-up buttons and similar items

Pop-up, radio button, checkbox, and scrolling value lists fields work exactly the same way, only the screen appearance is different. They allow you to create a list of items, then automate data entry by choosing one of these field appearance options.

1. Choose the Define Fields command from the Layout menu, or press ⇧⌘-**D**.

2. Select a field you have created or create a new field by typing a name in the name box.

3. Select the field type (pop-up, radio button, checkbox, or value list) from the Field type list.

4. Click on the Options button from the Define Database Fields dialog box.

5. In the Item Label box, type the name of the first item you want in your list.

6. Click on the Create button. Continue entering items until your list is complete, clicking on Create after each one.

7. If you need to change any item, select the item from the Items for control text list, then click on the Modify button.

8. If you need to delete an item on the list, select the item, then click on the Delete button.

9. When you are finished, click on the OK button.

Item list

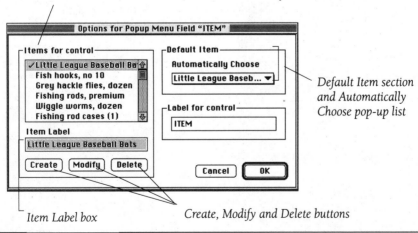

Default Item section and Automatically Choose pop-up list

Item Label box   *Create, Modify and Delete buttons*

Options with serial number field

The serial number field will let you create a unique number for every record in the database.

An example of the usefulness of this option is if you want to create invoice forms, each with its own number.

1. Choose the Define Fields command from the Layout menu, or press ⇧⌘-**D**.
2. Create your field with the proper field name and field type (serial number).
3. Click on the Options button.
4. In the Next Value box, type the first number you want to use for your serial numbers.
5. In the Increment box, type the number you wish each serial number to be increased by (normally the number one).
6. Click on the OK button, then click on the Done button in the Define Database Fields box.

Note: If you have already entered records, the serial number field will not automatically number these records. Be sure to go back and renumber each of your preexisting records manually.

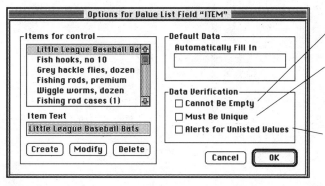

Automatic creation—This choice will let you set a starting number. You might need to do this if you want to create invoices, for example, and want the very first invoice to be numbered 1000. The increment box is where you type the number you want the invoices to be increased by.

Cannot Be Empty—the field must contain some type of data.
Must Be Unique—the field must have unique information (in which case you probably wouldn't want to use a value list field type).
Alerts for Unlisted Values—alerts you if data that is not on the value list is entered.

■ Calculations and summary fields

Just like spreadsheets, databases can use almost all of the same functional formulas.

Using simple algebraic formulas

1. Start by creating all of the fields you will need to input data such as invoice amount.
2. Create a new field called the total due field and make that field type a Calculation field. You will see an Enter Formula for Field dialog box. The left-hand side of this dialog box lists all of your fields in this database.
3. Click on the field you want to use first to create the calculation such as invoice amount.
4. Click on the operator you wish to use to perform the calculation (in this example the "-" or minus sign). That operator will appear after the field name in the Formula box.
5. Select the field name you wish to subtract (in this example, amount paid).
6. When you are finished, select the Formula result as pop-up menu and make sure the word Number has a check mark beside it.
7. When you are finished, click on the OK button.

Make sure any fields you want to perform calculations on are specified as numeric type fields.

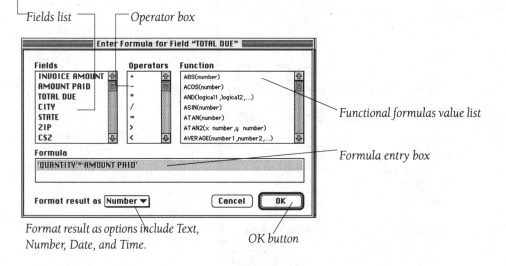

Fields list ⌐ ⌐ Operator box

Functional formulas value list

Formula entry box

Format result as options include Text, Number, Date, and Time.

OK button

Operators

Operators are the signs that add numbers or text together. The chart below shows you the operators used in databases. Sample field names appear in single quotation marks while actual numbers are typed without the quotation marks.

Logical or Boolean operators

Operation	Symbol	Explanation	Example
Addition	+	Used to add two numeric fields together	'Total amount'+'Shipping'
Subtraction	-	Used to subtract one numeric field from another	'Total amount'-'Amount paid'
Multiply	*	Used to multiply one numeric field by another numeric field or by a constant number	'Item'*'Price'
Divide	/	Used to divide one numeric field by another numeric field or by a constant number	'Price'/'Months'
Equal	=	Denotes two or more fields that are equal	'Item'='Description'
Greater than	>	Denotes a field that is larger than another field	'Total amount'>0
Less than	<	Denotes a field that is smaller than another field	'Amount paid'<'Total amount'
Greater than or equal to	>=	Denotes a field that is larger than or equal to another field	'Year'>=1966 1996 or later
Less than or equal to	<=	Denotes a field that is smaller than or equal to another field	'Year'<=1966 1966 or earlier
Not equal to	<>	Denotes two fields that should not be equal to one another	'State'<>'CA'
Exponentiation	^	An algebraic symbol that denotes raising a number to a power	'Measurement'^2
And	&	Used to add two text fields together, called concatenating two fields	'First name'&" "&'Last name' Notice the blank space between the &" "&—this results in a space between the first and last names.

`'CITY'&"CA"&" "&'ZIP'`

Field names are in single quotes, while text appears in double quotes. In this sample, notice the &, which is used to add both the fields and text together.

Instead of using a pair of quotation marks with a space between, you could also use a pair of quotation marks with a comma and a space between. For example:
'CITY'&", "&'STATE'&" "&'ZIP'

Adding text together

You can certainly add text or text fields together— this is called concatenating. The result is a phrase or sentence. The phrase Dr. Karen Shaol consists of three words separated by spaces, or in computerese "Dr."&" "&"Karen"&" "&"Shaol"—the spaces are indicated by a pair of quotation marks separated by a space. Field names are enclosed by single quotation marks.

Typed text must always be enclosed in quotation marks. Notice the "&" (ampersand) was used to add the phrases together instead of the + (plus).

Adding two text fields together

1. Click in the cell you wish to contain the formula and choose Paste Function from the Edit menu. The Enter Formula dialog box will appear.
2. In the Enter Formula dialog box, click on the first field containing textual information (for example, city in the fields list).
3. Choose the & operator from the bottom of the Operators scrolling list.
4. Click in the Formula entry box and type " " (quote space quote)—this will give some space between the city field and the state field.
5. Select another & from the Operators scrolling list.
6. In the Enter Formula dialog box, click on the state field from the fields list.
7. When you are finished click on the OK button.

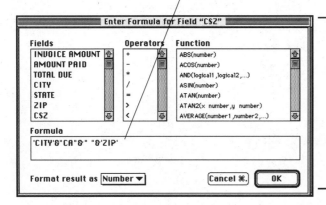

Enter Formula for Field "CSZ"

Fields	Operators	Function
INVOICE AMOUNT	+	ABS(number)
AMOUNT PAID	–	ACOS(number)
TOTAL DUE	*	AND(logical1,logical2,...)
CITY	/	ASIN(number)
STATE	=	ATAN(number)
ZIP	>	ATAN2(x number,y number)
CSZ	<	AVERAGE(number1,number2,...)

Formula
`'CITY'&"CA"&" "&'ZIP'`

Format result as [Number ▼]   [Cancel ⌘.]   (OK)

✔ **Tip**: *You can add text that does not appear in a field. For example, if your mailing list consists entirely of people in California, but you didn't create a state field, you can now make mailing labels with the state appearing on the label. When you want to add text you have typed together, type the words out between double quotes.*

Functional formulas

Functional formulas work in much the same way. You can add text, numbers, or fields within any functional formulas—but you cannot add text and numbers together. To check how to use the most common functional formulas, see "Math" on page 115.

Using the IF functional formula

1. Click once in the cell you wish to contain the formula and choose Paste Function from the Edit menu. The Enter Formula dialog box will appear.

2. In the Function scrolling list of the Enter Formula for Field dialog box, select the function you wish to use. In the case of the IF functional formula, your Formula text box will now read: IF(logical,true-value, false-value).

3. The logical statement will be highlighted. Select the field that you first want to test in the Fields list (for example, state, as in state="CA").

4. That field will now replace the word logical. Type in the rest of the text, including inserting the proper operator from the Operators scrolling list and the condition you wish to examine. In the example in step 3, the condition is that entries in the state field match the code CA.

5. Select true-value and type in what you want the results to be if the logical condition is true.

6. Select false-value and type in what you want the results to be if the logical condition is false.

7. Click on the OK button when you are finished.

Functional formulas first appear in the Formula box with placeholders. You are to fill in the placeholders with fields or text.

Formula
IF(logical,true value,false value)

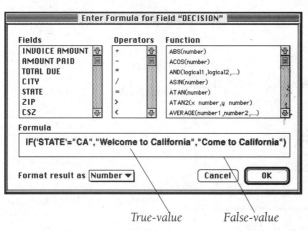

Fields	Operators	Function
INVOICE AMOUNT	+	ABS(number)
AMOUNT PAID	–	ACOS(number)
TOTAL DUE	*	AND(logical1 ,logical2,...)
CITY	/	ASIN(number)
STATE	=	ATAN(number)
ZIP	>	ATAN2(x number ,y number)
CSZ	<	AVERAGE(number1 ,number2,...)

Formula
IF('STATE'="CA","Welcome to California","Come to California")

Format result as [Number ▼]   [Cancel] [OK]

True-value   *False-value*

Notice that if you are looking for text, the text must be enclosed in double quotes. Numbers can be typed in without any quotation marks. In the figure on this page, the true value is "Welcome to California." In the figure on this page, the false value is "Come to California."

Summary vs. calculation fields

Summary fields are calculation fields that appear in the summary section of a layout and add up calculation fields. For example, if you were creating an invoice form, the invoice items, item prices, and extensions would all be placed in the body of the layout format. Summary fields would be placed in a summary section of the report.

Summary sections are subsections of a layout, rather like a footer. If you place a formula in this field, it will summarize all of the data in the database or the selected portion of the database. To find out more about summary sections, see "Layout screen parts" on page 157.

Sorting data *(side tab)*

✔ **Tip**: *Any blank records will be sorted to the beginning of the database, so you will be able to easily tell if you've accidentally added in blank records. You can then quickly delete these records.*

The Sort Records command has a shortcut of ⌘-J.

■ Sorting data

Arranging your data into alphabetical or numerical order is called sorting. To do a simple sort of the database:

1. Choose Sort Records from the Organize menu, or press ⌘-J. You will see a Sort Records dialog box.
2. In the Fields List on the left-hand side of the dialog box, click once on the field you want to sort by.
3. Click on the Move button in the center of the Sort Records dialog box. You will see the field name appear in the Sort Order list on the right.
4. Click on either the Ascending (A to Z) radio button or the Descending (Z to A) radio button in the lower right-hand corner of the dialog box.
5. Click on the OK button to perform the sort.

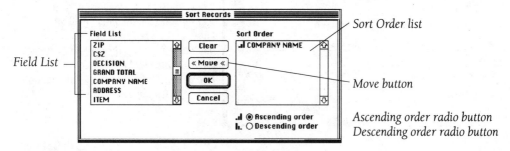

Field List

Sort Order list

Move button

Ascending order radio button
Descending order radio button

Changing sort order information

If you want to do a completely different sort, you can change which fields the database uses to sort:

1. Choose Sort Records from the Organize menu, or press ⌘-J. You will see a Sort Records dialog box.
2. In the Sort Order list, you will see the field(s) you are currently sorting by.
3. Select any field you wish to remove from the Sort Order list.
4. Click on the Clear button to remove any selected fields from the Sort Order list.
5. Add in the correct field you wish to sort by.
6. Perform the sort by clicking on the OK button.

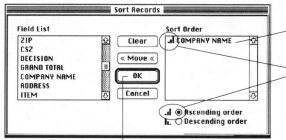

Notice the field listed in the Sort Order box. This database will be sorted by company name, and the icon for ascending order appears by the name. This means the database will be sorted from A to Z.

The OK button is what actually starts the sort working.

Multiple sorts

Multiple sorts are performed on two or more database fields. For example, if you want to create a mailing list from customer information in your database, you might sort first by state, then within the state by zip code. This is a multiple sort.

Performing a multiple sort

1. Choose Sort Records from the Organize menu, or press ⌘-J. You will see a Sort Records dialog box.
2. Clear any fields you do not want to sort by.
3. Select the first field you want to sort by and enter it into the Sort Order list—the state in the mailing list example and the figure to the right.
4. Now select the the second field you want the database to be sorted by—the zip code in the mailing list example.
5. Add in all of the multiple sort items, making sure the Sort Order list is in the correct order.
6. Perform the sort by clicking on the OK button.

The Sort Order list contains two fields: state and zip.

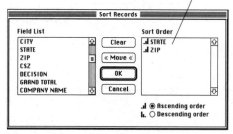

This database will sort first by state, then within the state field, by zip code. The field listed first in the Sort Order list (state) is the field that is sorted first. Once that sort is finished, the second field in the Sort Order list (Zip) is sorted sequentially.

Sorting data

■ Viewing your database

There are four ways to look at your database:

▲ Browse without the Show Multiple choice; you will see one record at a time.

▲ Browse with Show Multiple chosen from the Layout menu shows you as many records as will fit on your screen.

▲ List shows the records arranged in rows and columns.

▲ Page view shows the records as they will print out on your printer.

Using the browse view

ClarisWorks starts in the browse view with the Show Multiple records command when you first begin to enter records. To see only one record at a time:

▲ Choose Show Multiple from the Layout menu. This will remove the check mark and deactivate this menu choice.

▲ To see more than one record at a time, reselect Show Multiple from the Layout menu.

Layout	Organize	View
✓Browse		⇧⌘B
Find		⇧⌘F
Layout		⇧⌘L
List		⇧⌘I
Define Fields...		⇧⌘D
Insert Field...		
Insert Part...		
Tab Order...		
✓Show Multiple		
New Layout...		
Edit Layouts...		
✓Layout 1		

List, or ⌘-I, will show your records arranged in rows and columns across the screen.

The Show Multiple menu choice will show you as many of your records as will fit on the screen at the same time.

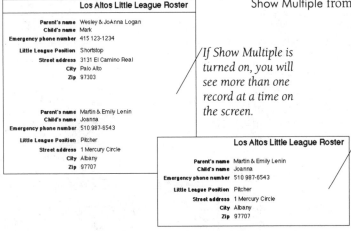

Los Altos Little League Roster

Parent's name	Wesley & JoAnna Logan
Child's name	Mark
Emergency phone number	415 123-1234
Little League Position	Shortstop
Street address	3131 El Camino Real
City	Palo Alto
Zip	97303

Parent's name	Martin & Emily Lenin
Child's name	Joanna
Emergency phone number	510 987-6543
Little League Position	Pitcher
Street address	1 Mercury Circle
City	Albany
Zip	97707

If Show Multiple is turned on, you will see more than one record at a time on the screen.

Los Altos Little League Roster

Parent's name	Martin & Emily Lenin
Child's name	Joanna
Emergency phone number	510 987-6543
Little League Position	Pitcher
Street address	1 Mercury Circle
City	Albany
Zip	97707

If you turn Show Multiple off by removing the check mark, you will see one record at a time on the screen.

Viewing your database

Using the list view

List view places the database fields across the screen from left to right in rows and columns. To change into the list view:

1. Choose List from the Layout menu, or press ⇧⌘-I. Your data will extend in columns from left to right with the field names above each column. Records will appear in rows running across the screen from left to right.

2. Use the Tab key to move to the right or Shift-Tab to move to the left between fields in this view.

✔ **Tip**: *If you need to select the records in the list view you can:*
▲ *Click just to the left of the first column to select the one row.*
▲ *Drag the pointer down the left of the first column to select multiple rows.*
▲ *Select the column label to select the entire column.*
▲ *Select one column label then hold the shift key down and click on other column labels to select more than one column.*

Parent's nan	Child's name	Emergency p	Street addre	Little Leagu	City	Zip
Wesley &	Mark	415 123-	3131 El	Shortstop	Palo Alto	97303
Martin &	Joanna	510 987-	1 Mercury	Pitcher	Albany	97707

league (DB)

List view—The data runs from left to right in this view, with the names of the fields appearing as the column headings.

City ◀◇▶	Zip
Palo Alto	97303
Albany	97707

The double-sided arrow will help you move the position of a column from left to right on the screen.

Moving columns in list view

When using the list view, you will see a double-sided arrow as the pointer moves into the column headings. You can use this unusual pointer to move the columns on screen to either the left or right:

1. Move the pointer into a column—column three, for example.

2. Drag the column to the left or right.

Using Page View

Using this option does not affect the field order in the Browse view from the Layout menu. Page View shows you how your information will look when it prints.

1. Make sure you are in the Browse view.

2. Select Page View from the View menu, or press ⇧⌘-P.

The Find command appears on the Layout menu.

Layout	Organize	View
✓Browse	⇧⌘B	
Find	⇧⌘F	
Layout	⇧⌘L	
List	⇧⌘I	
Define Fields...	⇧⌘D	
Insert Field...		
Insert Part...		
Tab Order...		
✓Show Multiple		
New Layout...		
Edit Layouts...		
✓Layout 1		

▪ Finding data

There are three ways of looking for information:
- ▲ Looking at everything in the database.
- ▲ Looking at selected data.
- ▲ Looking at the records that remain not found after you use selection criteria.

Setting up a simple selection

1. Choose Find from the Layout menu, or press ⇧⌘-**F**. You will see a screen that looks exactly like a data entry screen.

2. Type the information you want to find in the proper field.

3. Click on the Find button. Your selected information will appear and your Rolodex record number will show you how many records match the criteria you used.

Here is a list of sample search criteria—in the parent's name field notice the name martin. This search will look for the first name or the last name martin.

You can search through all records by using the All radio button on the right side of the screen, or search through the results of a previous search by clicking on the Visible radio button on the right side of the screen.

```
                                    league (DB)
                              Los Altos Little League Roster

                    Parent's name  martin
                     Child's name
           Emergency phone number
            Little League Position
                   Street address
                             City
                              Zip

Requests:
1

Find from
○ Visible
● All

☐ Omit

  Find
```

Find screen—

▲ *Whenever you use the Find command, you will see a blank form. Type what you are searching for in the field the information was input.*

▲ *This program is not case-sensitive. You don't have to worry about capitalization—it will find Martin or martin.*

▲ *You also do not have to type the entire name in—it would find Martin if the only text that is typed is mar. It would also find the phrase mar buried inside of words such as marvelous, remarkable, and so on.*

Found records indicator— The number in parentheses is the total number of records in the database. The number to the left that does not appear in parentheses tells you how many records were found.

Selecting just one record

If you want to select just one record in order to print, delete, or copy it:

1. From the regular database screen, click anywhere outside of the fields on the screen but near the record. The entire record will become selected.

2. Print (⌘-**P**), Cut (⌘-**X**), or Copy (⌘-**V**) the record.

3. Click inside a field on the screen to return to the editing mode.

The perfect place to click is outside the field but near the record.

Deleting a group of found records

1. Perform a Find operation (see "Finding data" on page 152 if you need to review this operation).

2. Choose Select All from the Edit menu, or press ⌘-**A**.

3. Choose Cut from the Edit menu, or press ⌘-**x**.

Edit	Format	Layout
Can't Undo		⌘Z
Cut		⌘H
Copy		⌘C
Paste		⌘U
Clear		
Select All		⌘A

The Select All command in the Edit menu will select all of your records. You can then delete all of the visible records (the records that you just found).

Refinding hidden data

When you find information, you hide information that did not match the selection criteria. You need to refind or show records that are hidden if you want to be able to edit or print them.

▲ Choose Show All Records on the Organize menu, or press ⇧⌘-**A**.

Finding hidden information

Another way of looking at information is to find everything that did not meet your selection criteria—an example of this option is if you looked for anyone living in California and found 252 people.

You might want to then see the rest of the people in the database who did not live in California. In this case, you would want to hide the found set and expose the hidden set.

1. Perform a Find operation (see "Finding data" on page 152 if you need to review this operation).

2. To see just the records that were not selected, choose Hide Unselected from the Organize menu, or press ⌘-**)**.

Organize	View
Show All Records	⇧⌘A
Hide Selected	⌘(
Hide Unselected	⌘)
Go To Record...	⌘G
Sort Records...	⌘J
Match Records...	⌘M

The Organize menu gives you three useful commands: Show All Records, Hide Selected, and Hide Unselected.

✔ **Tip**: *If you choose Hide Selected or press ⌘-(, both your found set and your hidden set will disappear from the screen. Use Show All Records to get your records back.*

Finding data

Visible and all records

When you first perform a search you will be looking through all records. Once you have completed a search and have selected some records, you have visible records that are the result of your search.

▲ If you want to search just through those records you recently found, select the Visible Records radio button on the left-hand side of the screen before you perform the next search.

For example:

1. You perform a search for everyone living in California who has purchased rubber widgets from you in 1995.

2. Your database shows that 1,256 customers from California have purchased rubber widgets from you in 1995.

3. Now you want to know how many of these customers live in Kensington, California, so you make a second search looking only in the visible records for those customers in Kensington.

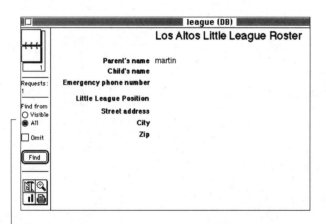

Visible and All radio buttons—Use the Visible radio button when you want to do a second search through your found, or "visible," records, and do not want to look through the hidden, or "not found," records.

Saving searches

If you have set up a search and it works for you, you can save the search under a name. Later on you'll just recall your previous search.

1. Choose Find from the Layout menu, and type in the criteria—what you are looking for— in the correct fields.
2. Select the search pop-up from the status panel on the left-hand side of the screen. The Search pop-up menu appears.
3. Select New Search from the Search pop-up menu.
4. You will see the New Search dialog box.
5. Type a short name in the Name for this search box.
6. Click on the OK button or press the Return key when you are finished.

Don't forget about the database pop-up tools on the lower left-hand part of the status panel.

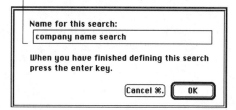

This is the Search pop-up from the status panel. You use this pop-up to save a search.

Saved search pop-up with a name for a search typed in the Name for this search box.

> **Name for this search:**
> company name search
>
> **When you have finished defining this search press the enter key.**
>
> Cancel ⌘.   OK

Search pop-up with a named search (company name search) on the bottom of the pop-up menu.

Recalling a saved search

1. Select the search pop-up from the status panel on the left-hand side of the screen. The Search pop-up menu will appear.
2. Select the named search on the bottom of the list.

Deleting a search

1. Select the search pop-up from the status panel on the left-hand side of the screen. The Search pop-up menu appears.
2. Choose Edit Searches from the Search pop-up menu. The Edit Searches dialog box will appear.
3. Select the name of the search you wish to delete from the Edit Searches dialog box.
4. Click on the Delete button.
5. When you are finished, click on the OK button.

The Edit Searches dialog box with a list of Named Searches

Finding data

Boolean searches

Boolean searches are a more precise way of looking for information in your database.

There are six operators with Boolean logic that can be added to a simple search statement.

▲ Equals or =—used to find precise matches.

▲ Not equal to or<>—used to find information that does not equal the selection criteria.

▲ Less than or <—used to find information that is precisely less than the criterion number.

▲ Less than or equal to, or =<—used to find any number equal to the number typed in the selection criterion and any number that is less than the selection criterion.

▲ Greater than or >—used to find information that is larger than the criterion number.

▲ Greater than or equal to, or =>—used to find any number equal to the number typed in the selection criterion and any number that is greater than the selection criterion.

Using Boolean logic in a simple search

1. Choose Find from the Layout menu.
2. Click in the field in which you want to search.
3. Type in the symbol for the Boolean search followed by the criteria—for example, when looking for a number that is smaller or equal to 100, type =<100.
4. Click on the Find button.

Examples of Boolean searches

Company="Toybox"
   State<>"Texas"
   Amount due<100
   Amount due=<99.95
   Past due>0
   Past due=>10
Notice that text is enclosed in double quotes and numbers are not enclosed.

Parent's name
Child's name
Emergency phone number
Little League Position
Street address
City
Zip
Age <9

The Age field in this example has the Boolean search statement that means any age less than 9 (but not equal to 9), or <9.

Finding data

■ Creating a report

Using the layout view

The layout view is used to create screen layouts and printed reports. In this view you can:

▲ Select the font, size, style, and text color of both the field labels and the field text.

▲ Show all or some of the fields.

▲ Move the fields and field labels.

▲ Fill the fields with color, add colored borders, or eliminate borders.

▲ Add text, background colors, pictures, gradations, patterns, and decorative lines.

▲ Change the tab key order of the fields.

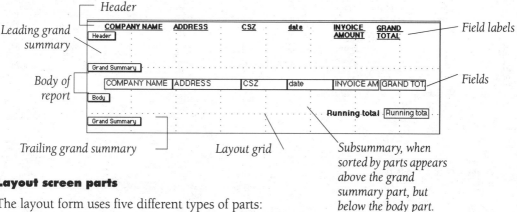

Layout screen parts

The layout form uses five different types of parts:

▲ Header part, which includes any information you want printed at the top of every page.

▲ Leading grand summary part, which is used to place fields that will form report sections, for example, an employee field when tracking sales by employee.

▲ Subsummary when sorted by part, which is used to add up subtotals.

▲ Trailing grand summary part, which is used to add up calculated fields using Summary field types, for example, as when tracking sales by employee, giving the total sales for all employees.

▲ Footer part, which contains information such as page numbers, or text, that you wish to repeat at the bottom of every page.

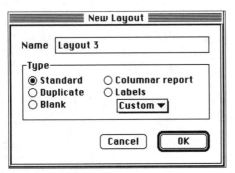

Layout	Organize	View
✓Browse	⇧⌘B	
Find	⇧⌘F	
Layout	⇧⌘L	
List	⇧⌘I	
Define Fields...	⇧⌘D	
Insert Field...		
Insert Part...		
Tab Order...		
✓Show Multiple		
New Layout...		
Edit Layouts...		
✓Layout 1		

Use the New Layout command from the Layout menu to create a new report layout. These layouts can be used both for displaying the information on the screen and for printing directly on your printer.

New Layout dialog box:

Name: Layout 3

Type
- ◉ Standard
- ○ Duplicate
- ○ Blank
- ○ Columnar report
- ○ Labels
- Custom ▼

[Cancel] [OK]

Creating a simple layout

1. Choose New Layout from the bottom of the Layout menu. You will see the New Layout dialog box.
2. Type a name for the layout in the Name box of the New Layout dialog box—for example, invoice.
3. Select the radio button for the type of report you want in the new layout.
4. Click on the OK button.

Report types

There are five report types:

▲ Standard report creates a blank page containing all of the field names and field labels.

▲ Duplicate report will duplicate the current report you have on the screen.

▲ Blank report will give you a completely blank piece of paper.

▲ Columnar report displays fields in columns.

▲ Labels report gives you a choice of all of the Avery label sizes or you can create a custom-sized label.

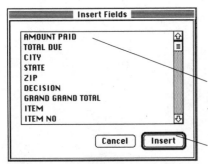

Define Fields...	⇧⌘D
Insert Field...	
Insert Part...	
Tab Order...	
✓Show Multiple	

The Insert Field and Insert Part commands are used when adding fields and parts to a new layout.

Insert Fields dialog box:

- AMOUNT PAID
- TOTAL DUE
- CITY
- STATE
- ZIP
- DECISION
- GRAND GRAND TOTAL
- ITEM
- ITEM NO

[Cancel] [Insert]

The Insert Fields dialog box shows you a list of fields that have not been used in your layout.

Insert button

Deleting and adding fields to a report

▲ To delete a field or a field label while you are in the layout view, click once on the item and tap the Delete or Clear key.

1. To add a field to a layout, choose Insert Field from the Layout menu. You will now see the Insert Fields dialog box that contains a list of all of your unused fields.
2. Select the field you want to add.
3. Click on the Insert button and the field will now appear in the report.

Moving fields

▲ In the layout view, select the field you want to move and drag it into the desired position.

Lining up the fields or field labels:

1. In the layout view, select all of the fields and field labels that need to be aligned on either the horizontal or vertical axis by clicking on each field while holding down the Shift key.

2. Choose Align Objects from the Arrange menu, or press ⇧⌘-κ.

3. There are two categories of alignment: Top to Bottom and Left to Right. Select the radio button in each category that best describes how you want the fields and field names to align.

4. Click on the OK button when you are done.

Watch the Sample box to see how your alignment will work. If the sample boxes are lined up on top of one another, change one of your selections.

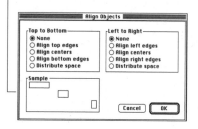

Changing tab order

Pressing the Tab key moves you between fields, but you can change the order the Tab key uses.

Changing the Tab order

1. In the layout view, choose Tab Order command on the Layout menu. You will see the Tab Order dialog box.

2. In the Tab Order list on the right of the Tab Order dialog box, click on any fields that are in the incorrect order, then click on the Move button.

3. In the Tab Order list on the right of the Tab Order dialog box, select the field that is just below where you want your field to be.

4. In the Field List on the left of the Tab Order dialog box, select the field you want to insert, and then click on the Move button. The field will appear just above the field you selected in step 3.

5. Click on the OK button when you are done.

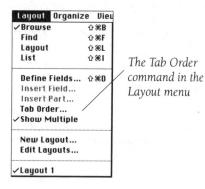

The Tab Order command in the Layout menu

The Tab Order list must have the fields appearing in the order you want to tab between them.

The Field List shows you a complete list of all of your database fields.

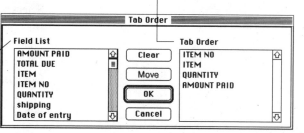

Creating a report

Creating a report

Changing text and text color

Changing text and text color in database program mode is identical to changing these items in the Word Processing program mode.

You might need to change field labels, which are the text that appears on the layout and that describes or labels the fields. To begin changing field label text:

1. In the layout view, double-click on any single word in the field label or triple-click to select the the entire field label.

2. Select any of the following options in the Text Style dialog box and make your changes in the same way you did in Word Processing:

▲ Font   ▲ Paragraph Format

▲ Size   ▲ Tabs format

▲ Style

To review changing regular text, see "Changing the font and font styles" on page 38.

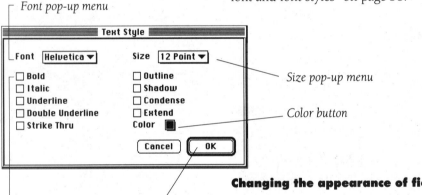

Font pop-up menu

Size pop-up menu

Color button

Enhancements   *OK button*

Changing the appearance of field text

1. In the layout view, double-click inside of a field. You will see a Text Style dialog box.

2. To change the font, hold down on the Font pop-up menu button and select your font from the list.

3. To change the size, hold down on the Size pop-up button and select the size you want.

4. Select any enhancements you want to use from the checkboxes such as Bold, Underline, Shadow, or Outline.

5. To change the color, click and hold down on the Color button. A pop-up color palette will appear. Select the color you want to use.

6. When you are finished, click on the OK button.

Adding lines, fills, and gradients to fields

1. In the layout view, click inside of the field you wish to change.
2. Select the color fill tool and then select the color to fill the field from the color palette that appears.
3. Select the pattern tool and then select the pattern you want to use in the field from the pattern palette that appears.
4. Select the gradient tool and then select the type of gradient fill you want to use from the gradient palette that appears.
5. The color, pattern, or gradient you choose will fill the field and the text in the field is displayed on top of the chosen fills.

Lines and shapes

The pen palette has three of the same tools that are available to fields, but also has an additional tool, the arrow tool.

Drawing a line

1. Select the line tool or shape tool you want to use in the drawing palette
2. Select the line thickness tool in the status panel.
3. From the Line Thickness pop-up list that appears, scroll through the line choices and select the thickness of the line you want.
4. If you want to make the line a color, pattern, or gradient, make those choices in the Line tools palette by clicking and selecting them.
5. Drag the pointer into the layout and draw the shape or line by holding the mouse button down.
6. Let go of the mouse button when the shape is finished.

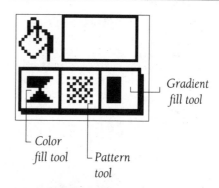

Gradient fill tool

Color fill tool

Pattern tool

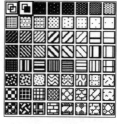

Pattern palette— These are patterns in the pattern palette. If you use a pattern, your text in front of the pattern might have to be bold for you to see it.

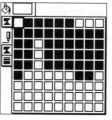

Color palette—The gradient palette resembles the color palette. You select colors or gradients by dragging then selecting your choice.

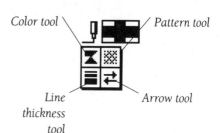

Color tool   *Pattern tool*

Line thickness tool   *Arrow tool*

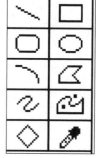

Drawing tools (top to bottom)
Straight line
Lozenge
Curved line
Freehand line
Polygon

Drawing tools (top to bottom)
Rectangle
Oval
Irregular polygon
Bezier tool
Eyedropper

Creating a report

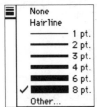

In the line thickness pop-up menu, the best line choice is Hairline, which makes a neat but narrow line that is .03 inches wide. The Other choice will let you make up a line-width in points. Remember, there are 72 points to one inch.

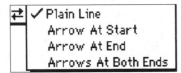

The term Start refers to the place where the mouse is first held down. The End is the place where you finally let go of the mouse button.

Changing line thickness

1. In the layout view, click on a line you have already drawn, then select the line thickness tool.
2. Scroll down the line thickness pop-up list until you see the line you want to use.
3. Select the line you want to use.

Note: If the line thickness you want to use does not appear in this dialog box, select the the Other choice at the bottom of the line thickness pop-up list. You will then be able to type in a line thickness in the Other dialog box.

Creating a line with an arrow

1. Follow steps 1 through 3 in "Drawing a line" on page 161, then click and hold down on the arrow tool button.
2. Click on one of the four arrow shape choices in the arrows pop-up list.
3. Now draw the line. When you finish drawing the line the arrow(s) will appear.

Adding artwork

You can use the Libraries command from the File menu to add artwork to any portion of the layout. Refer to "Libraries" on page 71 to review this procedure.

The Arrange menu

The Arrange menu helps you change the shape or relative position of artwork, fields, and field labels.

Arranging drawn objects

Action	Key	Explanation/Directions	Sample
Move Forward	⇧⌘-+	Move Forward will move that object on top of any single object, such as this lozenge shaped object on the right.	
Move To Front		Move To Front will move an object that is behind two or more objects to the top of the stack.	
Move Backward	⇧⌘-	Move Backward will move an object behind another object.	
Move To Back		Move To Back will move an object behind all other objects in the stack.	
Reshape	⌘-R	These tools are covered in "Drawing" on page 173.	
Free Rotate	⇧⌘-R		
Transform			
Group	⌘-G	Group combines two or more objects into one object.	
Ungroup	⇧⌘-G	Ungroup breaks a group of objects apart if they were formed into one group using the Group command.	
Lock	⌘-H	Lock keeps an object from being changed.	
Unlock	⇧⌘-H	Unlock removes a previous Lock command so you can make changes to an object.	

You can also use the tool bar on the left-hand side of the screen. Click and hold down on the report pop-up, then select New Report from the pop-up menu to begin creating a report.

Using the tool bar to create a menu of reports

1. Click on the Report pop-up in the tool bar. The Report pop-up submenu will appear.
2. Choose New Report from the pop-up menu.
3. Type the name you want to give the report in the Report Name box in the New Report dialog box.
4. Click on the Layout pop-up in the New Report dialog box. You will see a pop-up menu of all of your layouts for that database.
5. Select the layout you wish to use.
6. If you have saved searches, click on the Search pop-up. You will see a pop-up menu of all of your saved searches.
7. Select the saved search you want to use from the pop-up list.
8. If you have saved sorts, click on the Sort pop-up. You will see a pop-up menu of all of your saved sorts.
9. Select the saved sort you want to use from the pop-up list.
10. If you want to print the report when you select this report pop-up in the future, click in the checkbox labeled Print the report.
11. Click on the OK button when you are finished.

New report box

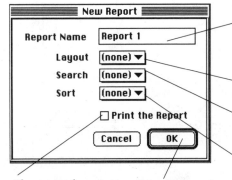

Type the name for the report in the Report Name box of the New Report dialog box. Later, selecting this name from the report pop-up in the Status panel will activate your Layout, Search, Sort, and Print options from this dialog box.

Select the Layout pop-up menu to see a list of all available layouts.

Select the Search pop-up menu to see a list of all available saved searches.

Select the Sort pop-up menu to see a list of all available saved sorts.

If you want the report to print automatically when this saved report pop-up is chosen, click in the Print the Report checkbox.

Click on the OK button when you are finished.

Creating a report

Mailing labels

1. Choose New layout from the Layout menu.
2. Select the Labels radio button from the New Layout dialog box.
3. Click on the Custom pop-up menu in the New Layout dialog box.
4. Select the Avery label type you want to use from the list.
5. Click on the OK button from the New Layout dialog box. The Set Field Order dialog box will then appear.
6. In the Set Field Order dialog box, select each field you want to use, one at a time, clicking on the Move button after you select each field.
7. Click on the OK button when you are finished selecting all of the fields you want to use.
8. Do any rearranging, adding art, changing text style and size and other enhancements when the layout appears on the screen.

Finishing up mailing labels

1. Choose Edit Layouts from the Layout menu.
2. In the Edit Layouts dialog box, select the database layout you are currently creating. The layout name will be the name of the label number.
3. Click on the Modify button.
4. You will see a Layout Info dialog box. Make sure that Slide objects left and Slide objects up both have a check mark in the checkboxes.
5. Click on the OK button in the Layout Information dialog box and in the Edit Layouts dialog box.
6. Choose Page Setup from the File menu.
7. Click in the box labeled No gaps between pages so that you won't print just one label per page.
8. Click on the OK button.

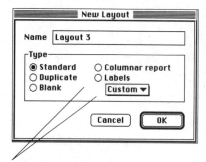

Labels radio button and Custom pop-up menu

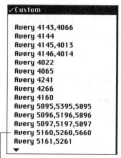

Avery labels—The Avery 5160 is the most common laser-printed address label.

The Set Field Order dialog box will automatically appear once you choose the label type you want to use.

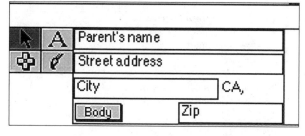

Sample label layout—notice that after the City field, the text phrase CA appears. You can combine fields and text on a label layout in this manner by typing the text after the field is placed in position.

Creating a report

Creating a report

What happens if you don't have any information entered for the contact name? You need to have the street address, city, state, and zip code information all slide up to fill in the blank.

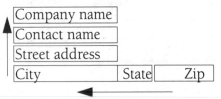

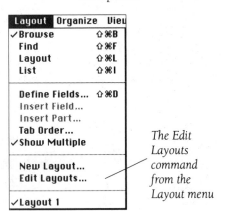

The city, state, and zip code fields need to slide to the left so that there will not be extra blanks between the city, state, and zip code.

The Edit
Layouts
command
from the
Layout menu

Slide objects

Sliding objects are a way of closing up gaps in a layout, particularly with label layouts.

For example, when a label layout is created, typical fields include:

▲ Company name
▲ Contact name
▲ Street address
▲ City
▲ State
▲ Zip code

Creating sliding fields

1. In the layout view, click on each one of the fields while holding down the Shift key. You should see small dots on the corner of each field—these dots are the field handles.
2. Choose Edit Layout from the Layout menu.
3. In the Edit Layouts dialog box, click once on the name of your layout.
4. Click on the Modify button.
5. In the Layout Info dialog box, click in the checkboxes labeled Slide objects left and Slide objects up.
6. Click on the OK button from the Layout Information dialog box.
7. Click on the OK button in the Edit Layouts dialog box.

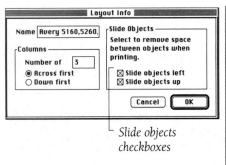

Slide objects checkboxes

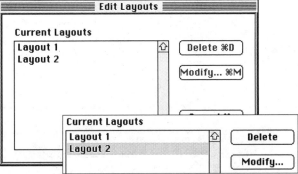

When you click on a file name in the Edit Layouts dialog box, you will see a Modify button on the right-hand side of the dialog box. Use this button to open the Layout Info dialog box.

Advanced reports: Using parts

1. In the layout view, choose Insert Part from the Layout menu. The Insert Part dialog box will appear.

2. Select the radio button in the Insert Part dialog box that describes the type of part you want to use.

3. Click on the OK button from the Insert Part dialog box when you are finished. Refer to "Layout screen parts" on page 157 for descriptions of each part.

4. To resize a part, select the solid line that defines the bottom of the part and has the part label on the right-hand side of the layout.

5. Drag up or down until the part is the size you want it to be.

Note: You cannot move fields at the same time you resize a part. If you have fields that are at the bottom of a part, they will not move up when you try to make that part shorter. First move the fields to the top of the part, then resize the part itself.

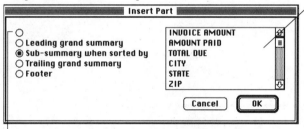

Field list in the Insert Part dialog box displays fields you might need to sort the database before you print out the report.

Part radio buttons with the Sub-summary when sorted by radio button selected. This particular part will require you to pick a field from the field list on the right.

Part lines appear as thin lines extending across the page. These lines do not print, but if you need to re-size a part, you select the line, then drag up or down to make the part shorter or longer.

Part label for the Body part in this report example

Creating a report

■ Shortcuts

The Database mode has additional shortcut keys you can use at any time. These tools appear in the same position that the special text tools appeared in the Shortcuts palette (bottom row, left-hand side).

Shortcuts palette in the browse view

Sort ascending order   Sort again   Show records that do not match value   Show records greater than value   Show all records

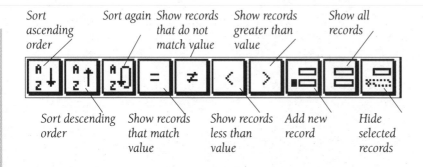

Sort descending order   Show records that match value   Show records less than value   Add new record   Hide selected records

Shortcuts palette in the layout view

Align top edges   Align bottom edges   Align horizontal centers   Bring forward   Irregular wrap

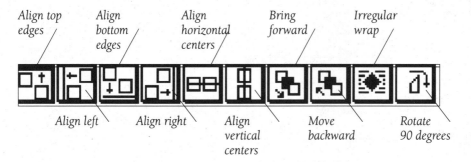

Align left   Align right   Align vertical centers   Move backward   Rotate 90 degrees

■ Working with other files

You can use databases that are created in several other database types directly in ClarisWorks. ClarisWorks will not disturb the original database, but will smoothly bring them into the database program.

1. Choose Open from the File menu and select the borrowed database in the scrolling list in the dialog box that appears.
2. From the Document Type pop-up list, select the type of database the borrowed database is.
3. Click on the OK button.

Acceptable database formats

Name of format	Program
AppleWorks Database	AppleWorks
ASCII	Any program can convert data into ASCII, which is plain text
DBF	Almost all databases, IBM and Macintosh, can create DBF files
DIF	Spreadsheets, some databases, AppleWorks
MSWorks 2.0 DB	Microsoft Works 2.0
SYLK	Spreadsheets

Adding to current file

1. Open the database that you wish to add files to.
2. Choose Insert from the File menu and select the file you wish to add from the scrolling list in the dialog box that appears on screen.
3. Choose the appropriate file type from the Document type pop-up menu.
4. Click on the OK button.

Exporting to another file format

1. Choose Save As from the File menu.
2. In the Save As pop-up list, choose the file type you want the new file to be.
3. Type a new name in the Save As text box.
4. Click on the Save button.

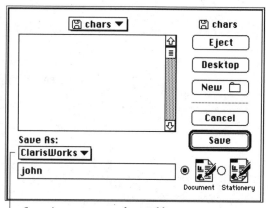

Save As type pop-up list and list contents

■ About the potential of databases

Databases are the last thing computer users think about learning and the first thing that intimidates them when they do think about using them.

You are probably familiar with databases that are used to track names and addresses or to track inventory and customer sales—all very practical business applications of databases.

But stop and think for a moment about how a database can work for an individual or family:

For teachers

▲ A list of student's names and grades with a grade calculation field can make end-of-the-term frenzy last only 15 minutes instead of the usual hours or days.

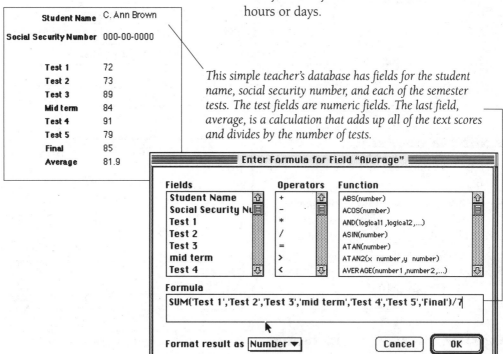

Student Name	C. Ann Brown
Social Security Number	000-00-0000
Test 1	72
Test 2	73
Test 3	89
Mid term	84
Test 4	91
Test 5	79
Final	85
Average	81.9

This simple teacher's database has fields for the student name, social security number, and each of the semester tests. The test fields are numeric fields. The last field, average, is a calculation that adds up all of the text scores and divides by the number of tests.

Enter Formula for Field "Average"

Fields
Student Name
Social Security Nu
Test 1
Test 2
Test 3
mid term
Test 4

Operators
+
−
*
/
=
>
<

Function
ABS(number)
ACOS(number)
AND(logical1 ,logical2 ,...)
ASIN(number)
ATAN(number)
ATAN2(x number ,y number)
AVERAGE(number1 ,number2 ,...)

Formula
SUM('Test 1','Test 2','Test 3','mid term','Test 4','Test 5','Final')/7

Format result as Number ▼   Cancel   OK

About the potential of databases

For the gourmet—A recipe book!

▲ You can have fields such the name of the recipe, how many it serves, what type of recipe it is (hors d'oeuvres, salads, etc.), a big field for the ingredients, another field for cooking time and temperature, and a field for instructions. With ClarisWorks' outstanding ability to incorporate graphics and fancy fonts right into a database—voila, you have holiday gifts for all of your friends and family.

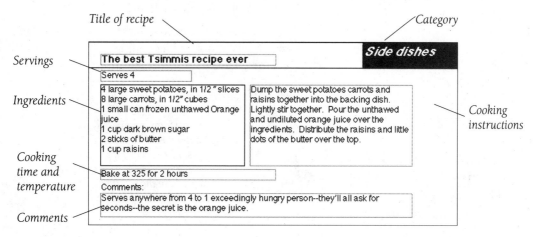

Title of recipe *Category*

Servings

Ingredients

Cooking instructions

Cooking time and temperature

Comments

Side dishes

The best Tsimmis recipe ever

Serves 4

4 large sweet potatoes, in 1/2" slices
8 large carrots, in 1/2" cubes
1 small can frozen unthawed Orange juice
1 cup dark brown sugar
2 sticks of butter
1 cup raisins

Dump the sweet potatoes carrots and raisins together into the backing dish. Lightly stir together. Pour the unthawed and undiluted orange juice over the ingredients. Distribute the raisins and little dots of the butter over the top.

Bake at 325 for 2 hours

Comments:
Serves anywhere from 4 to 1 exceedingly hungry person--they'll all ask for seconds--the secret is the orange juice.

These recipe database fields include a recipe category list in the form of a pop-up list of items such as side dishes, main dishes, and desserts. Other fields include the recipe title, servings, ingredients, instructions, time and temperature, and comments.

If you create this type of database, you can then sort the database out first by category—so that all of the side dishes will appear together. The second sort criteria should be recipe title, so the recipes will be in title order. Print out the database and you'll have an instant recipe book.

For the hobby enthusiast

▲ I collect rubber stamps and I have a database on my computer that lists all of my favorite rubber stamp companies, along with a brief description of their products (remarks like "Cool stuff," or "Definitely not my style"). I've even left a place where I can stamp my stamps and have a record of what I've bought from various stamp companies. If your hobby is like mine, it grows like crazy and I no longer have to wonder what rubber stamp image I have on hand.

The uses of databases are limitless—break out of the mailing list mold and let your imagination soar—you only have your disorganization to lose.

About the potential of databases

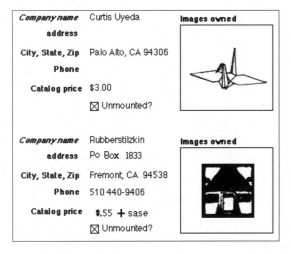

This rubber stamp database lets me find out if companies sell unmounted stamps and shows me what stamps I have purchased. You could either stamp the stamp directly in the square, or if you have a scanner, place the image inside of the database itself.

*All images copyrighted by
Rubber stamps by Curtis Uyeda, Palo Alto, CA;
Rubberstilzkin, Fremont, CA*

Drawing

■ Drawing or Painting

What's the difference?
Both the Drawing and Painting modes share a group of tools, and many tasks are performed in the same way. However, each mode has specialized uses.

Draw
▲ Uses simple shapes
▲ Creates lines that are solid lines not lines that re made up of pixels
▲ Easily creates flow charts, floor plans, and other architectural schematics
▲ Works best in creating forms and documents
▲ Works great for borders and signs

This Drawing document uses three geometric shapes and text to create a basic logo.

■ Creating a new Drawing document
▲ Choose New from the File menu if you have been working in ClarisWorks, or double-click on Drawing in the scrolling list.

Drawing or Painting

■ Drawing

The Drawing tools work exactly the same way inside Drawing, Painting, and other ClarisWorks modes. The tool bar has a variety of shapes and lines, as well as the fill tools that provide you color, patterns, and gradients.

The Drawing menus include File, Edit, Format, Arrange, Options, and View. These menus are accessed the same way and contain many of the same functions as other ClarisWorks program modes.

The Format menu now contains the text options such as font, size, and style.

The Arrange menu has options that help you stack up objects and rotate them.

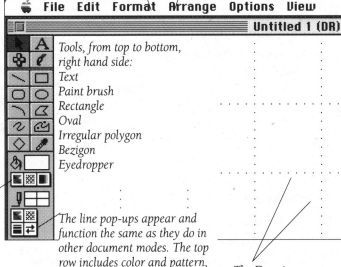

Tools, from top to bottom, left hand side:
Pointer
Spreadsheet
Line
Rounded rectangle
Arc
Freehand
Regular polygon

Tools, from top to bottom, right hand side:
Text
Paint brush
Rectangle
Oval
Irregular polygon
Bezigon
Eyedropper

The fill pop-ups appear and function the same as they do in other document modes. From left to right they include color, pattern, and gradient.

The line pop-ups appear and function the same as they do in other document modes. The top row includes color and pattern, while the bottom row includes line thickness and line endings.

The Drawing screen contains grids that will help you align objects. The grids may be turned on and off.

✔ *Tip: Double-click on any pop-up to use that tool multiple times without having to reselect it each time. To unselect the tool, click on any other tool in the tool bar.*

■ Creating a first drawing

1. Choose New from the File menu.

2. Select the Drawing menu program mode.

Changing paper size and margins in Drawing

1. Choose Page Setup from the File menu.

2. Select the paper you want to use from the Paper pop-up menu in the Page Setup dialog box.

3. Select the layout you want to use from the Layout pop-up menu in the Page Setup dialog box. You have three choices:

▲ 1 Up, which is suitable for single documents such as a letterhead with logo

▲ 2 Up, which is suitable for two documents that are exactly alike or a folded brochure

▲ 4 Up, which is suitable for four documents such as business cards or a folded greeting card.

4. Click on the OK button when you are finished.

5. Choose Document from the Format menu and in the text boxes in the Document dialog box, type the proper margins for the document.

6. Click on the OK button when you complete your page setup changes.

The Paper pop-up menu will contain other paper choices that are dependent on the type of printer you are using. This LaserWriter Page Setup dialog box gives six choices: US Letter, US Legal, A4, B5, and two different envelope setups.

| File | Edit | Format | Arrange |

New...　　　　⌘N
Open...　　　　⌘O
Insert...

Close　　　　　⌘W
Save　　　　　　⌘S
Save As...　　⇧⌘S
Revert
Document Summary Info

Shortcuts　　　　▶
Library　　　　　▶
Mail　　　　　　　▶

Mail Merge...　⇧⌘M
Page Setup...
Print...　　　　⌘P

Quit　　　　　　⌘Q

The Page Setup command in the File menu

The LaserWriter Page Setup dialog box

OK button

Options button

The Options button contains checkboxes that perform special effects such as inverting or reversing your picture's color scheme.

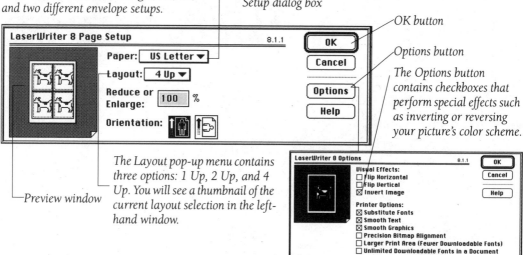

The Layout pop-up menu contains three options: 1 Up, 2 Up, and 4 Up. You will see a thumbnail of the current layout selection in the left-hand window.

Preview window

Creating a first drawing

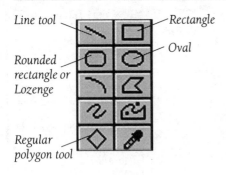

Line tool

Rectangle

Oval

Rounded rectangle or Lozenge

Regular polygon tool

✔ **Tip**: *To draw a straight line, a true square, or perfect circle, hold the Shift key down while you draw the object.*

Drawing objects

Drawing objects

Handles appear as small square dots

Drag the cursor to the left and down until the object is the correct size.

■ Drawing objects

Five of the drawing palette tools draw objects that are either regular in shape or are lines that enclose a space. These five objects are the straight line, rectangle, rounded rectangle, regular polygon, and oval.

Drawing a straight line

1. Select the line tool, move the pointer where you want the line to begin, and click.
2. Drag in the direction you want the line to go.
3. Let go of the mouse button.

Drawing a simple solid object using the rectangle tool

1. Click once on the rectangle tool, move the pointer to the upper left-hand position of the rectangle, and click.
2. Drag to the right and down until the rectangle is the size you want it to be. If you want a perfect square, hold the Shift key down while you are dragging.
3. Let go of the mouse button.

Changing the shape of a solid object

1. Click once inside of the rectangle or other solid object. You will see four square dots or object handles on the outside of the object.
2. Position the pointer over one of the dots.
3. Drag to the left to increase the vertical size or drag down to increase the height of the object.
4. Let go of the mouse button.

Moving an object

1. Click inside the rectangle or other filled object or click in the middle of a line.
2. Drag the object to the desired position. Notice the ghost or faintly dotted image that indicates where the object is going.
3. When the object is in position, let go of the mouse button.

✔ **Tip**: *To move an object in small jumps, click once on the object, then tap the up, down, left, or right arrows on the keyboard.*

When you move an object you will see a faint ghostlike image of that object. Use this image as a guideline to determine when the object is in position.

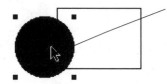

When you are moving an object, keep the pointer in the middle of the object and hold the mouse button down firmly.

■ Creating irregular objects

Drawing program mode uses several types of irregular objects and irregular line tools:

- ▲ Arc tool
- ▲ Freehand tool
- ▲ Irregular polygon tool
- ▲ Bezigon tool

Using the arc tool

1. Select the arc tool and click in the document where you want your arc to begin.
2. Drag in the direction you want the arc to swing.
3. Let go of the mouse button when the arc is finished.
4. To change the arc, click on one of the handles and pull the arc up or sideways.

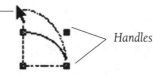

Direction of arc and pointer movement

Handles

As you move your pointer up the screen, the arc becomes taller. As you move your pointer to the right, the arc becomes wider.

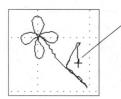

Use the freehand tool exactly the same way you would use a pencil.

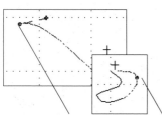

The Polygon Sides dialog box determines how many sides a regular polygon has—a triangle, for example, has three sides.

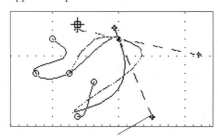

When you first create a Bezier drawing, you will see a handle appear at the beginning of the line. As you click to make the line curve, you will see the round nodes appear as open dots.

Right-hand handle in the process of being moved down. Notice the ghostlike image indicating the handle's previous position.

Using the freehand tool

1. Select the Freehand tool from the tool panel and click in your document where you want your drawing to begin.
2. Drag the pointer as you would drag a pencil and draw your object.
3. When the drawing is finished, let go of the mouse button.

Using the regular polygon tool

1. Select the regular polygon tool from the tool panel at the left side of the screen.
2. Choose Polygon Sides from the Options menu.
3. In the Polygon Sides dialog box, type the number of sides for the regular polygon.
4. Click on the OK button.
5. Click in your document where you want the polygon to start.
6. Drag the mouse until the polygon is the correct size in the document.
7. Let go of the mouse button.

Bezier drawing

Bezier drawing creates curves and shapes using a bezigon tool from the tool panel, which creates a handle that can be used to alter the curve of the line.

1. Select the bezigon tool and click in your document where you want the line to begin.
2. Click at each point where the line curves.
3. To end the line, double-click.

Reshaping a Bezier drawing

1. Using the pointer tool from the tool panel, click once on your Bezier line drawing.
2. Choose Reshape from the Arrange menu, or press ⌘-R. Your line appear with nodes or round dots where the line curves.
3. Click and hold down on one of the dots and a handle will appear.
4. Click on one of the ends of the handle and tug upward. The line will be pulled upward.
5. Double-click away from the line to finish.

Creating irregular objects

■ Making changes

You can stack up the objects you have drawn to create an image. In order to do that, you must place the objects in the proper order.

Restacking graphic objects

1. Select the object you want to appear on top.

2. Select one of the four following choices from the Arrange menu:

▲ Move Forward or ⇧⌘-+ lets you move the object to the absolute top of the stack.

▲ Move To Front lets you will move the object forward one position.

▲ Move Backward or ⇧⌘--(HYPHEN) lets you move the object to the absolute back of the stack.

▲ Move To Back lets you move the object back one position or object.

Making a coffee cup

This exercise will show you how to stack objects and create your own fancy virtual coffee cup.

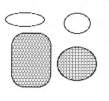

Step 1

1. *Create the four shapes illustrated to the left using the tools on the tool panel.*

2. *Fill the lozenge shape and the larger circle with the same pattern or color of your choice.*

3. *Fill the smaller circle with white and fill the oval with white for an empty cup, or black for a full cup of coffee.*

Step 2

1. *Move the larger circle on top of the lozenge.*

2. *Move the small white circle on top of the large filled-in circle and center it.*

3. *Click on the lozenge, and select Move To Back from the Arrange menu.*

4. *Place the oval for the coffee cup opening over the top of the lozenge.*

There you are—a full or empty cup of coffee!

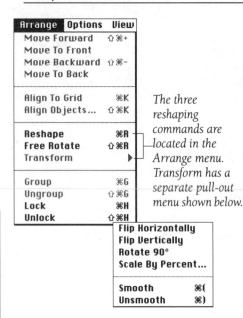

The three reshaping commands are located in the Arrange menu. Transform has a separate pull-out menu shown below.

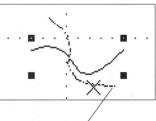

Notice the ghostlike image that indicates the new position of the object. As soon as you let go of the mouse, that is where your object will appear.

Reshaping objects

You can reshape objects one of three ways:

▲ Using the file handles

▲ Using Free Rotate to rotate an object

▲ Using Transform to flip an object horizontally or vertically, rotate it by exactly 90 degrees, or scale the object up or down. You can also smooth curves or make them more angular by using the Transform commands.

Reshape

See "Changing the shape of a solid object" on page 176 for how to use object handles to change an object's shape. Bezier objects are reshaped very differently from any other type of drawing. You can find that information in "Reshaping a Bezier drawing" on page 178.

Using Free Rotate

1. Click once on the object you wish to rotate.

2. Choose Free Rotate from the Arrange menu, or press ⇧⌘-R.

3. The pointer appears as a large X. Using this pointer, pull on one of the sides of the object, moving in the direction you wish the object to rotate. You will see a ghostlike image of the object that indicates the direction that the object is rotating.

Using Transform

1. Select the object you wish to transform.

2. Choose Transform from the Arrange menu.

3. Select the transformation choice you wish to use.

Note: The Smooth and Unsmooth menu choices can have extreme effects on your object, so use these choices with care.

■ Filling an object

1. Click in the middle of an object, making sure the object handles appear.
2. Select the color, pattern, or gradient pop-up you want to use.
3. Drag over the fill pop-up palette until you find the color, pattern, or gradient you want to use.
4. Let go of the mouse button.

You may select a choice from all three buttons so that your pattern will appear in color and with a gradation to that color.

When you hold the color, pattern, or gradient pop-up down, a palette will pop out to the right. Move your pointer over the choices and when you find the one you want, let go of the mouse button.

Color pop-up

Pattern pop-up   *Gradient pop-up*

The selected pattern appears surrounded by a darker line.

Changing the outline of a solid object

1. Click once on the object you want to change.
2. Click on the line thickness pop-up.
3. Select the proper line thickness from the line thickness pop-up list.
4. Let go of the mouse button.

Setting a unique line thickness

1. Click once on the object you want to change.
2. Click on the line thickness pop-up list.
3. Select Other from the line thickness pop-up list.
4. Type a line width in the Enter Line Width text box in the Line Width dialog box.
5. Click on the OK button.

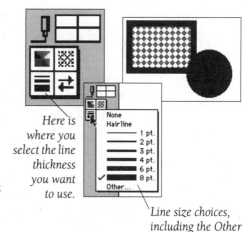

Here is where you select the line thickness you want to use.

| None |
| Hairline |
| 1 pt. |
| 2 pt. |
| 3 pt. |
| 4 pt. |
| 6 pt. |
| 8 pt. |
| Other... |

Line size choices, including the Other menu choice

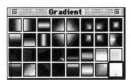

The Gradient palette shows you your current gradients.

The Gradient Editor dialog box appears to the right of the Gradient palette shown above.

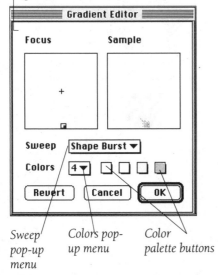

Sweep pop-up menu   Colors pop-up menu   Color palette buttons

■ Gradients

Gradients are combinations of colors that gradually fade from one color to the next color. Gradients can be used to fill an object, or a line can be colored with a gradient.

You fill objects with gradients the same way you select patterns or colors. However, gradients themselves can be changed. You can select new colors and new gradient patterns.

Changing gradients

1. Choose Gradients from the Options menu.
2. You will see a Gradient Editor dialog box. You can change the gradient colors, sweep, and focus point from this dialog box.

Changing gradient colors

1. From the Gradient Editor dialog box, select the Colors number button. A Colors pop-up list will appear. Select 2, 3, or 4 color combinations. To the right of the Colors number button, you will see the same number of Color palette buttons as the number of colors you want to use.
2. Select the first color palette button and select the first color you want to use in that button. You will see a preview in the Sample box at the top of the Gradient Editor dialog box.
3. Repeat step 2 for each color button to change all of the gradients.

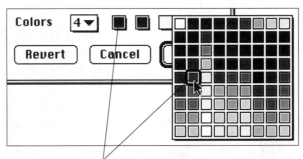

The color palette buttons will show a pop-up color palette. You choose the colors in this palette the same way you choose colors from the color pop-up in the tool bar.

Gradients

Changing the gradient pattern

The Sweep pop-up menu in the Gradient Editor dialog box contains three Sweep choices: Directional, Circular, or Shape Burst.

Using shapeburst and circular gradients

1. In the Gradient Editor dialog box, choose either the Shape Burst or Circular gradient commands from the Sweep pop-up menu.
2. Drag the small shape in the Focus box until the Sample box appears the way you want it to appear.
3. Click on the OK button when you are finished.

Using directional gradients

1. In the Gradient Editor dialog box, choose the Directional gradient command from the Sweep pop-up menu.
2. Drag the Directional pointer until the Sample box appears the way you want it to appear.
3. Click on the OK button when you are finished.

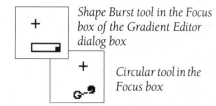

Shape Burst tool in the Focus box of the Gradient Editor dialog box

Circular tool in the Focus box

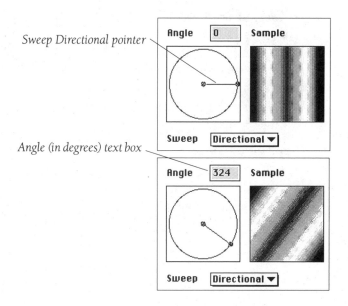

Sweep Directional pointer

Angle (in degrees) text box

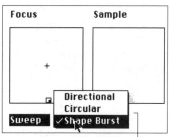

The Sweep pop-up menu gives you three variations for gradation.

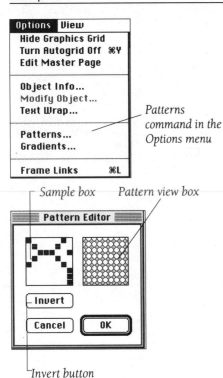

Patterns command in the Options menu

Sample box *Pattern view box*

Invert button

■ Using the Pattern Editor

1. Choose Patterns from the Options menu. You will see a Pattern Editor dialog box. In the left-hand sample box, the current pattern is shown as a series of square dots, or pixels.

2. To eliminate one of these black pixels, select that pixel and it will turn white, or to add a pixel, select a white pixel and it will turn black.

3. Click on the OK button when you are finished.

Using Pattern Editor Invert

Invert will make all of the black pixels white and all of the white pixels black. Just click on the Invert button in the Pattern Editor dialog box which you open by using the Patterns command in the Options menu.

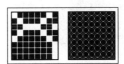

The pattern on the left has been inverted in this illustration.

■ Deleting and duplicating objects

Deleting an object or objects

1. Click on a single object.

2. Press the Delete or Clear key, or select Cut from the Edit menu.

Duplicating objects

1. Click on a single object, or hold down the shift key and click on multiple objects.

2. Choose Copy from the Edit menu.

Using the Pattern Editor

Using a marquee

If you want to select more than one object quickly, you can use a marquee.

1. In the tool bar, select the pointer tool.
2. Move the pointer just above and to the left of the group of objects you want to select.
3. Drag to the left and down until you see a moving dashed line.
4. Let go of the mouse button. All of your objects will appear with handles indicating they have been selected.

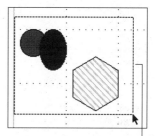

When you use the pointer tool to draw a marquee, you will see a shimmering dashed line indicating the objects have been selected.

■ Master pages

Master pages are template pages that contain text, color, or art. Each new page in a document will contain any element that is on a master page.

Master pages are useful for creating a uniform look for all types of documents such as slide presentations.

Creating master pages

1. Choose Edit Master Page from the Options menu.
2. Make your changes, adding text, art, and backgrounds to this master page.
3. When you are finished, reselect Edit Master Page from the Options menu.
4. To see the master pages while you are working on a document, choose Page View from the View menu, or press ⇧⌘-P.

Wilson Widget Company

Wilson Widget Company

Welcome to Wilson Widget

Wilson Widget Company

Our new health plan benefits YOU!

* Faster service
* Lower monthly rates
* No waiting in line
* Prescription plan too!

Master pages

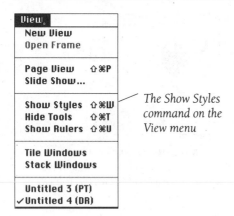

The Show Styles command on the View menu

■ Creating drawing styles

You can preserve your color and pen settings by creating a style from them.

1. Select the color, line widths, and fill patterns you want to use.
2. Choose the Show Styles command in the View menu, or press ⇧ ⌘ -**w**. The Stylesheet dialog box will appear.
3. Click on the New button at the bottom of the Stylesheet dialog box.
4. Type a style name in the Style name box of the New Style dialog box.
5. Click on the Inherit document selection format checkbox.
6. Click on the OK button in the New Style dialog box.
7. Click on the close box in the Stylesheet dialog box.

Editing styles

Drawing styles are edited much the same way Word Processing styles are edited.

1. Choose Show styles from the View menu. The Stylesheet dialog box will appear.
2. Click on the style you wish to change in the styles list of the Stylesheet dialog box.
3. Click on the Edit button from the Stylesheet dialog box.
4. Click on the item you want to change in the Properties list. Make the changes to color, lines, and patterns from the tool bar palettes.
5. Click on the Done button in the Edit Style dialog box when you are finished.

This is an example of the Edit styles dialog box from the View menu. The selected style has been created and is now being changed.

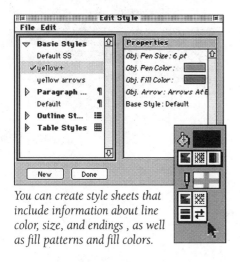

You can create style sheets that include information about line color, size, and endings , as well as fill patterns and fill colors.

■ Preventing changes

Once you have a document exactly the way you want, if you would like to protect your document from any future changes:

1. Select all of the objects you do not want to have accidentally changed, deleted, or moved. You can click on one object to select it, Shift-click on several objects to select them, or choose Select All from the Edit menu, or **⌘-A** to select everything on the page.
2. Choose Lock from the Edit menu. The locked objects will appear on the page slightly lighter than other objects.

Note: If you need to make changes later, just select all of the objects, and choose Unlock from the Arrange menu. If you need to add locked objects to objects that were previously locked, you will first have to unlock any locked objects. Then you can reselect all objects that need to be locked and use the Lock command from the Arrange menu.

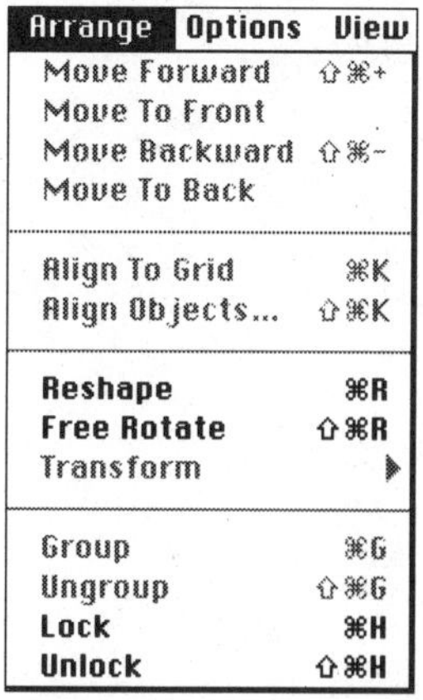
Arrange Options View
Move Forward ⇧⌘+
Move To Front
Move Backward ⇧⌘-
Move To Back
Align To Grid ⌘K
Align Objects... ⇧⌘K
Reshape ⌘R
Free Rotate ⇧⌘R
Transform
Group ⌘G
Ungroup ⇧⌘G
Lock ⌘H
Unlock ⇧⌘H

Lock in the Arrange menu prevents changes to objects in your drawing.

Painting

■ Painting

How is Painting different from Drawing

While many of the Drawing tools operate exactly the same way in the Painting program mode, Painting has other tools that are not available in Drawing.

Painting

▲ Uses freehand drawing

▲ Allows color gradations, tints, patterns, and spray can effects

▲ Gives you tools to alter scanned images

▲ Creates lines and objects that are pixel-based or created from dots on the screen

■ Creating a new Painting document

▲ Choose New from the File menu if you have been working in ClarisWorks, or double-click on Painting in the scrolling list.`

This Painting document combines geometric shapes with free-hand drawing for the coffee steam. The text is Bauhaus outlined and then filled with a color gradient.

■ Painting tools

While Drawing uses objects, Painting uses pixels, or dots, to form pictures on the screen. Art made up of dots is called bit-mapped, whereas art made up of solid lines is called object-oriented. Painting produces bit-mapped art, while drawing produces object-oriented art.

Painting tools

The Painting mode has several tools in addition to the tools that are available in the Drawing mode. These tools produce bit-mapped drawings that are made up of pixels, or dots.

Painting tools

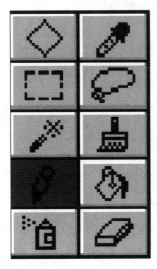

Regular polygon tool—creates regular polygons	*Eyedropper—used to pick up colors*
Rectangle selection tool—selects a regular area	*Lasso tool—used to select an irregular area*
Magic wand—selects similar colors	*Paint brush—used to paint freehand an area*
Pencil—freehand drawing with a pencil	*Paint bucket—used to fill an enclosed area with color*
Spray can—sprays a fine mist of color	*Eraser—used to erase an area*

■ Using Painting tools

Using the paint brush and spray can

These two tools operate the same way, but produce very different results.

1. Select the paint brush or spray can tool in the tool bar.
2. In the document, drag to create brush strokes or spray can effect.

The stroke size of the paint brush strokes is determined by the Brush Shape dialog box.

Editing brush shapes

You can use a fatter, skinnier, rounder, or squarer paint brush by editing the basic brush shape.

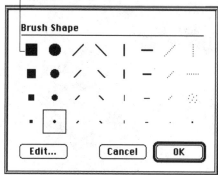

1. In the tool bar, double-click on the Brush tool. You will see a Brush Shape dialog box.
2. Select the brush shape you wish to use.
3. Click on the OK button.
4. Use your shape and line choices to draw an object using this new brush shape.

Using the pencil

The pencil can be used the same way that the brush and spray can are used—however, you can also use the pencil to edit the on-screen pixels individually.

1. Select the pencil tool from the tool bar.
2. Zoom in on your object by clicking on the increase size button at the bottom left-hand corner of the screen. Set the zoom as close as you can.
3. In the color fill palette on the left-hand side of the screen, select a color to use.
4. Select the pencil tool from the tool bar.
5. Click on a square pixel or dot to change the pixel to that color. If you click a second time, the pixel will change back to white.

Select the increase size button to zoom in on your picture and see the individual pixels.

The Options menu changes the appearance of lines and some painting tools through the Brush Shape, Spray Can, and Painting Mode choices.

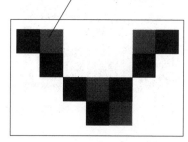

One click on a pixel will change it to your current color. The second click will turn the pixel to the color of the paper (in this case white).

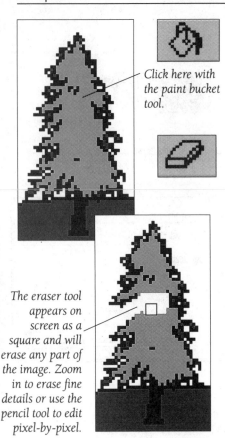

Click here with the paint bucket tool.

The eraser tool appears on screen as a square and will erase any part of the image. Zoom in to erase fine details or use the pencil tool to edit pixel-by-pixel.

Using the Paint bucket

1. In the color fill palette on the left-hand side of the screen, select a color to use.
2. Select the paint bucket from the tool bar.
3. Click inside of an enclosed area to change that area to your chosen color.

Using the eraser

1. Select the eraser tool.
2. Drag the eraser over the area you wish to erase. The area you erase will appear in the color of the paper.

Note: If you want to erase just a little tiny part of your image, zoom in close to your image using the increase size button on the bottom left-hand side of the window. The eraser size will stay the same, but the painting will appear bigger.

✔ **Tip**: *To erase the entire document, double-click on the eraser tool.*

Fill sample

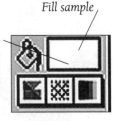

This is where the color shows up when you have selected a color using the eyedropper tool.

Using the eyedropper

The eyedropper tool is used to select colors that you want to use when these colors already appear on the screen.

1. Select the eyedropper tool and move the Eye-dropper to the color you want to pick up.
2. Click on that color. The fill sample in the tool bar on the left-hand side of the screen should show that color.

Using Painting tools

Selecting an area

You need to select an area if you want to cut, copy, or move part of an image. There are three tools that will help you:

- ▲ Rectangle selection tool
- ▲ Lasso tool
- ▲ Magic wand

Once you have selected an area you may:

▲ *Delete the selection by pressing the Delete or Clear keys*

▲ *Cut the selection by choosing Cut from the Edit menu*

▲ *Copy the selection by choosing Copy from the Edit menu*

▲ *Move the selection by tapping the right, left, up, or down arrow keys on the keyboard*

Using the rectangle selection tool

1. Select the rectangle selection tool.
2. Move the pointer just above and to the left of the area you wish to select.
3. Drag to the right and down until the entire area is surrounded by a shimmering line that indicates your objects have been selected.
4. Let go of the mouse button.

✔ **Tip**: *To create an illusion of motion, you can create multiple copies of the painting by selecting it with the rectangle selection tool. Then hold down the Option-⌘ keys and drag the picture. You will see repeated copies of the painting trailing behind the original image.*

Using the lasso tool

The lasso tool lets you select an irregularly shaped area.

1. Select the lasso tool from the tool bar.
2. Move the pointer just above and to the left of the area you wish to select.
3. Drag around the selection area in an irregular shape. You will see a shimmering line that indicates your objects have been selected.

Using the magic wand

The magic wand lets you select areas that are about the same color.

1. Select the magic wand.
2. Move the pointer over the colored area you wish to select.
3. Click with the mouse button.

This magic wand has selected the lawn beneath the trees. The lawn was moved using the arrow keys.

■ Using Transform

Transform combines backgrounds and pictures:

1. Create a simple drawing.
2. Create a background using the patterns fill palette.
3. Select the background using the pointer tool.
4. Choose Pick Up from the Transform menu. Your image will now be filled in with the background pattern and color you used.

■ Creating styles

You can preserve your color and pen settings by creating a style from them.

1. Select the color, line widths, and fill patterns you want to use.
2. Choose Show Styles from the View menu, or press ⇧⌘-w. The Stylesheet dialog box will appear.
3. Click on the New button at the bottom of the Stylesheet dialog box.
4. Type a style name in the Style name box of the New Style dialog box.
5. Click on the Inherit document selection format checkbox.
6. Click on the OK button in the New Style dialog box.
7. Click on the close box in the Stylesheet dialog box.

Editing painting styles

1. Choose Show Styles from the View menu. The Stylesheet dialog box will appear.
2. Click on the style you wish to change in the styles list of the Stylesheet dialog box.
3. Click on the Edit button from the Stylesheet dialog box.
4. Click on the item you want to change in the Properties list. Make the changes to color, lines, and patterns from the tool bar palettes.
5. Click on the Done button in the Edit Style dialog box when you are finished.
6. Click in the close box in the Stylesheet dialog box when you are finished.

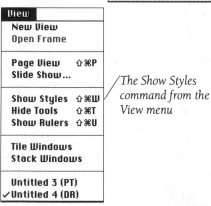

The Show Styles command from the View menu

This is an example of the Edit Styles dialog box. The selected style has been created and is now being changed.

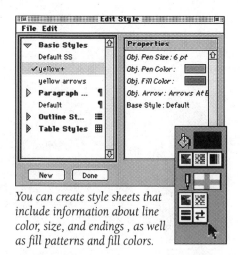

You can create style sheets that include information about line color, size, and endings , as well as fill patterns and fill colors.

■ Colors and patterns

The Painting Mode dialog box changes colors and patterns from solid color to transparent color. Transparent colors and patterns will then flow over any existing drawing and the existing drawing will show through the new color.

Using Paint Mode

1. Choose Paint Mode from the Options menu. You will see a Painting Mode dialog box.
2. Select one of three Painting Mode dialog box radio buttons.
   ▲ Opaque creates solid colors and patterns
   ▲ Transparent pattern creates transparent patterns
   ▲ Tint creates transparent colors
3. Click on the OK button when you are finished.

Note: When you change the Paint Mode radio buttons, the next time you select a color or pattern palette, it will display in that painting mode.

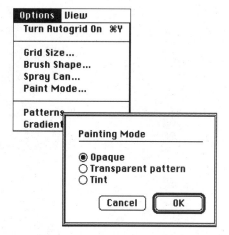

■ Document size and resolution

Drawing and Painting documents are created at 72 dots or pixels per inch. You can change the resolution in the Resolution and Depth dialog box. To open it, choose Resolution & Depth from the Format menu.

Changing the size of a document

1. Choose Resolution & Depth from the Format menu.
2. Type in the number of Pixels across and Pixels down you want to use or click on one of the preset Resolution radio buttons. Remember that the standard measurement is 72 pixels to the inch, so a 2 inch by 2 inch drawing would be 144 by 144 pixels.
3. The Depth radio buttons can be used to set how many colors you want to use. Click on the radio button that contains your choice.
4. Click on the OK button when you are finished.

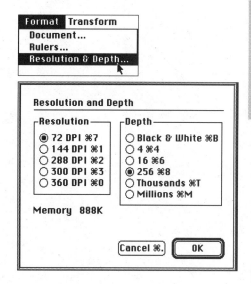

Communications

■ Basic communications

ClarisWorks can produce printed documents, but it can also send them into cyberspace through the communications features found in this rich package. With the ClarisWorks communications program mode, you can connect to services such as:

▲ The Internet

▲ Local bulletin board services (BBSs).

Many of these services have their own software they expect you to use, but the ClarisWorks communications program mode will allow you to connect with many communications providers.

So to begin with, you must have a modem to use this program mode.

Modem settings

When you want to start using ClarisWorks Communications, you must find out some information about your computer modem. The information should be on the box or the manual that came with the modem. You need to find the correct numbers for:

▲ Baud rate, which is the speed at which the modem will transmit data. Most new modems run at a minimum of 9600 baud, and some are even faster, running at 19200 baud or more.

▲ Connection is the place in the back of your computer where the modem plugs in—either the modem port or a printer port.

Limitations

If you are interested in faxing from your computer, you will have to purchase a fax modem, which will come with a fax-modem communications package. You can then use that package to dial regular services as well as send out faxes directly from your computer.

Communications window

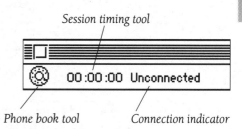

Session timing tool

Phone book tool   *Connection indicator*

The Communications screen will show you whether you are connected or not, and how long you have been connected. You can also use and create phone books using the phone book tool.

Basic communications

▲ Basic modem type refers to modems such as Hayes-compatible modems, Apple Data modems, Apple Personal Modem, Macintosh models, or Macintosh PowerBook modems.

Telecommunication services

Not only do you need to know those basic facts about your modem, you also need to know some basic facts about the type of service you are connecting to.

In the chart, "Basic communications information," shown below, you will see a summary of the four items you must learn about the service you wish to connect with. In particular, you need to know the baud rate (speed) your commercial provider uses. Sometimes services provide separate phone numbers for different baud rates.

Basic communications information for service providers

What you need to know	The details	Standard settings
Baud rate	The baud rate of the service you are connecting with.	9600 is the most common setting. Fax modems run at 9600 baud when communicating with a fax machine. Other services offer speeds higher than 9600 baud.
Parity	There are three choices: None, Even, and Odd.	Even is the most probable setting when connecting to mainframe computers. None is the setting when connecting to personal computers.
Data bits	Two common choices are seven or eight; two less common choices are, five or six.	Seven (7) is the most common setting when connecting to mainframe computers. Eight (8) is the usual setting when connecting to personal computers.
Stop bits	Again there are only a few choices: one, one-and-a-half, or two.	Usual stop bit setting is one (1).

Connections to large service providers such as universities are usually: Even 7 1
Connections to personal computers and commercial service providers are usually: None 8 1

■ Making that first connection

Making the correct connection settings

To connect, you need to fill out the Connection Settings dialog box for the service you are dialing. Collect the information from the service provider and proceed as follows:

1. Choose the Connection command from the Setting menu. You should see a Connection Settings dialog box.
2. Click on the Method pop-up menu, and select the method, which could be either the Apple Mode or Serial Tool.
3. Select the proper Baud Rate for the service you wish to dial—not the baud rate of your modem.
4. Select the Parity, Data Bits, and Stop Bits for the service you wish to dial.
5. You may or may not need to change the Handshake setting. It is set to None by default—which should work for most services. Once in a while a service will request XON/XOFF.
6. In the When dialing portion of the dialog box, inside of the Dial Phone Number box, type the number, including the area code, that the service has given you for access—no dashes, no parentheses, just a string of numbers as in: 14153568200.
7. Check the Modem options and make sure you are set to the correct type of modem.
8. Make sure the Modem Port or Printer Port icon is clicked so the computer knows where your modem is plugged in.
9. Click on the OK button when you are finished.

Settings Session Vie
> Connection...
> Terminal...
> File Transfer...
>
> Info...   ⌘I
> Show Scrollback   ⌘L
> Phone Book...   ⌘B

Settings menu: This menu is where you need to start setting up the specifications for both your modem and the service providers you will be calling.

✔ **Tip—About telephone numbers**: *Dialing from a centrex system like you find in many offices and hotels means you have to add codes in front of the telephone number in the Dial Phone Number box. Type a 9 followed by a comma (no spaces) and then your phone number. The number 9 will give you outside access and the comma will pause the modem long enough to make the outside connection.*

Method pop-up menu

Connection Settings dialog box

Connection Settings

Method: [Apple Mode... ▼]   [OK]   [Cancel]

When dialing
Dial Phone Number [   ] [▼]
Dialing Method: [Touch-Tone™ ▼]
☒ Redial [3] times every [10] seconds

When answering
Answer phone after [2] rings

Modem options
Modem: [Hayes-Compatible Modem ▼]
☐ Display Modem Monitor Window

Port Settings
Baud Rate: [2400 ▼]
Parity: [None ▼]
Data Bits: [8 ▼]
Stop Bits: [1 ▼]
Handshake: [None ▼]   1.5.3

Modem Port   Printer Port

Phone Number box

Modem options

Baud Rate, Parity, Data Bits, and Stop Bit settings

Connection icons

Making that first connection

*Terminal command
from the Settings menu*

Terminal settings for your modem

Terminal settings are needed so that the party you are dialing understands how to display information on your screen.

When you choose the Terminal Settings menu choice, you will see four panels:

▲ General
▲ Screen
▲ Keyboard
▲ Character Set

Each menu must be filled out correctly.

General settings on the Terminal settings menu

*General options on the
Terminal Settings dialog box*

Emulation button

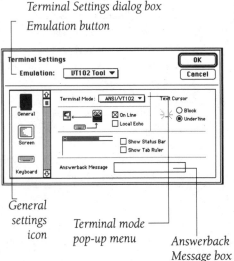

*General
settings
icon*

*Terminal mode
pop-up menu*

*Answerback
Message box*

1. Choose the Terminal command from the Settings menu. The Terminal Settings dialog box will appear.
2. Select the Emulation pop-up menu from the Terminal Settings dialog box. Select either VT102 or TTY in the Emulation pop-up menu.
3. Select the Terminal mode pop-up menu and select the correct mode, usually ANSI/VT102.
4. The On Line checkbox should probably be selected. If you can't see what you type on screen once you connect, go back to this choice and select Local Echo.
5. The Answerback Message box is a place where you can type a short phrase you will see on the

*The Terminal
Settings icons down
the left-hand side of
the screen give you
separate panels.
Each panel must be
filled out correctly for
your connection to
work properly.*

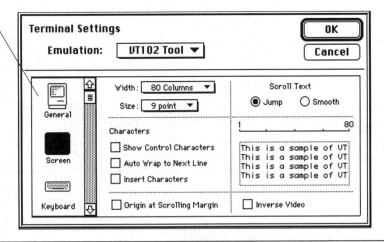

Making that first connection

screen when you are truly connected to the service.

Screen Terminal Settings

The automatic screen width is set to 80 columns with text appearing in 9-point type. You can change both of these items should you need to if you click on the Screen icon.

You also have a choice about scrolling text automatically—which makes any text on the screen move by at a rapid rate, instead of having to use scroll bars or mouse clicks to see additional or previous text.

Screen emulation pop-up menu

Screen options in the Terminal Settings dialog box

Screen icon

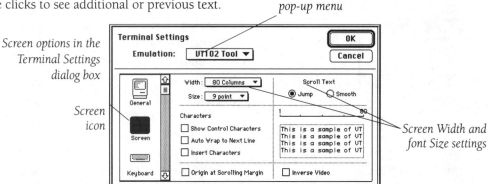

Screen Width and font Size settings

Keyboard Terminal Settings

You can temporarily reassign keys on your keyboard in the Keyboard panel of the Terminal Settings dialog box. You get to the Keyboard panel by clicking on the Keyboard icon.

1. Select the checkbox labeled Swap Backspace and Delete to exchange these two keys.
2. Select the checkbox labeled Keyclick Sound to turn on a keyboard click sound.
3. Select the checkbox labeled Auto Repeat Keys to have a key repeat itself when it is held down.

Character set terminal settings

Most computers understand ASCII (American Standard Code for Information Interchange). This panel is set to understand ASCII—which is a common way of representing characters for all computer systems.

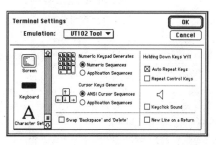

Settings in the Keyboard Terminal Settings dialog box with the default settings changed

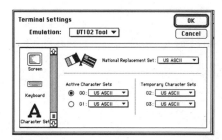

Character Set settings in the Terminal Settings dialog box

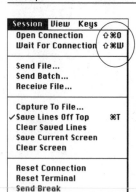

*Open Connection
and Wait For
Connection
commands in the
Session menu.
Notice the
shortcuts keys.*

Ready to dial? Here we go

Dialing is accomplished by:

▲ Choosing the Open Connection command from the Session menu, or pressing ⇧⌘-o. The modem will then dial the number you previously set up in the Connection Settings dialog box on page 199.

*/Phone Book
command from the
Settings menu*

Creating phone books

It's a good idea to keep a collection of commonly dialed modem numbers in the phone book. The phone book is created as follows:

1. Choose Phone Book from the Settings menu, or press ⌘-B. The Edit Phone Book Entry dialog box will appear.

2. In the Name box of the Edit Phone Book Entry dialog box, type the name of the service provider.

3. In the Number box of the Edit Phone Book Entry dialog box, type the phone access number including area code and the special 9-comma code if you need to connect through a centrex system, as in 9,14153332222.

4. In the Type box, it will say PhoneNumber. You don't need to change this as you will probably be dialing via phone, but if you are dialing within a network, you enter the word Network here.

5. Click on the OK button when you are finished.

*The Edit Phone Book Entry dialog box
contains Name, Number, and Type
boxes. This phone book can also be
accessed through the phone book tool
which appears as a small round icon at
the upper left-hand corner of the
Communications window.*

Making that first connection

Using the phone book

To use the phone book:

1. Choose Phone Book from the Settings menu, or press ⌘-B,
2. Select the name of the service you wish to dial.
3. Click on the Connect button.

Making changes to the phone book

To make changes or add more entries to the phone book:

1. Select Phone book from the Settings menu, or press ⌘-B.
2. Select the service you wish to change.
3. Click on the Delete button if you wish to delete the selected service.
4. Select the Edit button if you wish to make changes to the phone book such as changing the phone number or name of the service.
5. Click on the New button if you wish to add a new entry to the phone book and fill out the Edit Phone Book Entry Dialog box.
6. Click on the OK button when you are finished.
7. Click on the Done button in the Phone Book dialog box when you are finished.

Telephone book

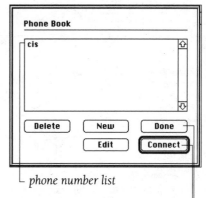

phone number list

Delete, New, Edit, Done, and Connect buttons. Use the Connect button to dial the service provider.

Hanging up

When you are finished you need to execute any termination procedure your service provider usually needs. This often means typing the word logout or exit. Make sure you do this so the main computer realizes you are hanging up. Then you must hang up the modem on your computer.

Connecting without modems over a network

You will need a null modem cable plugged into your serial port or other network cable connection. Contact your system administrator for the exact steps your network software requires.

Hanging up on-line

To hang up your modem connection:

1. Execute the procedure your service asks you to execute, such as typing exit or logout.
2. Choose Close Connection from the Session menu.

Making that first connection

Session	View	Keys

```
Open Connection        ⇧⌘O
Wait For Connection    ⇧⌘W

Send File...
Send Batch...
Receive File...

Capture To File...
✓Save Lines Off Top    ⌘T
Clear Saved Lines
Save Current Screen
Clear Screen

Reset Connection
Reset Terminal
Send Break
```

Capture To File from the Session menu: The Session menu will change slightly once you have opened a connection (dialed your service provider). Capture To File is useful in creating a log of activity so you can remember what you accessed from your service provider. Capture To File will keep track of everything you've typed.
Once you have dialed your provider and turned Capture To File on, you will have a new menu choice, Stop Capture. Use that choice to stop the computer from recording all of your keystrokes.

■ Capturing, sending, and printing information

Capture To File
Capturing to a file means that you are recording keystroke-by-keystroke what is happening on the screen—your typing, the screen that you see on the service you dialed, any e-mail you read, and so on.

You turn Capture To File on, and a file is created on your computer. When you are finished creating this log , use the Stop Capture command from the Session menu. You can then print or save this file.

Using capture
1. Choose Capture To File from the Session menu. You will see the Capture To File dialog box.
2. Enter a file name in the Save captured data as box.
3. Click on the Save button. You will be returned to the main Communications program mode screen.

Stopping capturing
▲ Choose Stop Capture from the Session menu. You will be returned to the main Communications program mode screen.

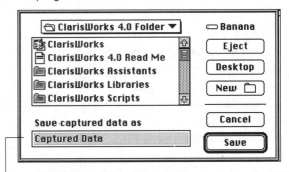

Use the Save captured data as box to give your capture session a title.

✔ **Tip**: *While you are using capture, you can also use Cut, Copy, and Paste to transfer data to a Word Processing or other type of document. Just highlight the part of the capture screen you wish to use and choose Copy or Cut from the Edit menu, then paste the information into your Word Processing document.*

■ Transferring files

Receiving or downloading a file

Receiving a file is called downloading a file, and involves taking a copy from the service provider's machine and saving the file on your computer.

This is very different from capture, as you won't see the file contents until you open the file directly on your Macintosh in a program such as ClarisWorks.

Setting up to receive or download a file

1. Choose File transfer from the Settings menu.
2. Click and hold down on the Protocol button, and select the proper transfer protocol.

Most services will work with the XMODEM tool, which is generally the most flexible setting. The Text tool setting will not allow you to transfer pictures or format commands within text such as special fonts—just ASCII text.

3. Select the Method pop-up menu.

Your choices are:
  ▲ MacBinary
  ▲ MacTerminal 1.1
  ▲ Straight XModem
  ▲ XModem Text

The MacBinary method can transfer formatted text like MicroSoft Word files or pictures.

4. Click on the button labeled Transfer Options.

The default setting is Standard, but the choice 1K Blocks will speed up file transfer. If you aren't sure, leave this button at the default setting.

5. Click on the OK button when you are finished.

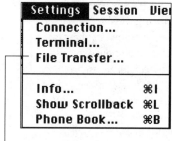

File Transfer from the Settings menu

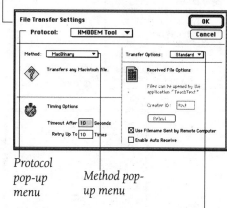

File Transfer Settings dialog box

Protocol pop-up menu

Method pop-up menu

Transfer Options pop-up menu

Transferring files

✔ **Warning**: *If you connect with a university computer, there is some chance that the university computer cannot transfer binary files. If that is true, change to the XModem Text setting or call the administrator of the computer system for tips in how to transfer binary files from their system.*

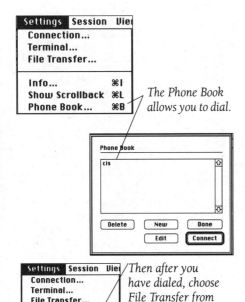

The Phone Book allows you to dial.

Then after you have dialed, choose File Transfer from the Settings menu.

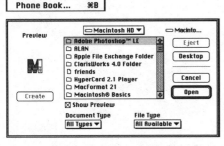

Once you have selected Send File from the Session menu, you must choose your file from a dialog box similar to the Open dialog box.

Receiving a file

1. Choose Phone Book from the Settings menu. Dial your bulletin board or other computer service where the file is going to go.

2. Choose Receive File from the Session menu, if you want to move a file from the main computer to your computer.

3. At this point, the instructions for finding your file on the service are going to be unique according to the type of service you have. Consult your service provider for the balance of the steps.

Sending a file

Sending a file is a standard procedure that will remind you of saving files. To send a file:

1. Choose Phone Book from the Session menu. Dial your bulletin board or other computer service where the file is going to go.

2. Each provider will have an e-mail system or upload system that is unique to its service, but you will start the Send File command from the Session menu.

3. You will see a dialog box that looks like your Open file dialog box. Click on the file you wish to send.

4. Click on the OK button, then follow the steps recommended by your service provider.

Sending a batch

Sending a batch of files means that you will be sending more than one file at a time. The procedures are almost identical to those for sending a file, but you will be selecting more than one file to send.

Printing files

To print a file, use the same steps you would to print a Word Processing file.

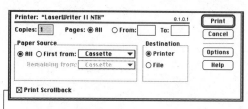

1. Choose Print from the File menu. You will see the Printer dialog box.
2. If you want to print your captured screen, click in the checkbox labeled Print Scrollback that appears on the bottom of the Printer dialog box.
3. Click on the Print button when you are ready to start printing.

When you want to print captured screens, the Print Scrollback checkbox must be selected. This checkbox appears only when you print from the Print command in the File menu while in the Communications program mode.

■ Acting as a host computer

While ClarisWorks isn't a good system for hosting a bulletin board, you can act as a host for a one-to-one computer connection. Host computers are those computers that users dial up and connect with—a commercial service or a small bulletin board service can be acting as a host computer.

1. Choose Connection from the Settings menu. You will see the Connection Settings dialog box.
2. In the Connection Settings dialog box, type the correct number of rings needed for your computer to answer—the default setting of two rings is fine unless you have a fax machine that answers on two rings on the same phone line.
3. Click on the OK button when you are finished.

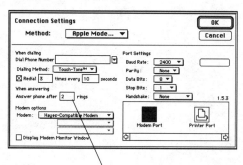

Host computer setup: Make sure you have enough rings for the computer to answer.

■ Automating tasks

You can create macros in the Communications mode using the same procedures you used in the Word Processing mode. These macros could be used to dial a service, type in a phone number, and turn on print, and screen capture. To review the steps for creating a macro, see "Macros" on page 94.

The open/close connection button is a toggle. When you need to dial, you can click on it. When you need to hang up, you can click on it.

Open/close
connection   Receive file

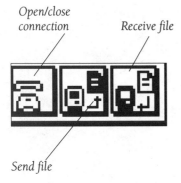

Send file

The send file button will send a file from your computer to your service provider.

The receive file button will download a file from your service provider to your Macintosh.

Shortcuts

The Communications program mode also has shortcuts keys available from the Shortcuts command on the File menu.

1. Choose Show Shortcuts from the Shortcuts submenu in the File menu.
2. The Shortcuts palette will appear. There are only three buttons for communications:
   ▲ Open/close connection
   ▲ Send file
   ▲ Receive file

■ About going on-line

Going on-line can be an adventure, but don't forget to observe "netiquette" by not spamming (sending unwanted files to multiple users) or flaming (sending vitriolic notes to other users). It might sound like fun and might be tempting, but we should all work on keeping the on-line world a friendly place.

Above all—go on-line and have fun!

Automating tasks

Putting It All Together

■ Assistants and Stationery

Assistants and Stationery are automated forms for Word Processing, Spreadsheets, Drawing, and the Database program modes in ClarisWorks. Stationery is a collection of premade forms that speed up creating documents.

These automated tools are divided into convenient categories:

▲ Business includes annual report stationery that works for both big and small businesses.

▲ General includes calendar and envelope forms.

▲ Home includes forms for home and school use, such as a name and address list, certificates, newsletters, stationery, and party invitations.

▲ Internet forms are for those yearning to get on the World Wide Web. ClarisWorks has made it easy by creating documentation and stationery that work with the Web's text tagging tool.

▲ Registration automates registration and includes a form you can use to send in via fax or mail.

▲ Small Business has big needs and ClarisWorks gives you all of the tools and templates you need to become your own entrepreneur. See "Assistants contents" on page 237 for more details.

Categories

Description of form

Assistants information: The bottom of the All Assistants scrolling list gives you a brief description about each available form as you select the name of the form.

New command on the File menu

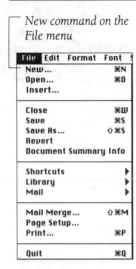

Using Assistants or Stationery

1. Choose New from the File menu. You will see the New Document dialog box.
2. Click in the Use Assistant or Stationery checkbox in the New Document dialog box.
3. To choose the form by category, select the Category pop-up menu. You will see a list starting with All Assistants and All Stationery. Below the solid line is a list of categories.
4. Scroll down the list until you come to the category you want to use.
5. Select the category you want to use. You will see just the forms for that category displayed in the scrolling list.

Typical Assistant walk-through

Some Assistants are automated, such as the calendar Assistant. Here is one example of this type of automated Assistant:

1. Choose New from the File menu. The New Document dialog box will appear.
2. Select the Use Assistant or Stationery checkbox at the bottom of the New Document dialog box.
3. Select the Calendar Assistant from the scrolling list of available Assistants. You will see the Welcome dialog box for the Calendar Assistant.
4. Click on the Next button at the bottom of the opening panel of the Calendar Assistant dialog box.
5. Choose the correct month for your calendar in the Month pop-up menu.
6. Click and type the year for your calendar in the Calendar year box.
7. Click and type the number of months you want in your calendar in the Number of months box.
8. Choose the font you want for the entire calendar in the Font pop-up menu.
9. If you want the weekends to be in bold, select the Bold Text radio button.
10. Click on the Create button. Your calendar will now appear on the screen.

The automated calendar assistant and the Next button

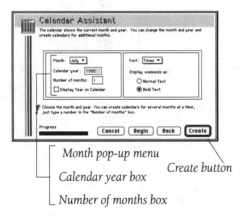

Month pop-up menu

Calendar year box

Create button

Number of months box

■ Publish and subscribe

Publish and subscribe is a way of linking two different types of documents together, such as a Word Processing document and a Painting document. The changes you make in one document will then be reflected immediately in the other document.

You can use an unlimited number of publish and subscribe links—and files that are used in this manner can appear in more than one document.

For instance, that same paint logo can be used in a Spreadsheet document, another Word Processing document, or a Database document—and all of these programs can be publish and subscribe clients.

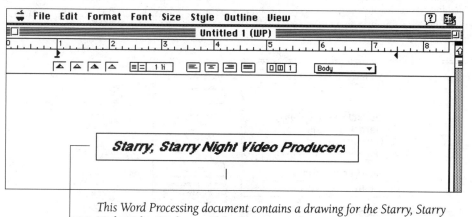

This Word Processing document contains a drawing for the Starry, Starry Night Video Producers. If the drawing needs some changes, once the changes are made in the Drawing mode, these changes will show up in the Word Processing document.

Publish and subscribe

This drawing was created in the Drawing program mode of ClarisWorks. The picture is selected by:

1. Clicking on the pointer tool in the tool box.

2. Clicking on the picture.

Writing Tools ▶	
Find/Change ▶	
Publishing ▶	**Create Publisher...**
	Subscribe To...
Preferences...	Publisher Options...
Show Clipboard	Hide Borders

The Publishing command showing the Create Publisher command on the Publishing submenu

Using publish and subscribe

1. Create the document you want to use, such as a logo or spreadsheet. This document will be called the Publish document.

2. Select the part of that document you will want displayed in a second document—for example, a logo created in the drawing or painting program mode.

3. Choose Publishing from the Edit menu. You will see the Publishing submenu.

4. Choose Create Publisher from the Publishing submenu. You will see the Create Publisher dialog box.

5. Type a name in this box for the document—it will appear with the default name ClarisWorks Edition 1, but each published document must have a unique name.

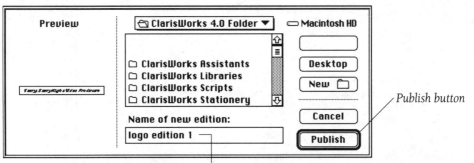

Name of new edition box

Publish button

6. Notice that your document has a light gray border around it. This border will not print. Save your document using the File menu.

7. Open a new document from the File menu.

8. In the second document, find where you want the Publish document to appear.

9. Choose Subscribe to from the Publishing submenu on the Edit menu. The Publish document will appear with the light gray border.

10. If you don't want to see the border, choose Hide Borders in the Publishing submenu on the Edit menu. The light gray border will then disappear.

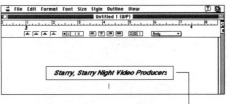

This new letterhead document in word processing contains the drawing that was created in the Drawing program mode.

■ Mail merge

Mail merge takes basic information about a group of people, such as their names and addresses, and inserts this information into a form letter. You work with three documents:

▲ A database that contains names and addresses or other information about each individual

▲ A form letter that you set up in Word Processing

▲ A third document that is created and sent directly to the printer when you actually perform the merge

Mail merge will also create envelopes—and even more complicated jobs, such as a mail merge for reports and brochures.

Creating the address database document for the merge

1. In the Database program mode, create your database of names, addresses, and any other information you might need to use in the mail merge. If you have forgotten how to create a database, see page 129.
2. Save the database and close it.
3. Open the Word Processing portion of ClarisWorks and start a new Word Processing document.

Sample database file that could be used in a mail merge. Not all fields need to be used; you can select which fields you want and ignore the rest of the fields in the database.

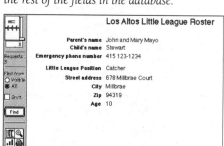

✔ **Warning**: *If you have set up the name field so that the names are entered last name first, for example, Brown, C. Ann, you will have to create a special field that lists the names the way you will want to use them in the merge letter. Similarly, if you want to address your letters to individuals by first name, as in Dear Sue, you will have to create a field for first names only. You might have two fields then: one field that will contain the entire name, as in Sue Jones, and a second field that will contain just her first name.*

✔ **Tip**: *If you are planning on sending out a number of letters, you may want the database to be sorted in zip code order. If that is true, when you set up the database, make sure you make the zip code a field by itself.*

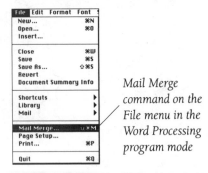

Mail Merge command on the File menu in the Word Processing program mode

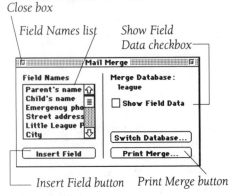

Close box

Field Names list

Show Field Data checkbox

Insert Field button   Print Merge button

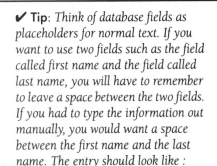

«Parent's name»
«Child's name»
«Little League Position»

Sample text file for a mail merge

✔ **Tip**: *Think of database fields as placeholders for normal text. If you want to use two fields such as the field called first name and the field called last name, you will have to remember to leave a space between the two fields. If you had to type the information out manually, you would want a space between the first name and the last name. The entry should look like : <<First Name>>space<<Last Name>>.*

✔ **Tip**: *To close the Mail Merge dialog box, click on the Close box.*

Preparing the form letter

1. In the Word Processing program mode, select Mail Merge from the File menu, or press ⇧ ⌘-M. The Mail Merge dialog box will appear.
2. In the Mail Merge dialog box, you should see the list of the fields you just created in your database. If you created the database at another time, you will need to switch databases by clicking on the Switch Database button.
3. You will see the File open dialog box. Scroll down until you see your Database file, and select it. This step will attach your database to the current Word Processing document and show a Mail Merge dialog box on your screen.

Adding fields to your form letter

Field names are used to substitute for information in the database.

1. Type your form letter, stopping where you want to add information from your database.
2. In the Mail Merge dialog box that appears on the screen, click on the field name you want to use first. If the Mail Merge dialog box is in your way on the screen, move the Mail Merge dialog box by clicking in the title bar and dragging the dialog box to a new position.
3. Click on the Insert Field button. The field should now appear in your letter.
4. Click back inside your form letter and continue typing text or pressing the Return key if you want the next piece of text or the next field to appear on a separate line.
5. When you have inserted all of the fields you need, make sure you turn on your printer and click on the Print Merge button in the Mail Merge dialog box.
6. Click on the Print button in the Print dialog box. All of the mail merge letters should now print.

Previewing the mail merge form file

1. Make sure you have your Word Processing form letter on screen, then choose Mail Merge from the File menu, or press ⇧⌘-M.

2. Click in the Show Field Data checkbox. In the Word Processing document screen, you should see the information for your first letter instead of the database field names.

3. To see the next letter, either type the record number in the Record box, or click on the arrow that points down on the right-hand side of the Record box.

Mail Merge dialog box

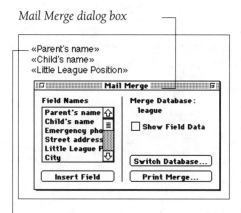

This is a view of the Mail Merge dialog box with the form letter just behind it. Notice the field names in the letter are entered between double brackets.

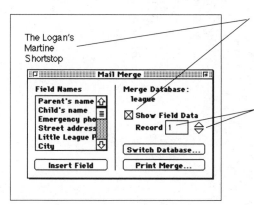

In this view, the Show Field Data checkbox has been checked and the field names in the Word Processing form letter have turned into actual field information.

Type the number of the record you want to see in the Record box, or click on the up or down arrow to scroll through all of the merged letters on screen.

Mail merge

Merge to envelope

Surprisingly, envelopes are not created in Word
Processing program mode, but are created in the
Drawing program mode of ClarisWorks. You can add
text, clip art, and merge fields to envelopes set up in
this manner.

Merging to envelopes is practical only if you have a
single-sheet-feeding printer such as a laser printer or
an ink-jet printer.

Setting up the printer

1. Choose New from the File menu.
2. Double-click on Drawing in the New Document
   dialog box to open a new Drawing file.
3. Choose Page Setup in the File menu in the Drawing
   mode.
4. In the Page Setup dialog box, select the horizontal
   Orientation icon.
5. In Paper options pop-up menu of the Page Setup
   dialog box, select the envelope type. The most
   common is Envelope-Center Fed—but the
   choices for your printer may vary.

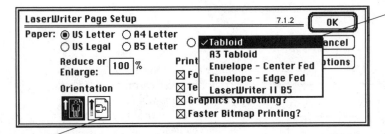

*Select the correct envelope
form from the paper type
pop-up menu.*

*Select the horizontal or landscape
orientation icon for most laser
printers that will print envelopes*

Working with the envelope

1. Turn on the rulers by choosing Rulers from the Format menu. The Ruler dialog box will appear.
2. Click on the OK button in the Ruler dialog box.
3. Allowing enough margin for your printer, and using the text tool from the tool bar, click in the drawing document and type the return address. Usually .33 of an inch from the top and side is sufficient.
4. Add any clip art you want to use with the Libraries command from the File menu.
5. With the ruler as a guide, use the scroll bars to move to approximately 4 1/2".
6. Choose Mail Merge from the File menu, or press ⇧⌘-M. The Mail Merge dialog box will appear.
7. Using the text tool, click about 2 1/2" down from the top of the envelope and about 4 1/2" from the left-hand side of the envelope.
8. Insert merge fields the same way you would for a regular document (see "Adding fields to your form letter" on page 214).
9. When you are finished, complete the merge by choosing the Print Merge button in the Mail Merge dialog box.

✔ **Tip**: *See "Using Assistants or Stationery" on page 210 to use ClarisWorks' automated envelope and label templates instead of creating an envelope or template from scratch.*

Merge to label

Merges to labels are accomplished when you set up a new layout that is designed to work with the Avery labels. Set up a mailing label according to the instructions in "Mailing labels" on page 165.

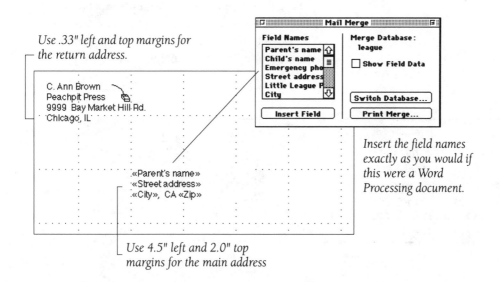

Use .33" left and top margins for the return address.

C. Ann Brown
Peachpit Press
9999 Bay Market Hill Rd.
Chicago, IL

«Parent's name»
«Street address»
«City», CA «Zip»

Use 4.5" left and 2.0" top margins for the main address

Insert the field names exactly as you would if this were a Word Processing document.

Mail merge

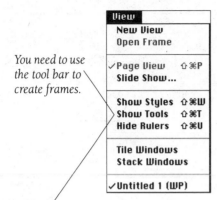

You need to use the tool bar to create frames.

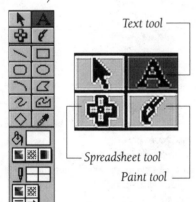

Text tool

Spreadsheet tool

Paint tool

■ Frames

Frames are the basic organizational tool for ClarisWorks documents that contain more than one type of document.

While you are inside of a document, you can insert a small spreadsheet, painting, or text block into your document using frames.

Creating frames

1. Open the document in which you want to create a frame.
2. Choose Show Tools from the View menu, or press ⇧⌘-T.
3. Select the tool you want to use to draw a frame.
   ▲ The text tool is for drawing text frames
   ▲ The spreadsheet tool is for drawing spreadsheet frames
   ▲ The paint tool is for creating painting frames
4. Click in your document where you want your new frame to be positioned.
5. Drag to the left and down until the frame is the size you desire.
6. Enter the text or spreadsheet data, or create a painting inside of the frame.

Moving frames

1. Select the pointer tool from the tool bar.
2. Select the frame and drag the frame to a new position just like you would drag a piece of clip art or a drawing or painting object.

✔ **Tip**: *You can tell if you have properly selected the frame for moving if you can see four small, square dots (called handles), one on each corner of the frame. If you don't see these handles, you need to reselect the pointer tool and try again.*

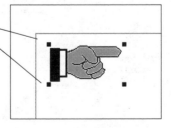

Adding borders and fills to frames

1. Select a previously created frame using the pointer tool from the tool bar.

2. Use the tools and select the fill, patterns, or gradient palettes you want to use in this frame.

3. Use the tools and select the border, color, or pattern palettes you want to use in this frame. Your frame will automatically change and include the fill patterns, gradients, borders, colors, and patterns you just selected.

Deleting frames

1. Select the frame you wish to delete.

2. Tap the Delete or Clear key. You may also select Cut or Clear from the Edit menu.

Creating text frames inside text documents or spreadsheet frames inside spreadsheet documents

1. Select the frame type you want to draw from the tool bar.

2. Press the Option key and drag until you have a new frame.

3. Type or enter spreadsheet data or text inside of this frame. Do not click outside of the text frame until you have typed something inside that frame or the frame will disappear.

4. Click outside the frame when you want to resume working in your main document.

Limitations of frames

There are three frame limitations that are related to the type of main document.

▲ You cannot create a painting frame inside a Painting document.

▲ You cannot create frames inside the Communications program mode.

▲ You must be in the layout view when you want to create a frame inside a database document.

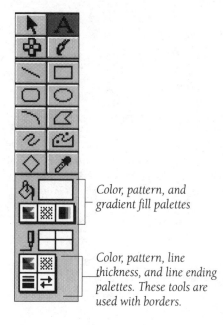

Color, pattern, and gradient fill palettes

Color, pattern, line thickness, and line ending palettes. These tools are used with borders.

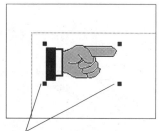

You can delete a frame when you can see the square frame handles. Use the pointer tool to click on the object and select it.

Frames

219

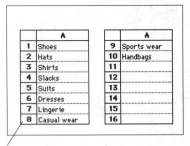

Linked frames are used to show pieces of a document, such as this spreadsheet inside of a second document, which is a Word Processing file.

The Frame Links command on the Options menu

If you want to delete any of these frames, select the frame. You will see the square frame handles. Then you can press the Clear or Delete key to erase the frame.

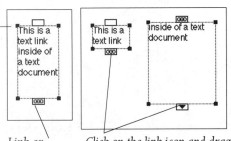

Link or continuation icon

Click on the link icon and drag it up or down. The text will flow between the first frame and the second frame.

■ Linking frames

Linking frames enables you to create a document that will flow from one frame to the next frame. For instance, you can create a story in a newsletter that starts in one frame, and continues in a second frame.

Similarly, you can create spreadsheets that start in one frame and continue in the next, or drawings that are linked in multiple frames.

Creating linked frames

1. In your main document, click on the frame you wish to link.
2. Choose Frame Links from the Options menu, or press ⌘-L.
3. Open the tools by choosing Show Tools from the View menu, or press ⇧⌘-T. Select either the text tool, spreadsheet tool, or paint tool for the type of frame you wish to create.
4. Draw your first frame and type in your text, insert a library clip-art file, or create a spreadsheet frame.
5. Using the pointer tool, select the Link icon on the bottom of the frame and immediately draw a second frame.
6. Your frame should then flow from the first frame to the second frame.

Unlinking frames

1. Using the pointer tool, click once on the frame you wish to unlink.
2. Choose Cut from the Edit menu. This will cause the frame to be erased from the document. The next step will put the frame back and unlink it from the other frames.
3. Choose Paste from the Edit menu. Pasting the frame back breaks the links between frames.
4. Check and make sure that the Frame Links command in the Options menu does not have a check mark by it and is turned off.

Creating framed text around pictures

1. Make sure that the Frame Links command in the Options menu is turned on by selecting it if it does not have a check mark indicating it is currently active.

2. Select the Option key if you are in a text document, create a text frame, then type the text you need inside of the text frame.

3. Select a picture from the Library clip-art collection using the Library command from the File menu. make sure you click outside of the document margins so that the picture will be placed as an independent graphic.

4. Drag the picture partially on top of the frame.

5. Choose Text Wrap from the Options menu. You will see a Text Wrap dialog box.

6. Select one of the two following options:
   ▲ Regular—to wrap the text in a rectangle around the picture
   ▲ Irregular—to wrap the text tightly in the shape of the picture

7. Click on the OK button in the Text Wrap dialog box. Your text will now wrap irregularly around the clip art, following the contours of the objects in the clip art.

The clip art is carefully placed on top of the text frame, then an irregular wrap is selected from the Text Wrap dialog box.

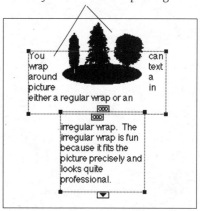

Text wrap dialog box with Regular and Irregular wrap icons

Linking frames

■ Slide shows

Slide shows are automatic documents that display document pages on your computer screen. You can choose:

▲ How quickly the pages will change

▲ The appearance the pages have as they move off of the screen

▲ Backgrounds that will be consistent throughout the entire slide show

▲ QuickTime movies that can be included in the slide show

Creating a slide show

1. Create each document page you want to include in the slide show. Your documents may be in most of the ClarisWorks modes: Word processing, Spreadsheet, Drawing, Painting, or Database.

2. Your documents should contain more than one page, but you will display them one page at a time—just like paging through a book.

3. Choose Slide Show from the View menu. You will see the Slide Show dialog box.

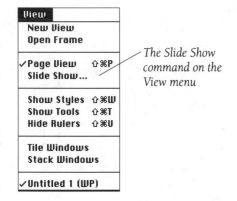

The Slide Show command on the View menu

Slide Show dialog box

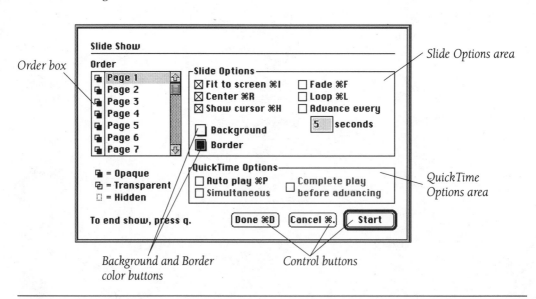

Order box

Slide Options area

Background and Border color buttons

Control buttons

QuickTime Options area

Slide shows

Changing order of pages

1. Choose Slide Show from the View menu.
2. In the Order panel of the Slide Show dialog box, drag the page you want to move to a new order. For example, drag page 4 so it follows page 1.
3. When you are finished, click on either the Done button to save your changes, or the Start button to immediately play the slide show back on the screen.

Changing Slide Options

1. Choose Slide Show from the View menu.
2. Select the page you want to change in the Order scrolling list in the Slide Show dialog box.
3. In the Slide Options area, click on how you want that page to be displayed.

   ▲ Fit to screen makes the entire page fill the screen from left to right.

   ▲ Center makes the page appear centered from top to bottom on the computer screen.

   ▲ Show cursor makes the pointer appear when the page is displayed so you can move the pointer around manually to point out items on the displayed page.

   ▲ Fade makes the page slowly fade out as the next page fades in for display.

   ▲ Loop makes the slide show play continuously until you stop it by pressing a Q or using the key combination ⌘-PERIOD.

   ▲ Advance every x seconds shows the number of seconds you want each page to be displayed on the screen. Place a check mark in the Advance every checkbox to run the slide show automatically.
4. Click on the Done button in the Slide Show dialog box to save your work or click on the Start button to run the slide show.

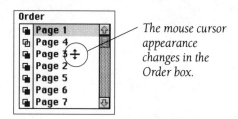

The mouse cursor appearance changes in the Order box.

You can view the pages of your document in any order you wish when you play a slide show.

Slide Options pane of the Slide Show dialog box

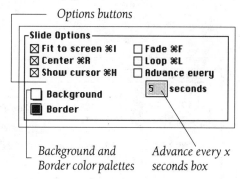

Options buttons

Background and Border color palettes

Advance every x seconds box

Slide shows

Changing the slide show's borders and background

1. Choose Slide Show from the View menu.
2. In the Slide Show dialog box, select the Background button.
3. You will see a pop-up palette of colors. Select the color you want your pages to have as a background color.
4. Select the Border button. You will see another pop-up palette of colors. Click once on the color you want to surround your pages in the desktop area outside of the actual pages.
5. Choose the Done button in the Slide Show dialog box to save your work or click on the Start button to run the slide show.

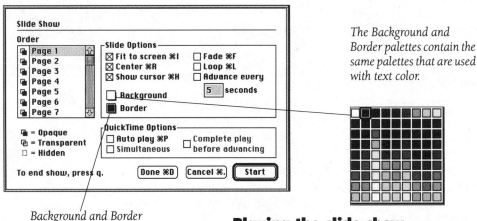

The Background and Border palettes contain the same palettes that are used with text color.

Background and Border color palettes

Playing the slide show

1. Choose Slide Show from the View menu.
2. Click on the Start button in the Slide Show dialog box, or press the Option key and choose Slide Show from the View menu. Using the Option key while choosing the Slide Show command causes the slide show to start without showing you the Slide Show dialog box.

✔ **Tip**: *Stopping an action: The emergency key combination that will stop any action from continuing is ⌘-period. If you have started a slide show and don't want to watch it all of the way through, this command will stop the slide show for you.*

Slide shows

■ Creating template documents

Template documents are documents that you will want to use over and over. The best example is a letterhead that is used more than once. Each time the letterhead is used, it is important that the letterhead itself isn't changed.

Creating a template or stationery document

1. Create your document, complete with graphics, text, and printer settings.
2. Choose Save As from the File menu. The Save As dialog box will appear.
3. In the Save As dialog box, select the Stationery icon and save the file in the ClarisWorks Stationery folder.
4. Type a document name in the name box.
5. Click on the Save button.

Stationery icon

■ AppleScript and WorldScript

Briefly, AppleScript and WorldScript are system software extensions that work with ClarisWorks. These software extensions can be found in System 7 of the Macintosh software. WorldScript requires system 7.1 or later and will work with symbolic-based languages such as Chinese or Japanese. See your system documentation for more information on AppleScript and WorldScript.

Appendix A
Functional Formulas

Functional formulas fall into several categories, including algebraic functions, business and financial functions, date and time functions, informational functions, statistical functions, text functions, and trigonometric functions

The formulas and examples below are typed exactly the way the formulas must be typed.

For example, a formula such as the payment formula PMT(rate,nper,pv{,fv}{,type}) has no spaces between information enclosed within the parentheses. This is the way the formula must be entered in the spreadsheet. The explanations similarly have no spaces between commas, as no spaces can be typed within the parentheses of any formula.

■ Algebraic functions

Name of formula	Function/Explanation	Formula format
ABS	Absolute value of a number	ABS(number)
	ABS(C13) where C13 is blank, gives the answer 0 (0 means blank).	
BASETONUM	Changes text to a base 10 number	BASETONUM(Text,base)
	Interprets numbers and text as a binary or other designated base value.	
EXP	Exponentiation	EXP(number)
	Raises a number to a given power.	
FACT	Factors a number	FACT(number)
	Gives the factorial of a number such as 3, or FACT(3) does the following: 1 x 2 x 3	
FRAC	Fractional part of numbers	FRAC(number).
	Returns fractionals that are the decimal part of a number, as in FRAC(2.95), where the answer is .95.	
INT	Integer	INT(number)
	Gives the closest number to the number in parentheses but not any number greater than the number in parentheses.	

Note: The term "number" when used in a cell formula means you can either type a number in that place or type a cell reference. For example, INT(number) could be INT(13.75) or INT(C1).

Algebraic functions, continued

Name of formula	Function/Explanation	Formula format
LN	Natural log	LN(number)
	Gives you the natural logarithm of the number in the parentheses.	
LOG	Logarithm	LOG(number)
	Gives you the natural logarithm of a number to a designated base.	
LOG10	Logarithm to base 10	LOG10(number)
	Gives you the natural logarithm of a number to base 10.	
MOD	Modulo	MOD(number)
	Calculates the decimal remainder portion of a division problem.	
NUMTOBASE	Converts base 10 numbers to an alternate base system.	NUMTOBASE(number)
	Converts to a string using both the numbers 0 to 9 and characters A to Z.	
PI	PI	PI()
	Gives you the value of PI,or 3.1415926.	
RAND	Random numbers	RAND(number)
	Generates random numbers.	
ROUND	Round	ROUND(number)
	Rounds numbers off to a specified number of digits or decimal places.	
SIGN	Sign (logical)	SIGN()
	Returns the number 1 if an answer is true and 0 if the answer is false.	
SQRT	Square root	SQRT(number)
	Gives you the square root of a number or a number in a cell.	
TRUNC	Truncate	TRUNC(number)
	Truncates a number to an integer or whole number.	

Algebraic functions

■Business and financial functions

Name of formula	Function/Explanation	Formula format
FV	Future value of an investment	FV(rate,nper,pmt{, pv}{, type})

Fill out this formula as follows: FV(Yearly interest rate,Number of periods,-How much the payments are,-Current worth of investment).
Note in particular some of the numbers have a hyphen (-) before the information to be entered. You must enter this hyphen if you want your answer to be a positive number.

| IRR (doesn't work in the Database mode) | Internal rate of return | IRR(Range {,guess}) |

IRR(Range of numbers,guess on percentage rate of return).

| MIRR | Modified internal rate of return | MIRR(Safe,Risk,Values) |

Fill out this formula as follows: MIRR(Rate of investment with negative cash flow,rate when positive cash flow can be expected,future cash flow).

| NPER | Number of periods | NPER(rate,pmt,pv {,fv} {,type}) |

Fill out this formula as follows: NPER(Interest rate by period—e.g. year or month,amount of payment,present value of investment,optional future value of investment).2

| NPV | Net present value | NPV(interest-rate, payment1,payment2,...) |

Fill out this formula as follows: NPV(Periodic interest rate,first payment,second payment,etc.).

| PMT | Payment | PMT(rate,nper,pv{,fv}{,type}) |

Fill out this formula as follows: PMT(Interest rate by year or month,number of payments,present value of money,future value of money after final payment,type where 0=due at end of month and 1=due at beginning of month).

| PV | Present value | PV(rate,nper,pmt{,fv}{,type}) |

Fill out this formula as follows: PV(Interest rate by year or month,number of payments or periods,payment to be made each period,future value of investment,type—see PMT).

| RATE | Interest rate needed for specific future value | RATE(fv,pv,term) |

Fill out this formula as follows: RATE(future value of investment,present value of investment,number of payments).

■ Date and time functions

Name of formula	Function/Explanation	Formula format
DATE	Changes a date to a serial number	DATE(year,month,day)
DATETOTEXT	Changes the serial number of a date to text	DATETOTEXT(Serial number of date,format number)
	Format numbers are as follows: format 0 = 1/15/95 format 1 = Ap 1, 1995 format 2 = April 1, 1995 format 3 = Mon,April 1, 1995 format 4 = Monday,April 1, 1995	
DAY	Changes a serial number to a day of the month	DAY(serial number)
DAYNAME	Changes the numbers 1 through 7 to a day of the week such as Monday	DAYNAME(number)
	Format numbers are as follows: 1 = Sunday, 2 = Monday, etc.	
DAYOFYEAR	Changes a serial number to the day of the year	DAYOFYEAR(Serial number) Starting with January 1, 1904
HOUR	Changes serial number time to the hour	HOUR(Serial number)
MINUTE	Calculates the minutes in a serial number	MINUTE(Serial number)
MONTH	Changes a serial number to the month	MONTH(Serial number)
MONTHNAME	Changes the numbers 1 through 12 to the month such as December	MONTH(Number)
	Format numbers are as follows: 1 = January, 2 = February, etc.	
NOW	Gives the current date or time	NOW()
	Gives current date and time setting picked up from the computer	

Date and time functions, continued

Name of formula	Function/Explanation	Formula format
SECOND	Gives the number of seconds of a serial number	SECOND(Serial number)
TEXTTODATE	Changes a date typed in text to a serial number	TEXTODATE(Date-text)
TIME	Changes time typed in 24-hour notation to a serial number	TIME(hour,minute,second)
TIMETOTEXT	Changes time serial number to text	TIMETOTEXT(Serial number,format)

Format numbers as follows:
format 0 = Hours:min AM or PM
format 1 = Hours:min:sec AM or PM
format 2 = Hours:min in 24 hour clock terms
format 3 = Hours:min:sec in 24 hour clock terms

Name of formula	Function/Explanation	Formula format
WEEKDAY	Changes a serial number to a day of the week	WEEKDAY(Serial number)
WEEKOFYEAR	Changes a serial number to a numeric designation of the week (1 to 52)	WEEKDAYOFYEAR(Serial number)
YEAR	Changes a serial number to a year	YEAR(Serial number)

A note about serial numbers:
Starting January 1, 1904, the very first second of the very first hour has a serial number. Each increasing second, minute, hour, day, and year has a serial number incrementing by one for each second. The computer figures this all out for you—you just need to know how to format the serial numbers.

Date and time functions

■ Informational functions

Name of formula	Function/Explanation	Formula format
ALERT	Displays a message you create	ALERT(message)
BEEP	Plays a beep	BEEP()
CHOOSE	Chooses an item out of a list	CHOOSE(Index of values,first value,second value,etc.)
ERROR	Types the response "Error"	ERROR()
HLOOKUP	Horizontal lookup table function	HLOOKUP(Lookup value,range containing values,index)
MACRO	Runs a macro	MACRO(text)
MATCH	Matches values in a range	MATCH(Lookup value,range to look in)
NA	States "Not available"	NA()
ROW	Tells you what row contains the cell you are referring to	ROW(cell)
TYPE	Tells you whether your information is blank, logical, number, or text in nature	TYPE(data location or expression)

Format answers appear as follows:
1 = Blank cell
2 = Logical information
3 = Numeric information
4 = Text information
5 = Numeric information as a result of a formula

| VLOOKUP | Vertical lookup table | VLOOKUP(Lookup value,range,index) |

■ Logical functions

Name of formula	Function	Explanation/Interpretation
AND	Checks conditions to see if they are all true	IF A1 AND A2 are blank
IF	Compares two conditions to see which is true	IF A1 is blank, say "blank, otherwise say "unknown"
ISBLANK	Checks to see if a cell or field is blank	ISBLANK(cell or location)
ISERROR	Checks for errors in an expression	ISERROR(cell or location)
ISLOGICAL	Checks for proper Boolean logic	ISLOGICAL(cell or location)
ISNUMBER	Checks to see if a cell or field contains a number and not text	ISNUMBER(cell or location)
ISTEXT	Checks to see if a cell or field contains text and not a number	ISTEXT(cell or location)
NOT	Looks for something that is not true	IF A1 NOT equal to A2
OR	Looks at two conditions, and if either is true, answers "True"	If either A1 OR A2 is equal or greater than 1

Logical functions

■ Statistical functions

Name of formula	Function/Explanation	Formula format
AVERAGE	Finds the average of a series of numbers	AVERAGE(A1..A4)

Finds the average of the four cells and gives you that number.

COUNT	Counts the number of records or fields	COUNT(A1..A4)

Counts how many cells have information in them.

COUNT2	Returns the average of a specific series of numbers	(COUNT,Search value,values or range)
MAX	Finds the maximum number in a series of numbers	MAX(A1..A4)

Gives you the largest number in a range, as in A1 = 4, A2 = 7, A3 = 1, and A4 = 12. The answer would be 12, or the largest number found in that range.

MIN	Finds the minimum number in a series of numbers	MIN(A1..A4)

Gives you the smallest number found in that range.

PRODUCT	Multiplies two fields or two numbers	PRODUCT(number or cell,number or cell)
STDEV	Calculates standard deviation of a series of numbers	STDEV(cell range) or STDEV(number 1,number 2,number 3,etc.)
SUM	Adds up a series of numbers or fields and acts as a container for a variety of basic algebraic formulas	SUM(cell beginning range..cell ending range)
VAR	Calculates variance of a series of numbers or fields	VAR(cell range) or VAR(number 1,number 2,etc.)

■ Text functions

Name of formula	Function/Explanation	Formula format
CHAR	Gives the ASCII character based on an input number	CHAR(number)
CODE	Gives the ASCII number based on an input character	CODE(text)
CONCAT	Concatenates or adds two text fields together	CONCAT(field 1,field 2)
EXACT	Gives the answer true if two fields match exactly	EXACT(field 1,field2)
FIND	Searches for text in a field	FIND(text,text expression to search in)
LEFT	Counts a specific number of characters in a text phrase from the left and gives those characters as an answer	LEFT(text,number of characters from left)
LEN	Tells you how many characters in the text of any specific field	LEN(text)
LOWER	Makes all uppercase characters lowercase	LOWER(text)
MID	Tells you the actual characters up to the middle of a text phrase	MID(text,starting position,number of characters)
NUMTOTEXT	Changes a number to a text number (as in a zip code)	NUMTOTEXT(number)
PROPER	Capitalizes the first letter of every word	PROPER(text)
REPLACE	Replaces an old text phrase with a new text phrase you specify	REPLACE(old text,starting,number of characters to replace,new text)

Text functions, continued

Name of formula	Function/Explanation	Formula format
REPT	Repeats text a specific number of times	REPT(text,how many times)
RIGHT	Searchs right for a specific number of characters and gives you those characters as an answer	RIGHT(text,number of characters)
TEXTTONUM	Counts a specific number of characters in a text phrase from the right and returns that as an answer	TEXTTONUMB(text)
TRIM	Removes extra spaces	TRIM(text) or TRIM(cell reference)
UPPER	Changes text to all uppercase	UPPER(text)

■Trigonometric functions

Name of formula	Function/Explanation	Formula format
ACOS	Arc cosine	ACOS(number)
ASIN	Arc sine	ASIN(number)
ATAN	Arc tangent	ATAN(number)
ATAN2	Arc tangent expressed in radians	ATAN(x-axis number,y-axis number)
COS	Cosine	COS(number)
DEGREES	Converts radians to degrees	DEGREES(number of radians)
RADIANS	Converts degrees to radians	RADIANS(number of degrees)
SIN	Sine	SIN(number)
TAN	Tangent	TAN(number)

Trigonometric functions

Appendix B
Assistants & Stationery

■ Assistants and Stationary

Check the categories to find documents that will help you save time with forms that have already been created for you. You can easily customize any of these ClarisWorks forms.

Assistants contents

Assistant	Category	Type of document	Use
Financial forms			
Annual Report	Small Business	Drawing	Provides text, graphics, and spreadsheets laid out for a narrative report
Home Budget	Home	Spreadsheet	Keeps track of income, stock dividends, and expenses by specific category.
Home Finance	Home	Spreadsheet	Answer questions about net worth, loan costs, and how much of a home you can afford to buy.
Mortgage Analyzer	Home	Spreadsheet	
Checkbook and Ledger	Home	Database	Prints out checks and standard information, such as the payee and amount, and calculates cash flow.
Expense Report	Small Business	Database	Details expenses, listed by category, set up for a weekly basis.
Lease vs. Purchase Analyzer	Small Business	Spreadsheet	Calculates analyses of lease versus purchasing capital equipment.

Assistants and Stationary

Assistants contents, continued

Assistant	Category	Type of document	Use
Fill-in-the-blanks forms			
In Case of Emergency	Home	Spreadsheet	Lists emergency numbers, such as hospitals, doctors, fire, police, and information on family members, such as work numbers and allergies.
Fax Cover Sheet	Small Business	Drawing	Contains a fax transmission cover sheet with room for graphics and messages.
Press Release	Small Business	Word Processing	Contains template for press release with embedded spreadsheet.
Meeting Agenda	Small Business	Word Processing	Contains meeting agenda, with graphics, time, speaker, and topic columns.
To-do List	Home	Word Processing	Gives you due dates and categories for your not-yet-completed items.
WWW HTML Document	Internet	Word Processing	Creates a World Wide Web home page. You need the HTML Primer document that comes with ClarisWorks to use this template. The primer will tell you how to tag your text files so you can create a World Wide Web home page; start by opening the file called HTML Primer that will be in your ClarisWorks folder.

Assistants contents, continued

Assistant	Category	Type of document	Use
Organizational tools and databases			
Music & Video Database	Home	Database	Keeps track of records, cassettes, CDs, and movies for home and hobby inventory.
Name & Address List	Home	Database	List format setup for personal, business, student information, family, and membership. Each type of list contains unique information such as parent/guardian phone numbers.
Family & Friends List	Home	Database	
Membership Database	Home	Database	
Recipe Database	Home	Database	Contains a database for categorizing and writing instructions for your favorite recipes. You can even input the calories per serving information.
Stationery and letters			
Holiday Letter	Home	Drawing	Includes fancy borders, scanned photographs, and colorful text that help create a special holiday letter.
Letterhead	Small Business	Word Processing	Provides a simple business letterhead with space for a graphic or logo.
Memorandum	Small Business	Drawing	Gives a memo form with graphics, automatic date, and subject sections.
Personal Stationery	Home	Word Processing	Shows a ready-made personal letterhead with a simple graphic.
Resume A	Home	Word Processing (all)	Include two resume styles and a sample resume cover letter you can tailor to fit your professional needs.
Resume B	Home		
Resume Cover Letter	Home		

Assistants contents, continued

Assistant	Category	Type of document	Use
Newsletters, certificates, signs, and invitations			
Border	Home	Drawing	Give you a jazzy border you can use to create posters and signs.
Notice	Home	Drawing	
Calendar	General	Spreadsheet	Contains a monthly or yearly calender that allows you to type information in the squares for each day.
Envelope	General	Word Processing	Shows how to type the return address and name address in dialog boxes and print a ready-made envelope.
Certificate	Home	Drawing	Contain formats for merit, appreciation, achievement, membership, diploma, or create-your-own certificates. Each style has different borders and contents.
Certificate A	Home	Drawing	
Certificate B	Home	Drawing	
For Sale Sign	Home	Drawing	Provides a pre-made sign that is designed for selling a car or house.
Invitation A	Home	Drawing	Give invitations that fold like a greeting card and contain art, along with borders and text.
Invitation B	Home	Drawing	
Newsletter	Small Business	Drawing	Provide a newsletter format for training or general information, and three layout styles: letter paper, folded booklet, and legal-size paper.
Club Newsletter	Home	Drawing	
Customer Newsletter	Small Business	Word Processing	
Presentation	Small Business	Drawing	Presents five different background and text styles for overhead presentations. There is even a special style just for kids.
Promotional Flyer	Small Business	Drawing	Shows a simple sale flyer.

Assistants and Stationary

Index

We'd like to hear from you!

Copy and mail or fax this page back to us
for more information about other Peachpit books.

I'd like to know more about Peachpit's:

- ☐ DOS books
- ☐ Windows books
- ☐ Mac books
- ☐ Books on other topics (specify):

_____

_____

Quantity discounts for:

- ☐ Dealers or school trainers
- ☐ Corporate/government use groups

Please tell us what you think of this book:

_____

_____

_____

_____

Name: _____

Organization: _____

Address: _____

City/State/Zip: _____

☐ Check here if you'd rather not receive computer-related
information from other companies.

Peachpit Press, Inc.
2414 Sixth Street
Berkeley, CA 94710
Phone 510/548-4393 ▼ 800/283-9444
Fax 510/548-5991

My Life Organizer

My Life Organizer

Take control for a happier, tidier and more fulfilled life

WENDY HOBSON

ARCTURUS

This edition published in 2020 by Arcturus Publishing Limited
26/27 Bickels Yard, 151–153 Bermondsey Street,
London SE1 3HA, UK

ISBN: 978-1-78950-792-8
AD006656UK

Printed in China

Contents

Why it's good to be organized

Do you envy those people who always remember everyone's birthdays, never turn up late, always have cakes to serve when you go round for a cup of coffee – freshly baked, of course – and are never put out by being asked to arrange a last-minute get-together or a big family event.

Some people are just natural organizers. If you are not one of those you can still learn from them how they do things and benefit from their logic, common sense and efficiency. If you are reading this, then I assume you are not a natural organizer. But don't despair. There are things you can do to help you improve on the organizational front.

You won't find all the answers here, but you will find many, and I hope you will be encouraged by the ideas, suggestions and information you discover that will help you be tidier, more efficient and generally more organized than you are now.

You should find you have more time because you're not constantly chasing your tail, trying to find your car keys or wondering how you are going to be in three places at once, having treble-booked your diary.

But before we start looking at practical ways to be more organized, let's address the modern mindset that we have to be invincible and that we have to do everything or we are somehow failing.

A quart does not go into a pint pot

Underlying many people's disarray is the feeling that they can do everything and shouldn't refuse to do anything in case they miss out. Here are a few truths to remember:

- you are only one person;

- you only have 24 hours in your day;

- and, to quote the old English adage: 'You can't get a quart into a pint pot'.

It is simply not possible for you to do everything that you would like to do. If you get two party invitations for the same evening, you can't go to both. The same applies to everything else and the sooner you accept that, the easier it will be to make decisions on what you can and cannot do. The more organized you are, the more you are likely to be able to fit things in, but even the most organized of people has to say 'no' sometimes.

What is the problem with saying 'no'?

There are many reasons why we find it hard to say 'no', from wanting to do something to not wanting to let someone down. What are your reasons?

Sometimes you will not be able to accept an invitation, volunteer for something, or get something done to a ridiculous schedule. Write down some honest reasons why you might say 'no'.

....

....

....

....

....

Ultimately it boils down to the same thing: you don't have the time, and you haven't prioritized it sufficiently to do it instead of something else. Tell yourself:

- there is nothing wrong with that.

Busy, busy, busy

On an advert for a famous gin, one woman is complaining how busy she is when her friend asks, 'Too busy for a gin and tonic?' Of course, the answer is: 'Oh no, not that busy.'

How infuriating are those who think they are the only people in the world with anything important to do! Organized people never compete as to how busy they are – they just get on with what they need to do and they learn to say 'no' when they have to.

Sometimes we also say 'yes' when we know a job is not going to take long. That's all very well, but it's not always the time it takes to do something that is important, it's the time it takes to get round to doing it. If something is going to take, say, two hours but you don't have a spare two hours until Thursday fortnight, then the answer to whether you will do it, is 'yes but.'

Compromise

Organized people also have to learn the sensible use of 'maybe', 'no, but …' and 'yes, but …', all of which have distinctive meanings and you must make sure that you and the person you are talking to have the same understanding.

- 'Maybe' doesn't mean 'yes' – but most children know it does when they ask for sweets, so be careful.

- 'No, but' doesn't mean 'yes' – it means 'no' unless something changes.

- 'Yes but' doesn't mean 'yes' – it is a qualified 'yes' if something can be changed.

Use them all to your advantage. Perhaps you can do something if you have a little more time or more information or maybe you can share the load with someone.

Think about things you have done that you should not really have taken on. What could you have done instead?

....

....

....

....

....

Selfish or self-aware?

There is an argument that I make regularly that selfishness is at the heart of everything that is wrong with our society. From discourtesy and littering to robbery and global warming, they are all motivated by selfishness, a disregard for the needs of anyone else.

On the other hand, self-awareness is essential if we are going to achieve a proper balance in life. How much can we do for other people and still have some time for ourselves? If we know something is just a step too far and will make us exhausted or even ill, we should be able to put our own needs on a par with those of others and say 'no.' We are all equally important.

Think about things you have not done that – had you compromised – you might have had time to do. Or things you did take on that could have been better organized.

....

....

....

....

....

....

Time to stand and stare

LEISURE

What is this life if, full of care,
We have no time to stand and stare?—
No time to stand beneath the boughs,
And stare as long as sheep and cows:
No time to see, when woods we pass,
Where squirrels hide their nuts in grass:
No time to see, in broad daylight,
Streams full of stars, like skies at night:
No time to turn at Beauty's glance,
And watch her feet, how they can dance:
No time to wait till her mouth can
Enrich that smile her eyes began?
A poor life this if, full of care,
We have no time to stand and stare.

William Henry Davis (1911)

I couldn't put it better. Slow down. Stop sometimes. Read a book. Have a cup of tea. Do nothing. Organized people can make time for that.

1

Introducing the Mess Spectrum

Now we move on to the practicalities, and how disorganized people differ from each other. They do differ, from those who are too well-meaning and want to do everything to those who are just haphazard and have no use for systems. Try to answer the questions in the left-hand column honestly, picking and choosing the ideas that best suit your individual profile.

Would you notice if the washing up hadn't been done as long as you could find a clean plate?	**10**	Your partner or flatmates will eventually get fed up of clearing up after you and find a more organized person to share with. Or you might end up with salmonella poisoning.
Are you almost always late?	**9**	Despite the fact that people make allowances for you, it is not only infuriating, it's unprofessional and unnecessary. It could lose you friends, jobs, tickets to a great show.
What percentage of floor is visible in the room you spend the most time in?	**8**	Completely covered? How deep? So what if the tickets to that sell-out gig are stuck to the bottom of the coffee cup?
Do you fly round with the vacuum cleaner when anyone is due to visit?	**7**	You know you'd like to be organized but it never quite works out.

Are you able to work a system but find those of your own devising always seem to be fatally flawed?	6	Ride on other shoulders, then. Borrow a system to organize yourself that you know will work.
Are you a compulsive list-writer but seem to add more than you cross off?	5	You have the motivation but not so much of the technique to put it into practice.
Do you have an active favourites bar on your computer?	4	Making use of the benefits of technology will help you be more organized.
Do you keep everything in one diary?	3	There's no chance of you missing an event or missing out.
Are your CDs in alphabetical order?	2	Precise order is a bit obsessive. Roughly in order is a good call as you can always find what you want.
Do you know exactly where you put the book you read three months ago?	1	Yes? That's because it had its place and you put it there. You don't miss a trick.
Do you measure the distance between items on your desk?	0	You are a very special person with hidden talents but probably the most annoying flatmate.

Now look at the right-hand column. Do you recognize any of the consequences of being up there in the 9s and 10s? In this spectrum I've focused on the basics because the state of your home often represents the state of your mind.

Where do you register?

So where did you score yourself on the Mess Spectrum? Most of us come somewhere around the middle, which means there's progress to be made. Use this page to jot down where you think your strengths and weaknesses lie, which will help you to decide on your priorities for change.

Register 10–7

If you take on board just some of the ideas in this book you will make some big improvements in your life.

Register 6–4

You split into three camps:

- you can work out a system but never stick to it;

- you can stick to a system that's in place but your own never seem to quite work out;

- you are full of good intentions and do your best in a rather haphazard fashion.

Whichever group you belong to, there's room for improvement and you'll really notice the difference. if you apply yourself.

Register 3–0

If you are down at the bottom of the scale, you are likely to be tidy, punctual and organized to the minutest degree. You would never have bought this book for yourself because you know it can't tell you anything so it must have been a gift or a joke. You don't need this book – pass it on to someone who does; perhaps the person who gave it to you.

10	Nothing is hopeless – remember that. But you do need to make some changes now.
9	Take it one step at a time because you have a long way to go.
8	This is still drastic-action territory, so don't expect too much too soon.
7	A bit of application will go a long way. Start small to encourage progress.
6	There is work to be done but you have an idea where you would like to be, which is a start.
5	Now we are in balance territory, so focus is the watchword here. Make improvements precisely where you need them.
4	Not a bad place to be because you know you have the ability to be more successfully organized.
3	You probably tend to binge organize, then relapse on a regular basis.
2	You are more likely to give this book to your untidy flatmate.
1	Don't lose sight of the bigger picture in your efforts to be exact.
0	You could teach me a thing or two about organization – but I might fall asleep.

Now make some notes on your strengths and weaknesses, which will help later on to work out the best ways to organize your life successfully.

I register ☐ on the Mess Spectrum

My strengths

....

....

....

....

....

My weaknesses

....

....

....

....

....

Moving down the Mess Spectrum

How disorganized am I
on a scale of 1 (good) to 10 (bad)

| 1 | 2 | 3 | 4 | 5 | 6 | 7 | 8 | 9 | 10 |

....

....

....

....

What I want to achieve

....

....

....

....

....

....

What am I worst at organizing?

....

....

....

....

....

....

....

....

....

....

....

....

Organized people I know and their
best and worst qualities

....

....

....

....

....

....

....

....

....

....

....

Disorganized people I know and their
best and worst qualities

....

....

....

....

....

....

My Mess Spectrum role models

....

....

....

....

....

Get your head in gear

If you are going to try to make changes to your life, you actually have to want to do it. You can sit with your feet up and a bowl of granola and think about going for a run – for all the good it will do you – or you can 'just do it.' And that is the hardest part.

So what is your motivation to organize your life?

The problems

First, think in terms of the problems you have now. You may be fed up with missing social opportunities because you lose invitations, fail to respond to emails or even forget to go. Perhaps your computer is on a go-slow because it is clogged up with unnecessary data.

....

....

....

....

....

....

....

....

....

The objectives

Now think about what you want to achieve by making improvements. A new job? A better work/life balance? Less time shuffling paper – literal or virtual.

....

....

....

....

....

....

....

....

....

....

....

....

....

....

The priorities

If there was just one thing you want to get out of reading this book, what would it be? And why?

....

....

....

....

....

....

....

....

....

....

....

....

....

Take the right approach

Take heart and remember that you are already making progress because you are thinking about where you are and where you want to be.

What you need to do next is to find the best route for you. To do that you need to combine and compare your personal qualities with what it is you want to achieve. And I deliberately used different terminology to make you think: all you have to do is compare the various bits of information you've jotted down so far.

Although I generally loathe marketing jargon, I do like their use of mnemonics so I am going to borrow the technique and SWOOP in on your ideal approach. (I'm assuming those who scored 0–3 have gone to tidy their filing cabinets by now.) As with any tick-box options, there won't be exactly the right combination but you can personalize it later.

S STRENGTHS	A	Better at working out systems and procedures	
	B	Better at implementing existing procedures	
	C	Find both hard	

W WEAKNESSES	A	Lack of staying power	
	B	Lack of motivation	
	C	Lack of patience	

O OBJECTIVE	A	Focused on social life	
	B	Focused on home	
	C	Focused on work	

O OBSTACLES	A	Not enough time	
	B	Not enough determination	
	C	Find organization very hard	

P PRIORITY	A	Improvement in one specific area	
	B	Improvement in several areas	
	C	General improvement	

What did you score?

Now look at your scores. What do they mean for your focus on how you actually grow your organizational skills? Think about how best to incentivize yourself to progress.

A ....

B ....

C ....

I scored mostly ....

Mostly A

You tend to be a starter rather than a finisher, so setting up systems works with your skills, but keeping them going will be harder. Concentrate on implementing one system in parallel with developing another so that you can switch between what you enjoy and what you find harder. It's called 'slow motion multi-tasking' and was popular with Einstein, I understand, as a way of overcoming stalling points in a project. Incentives could be the key to your success, so make a note of some things you'd like to treat yourself to at particular progress points.

I need to work first on

....

I should find it easier to

....

Rewards for progress

....

Mostly B

The blank page is your bête noire so you'll be better served by utilizing systems created by someone else. Once they are established, you'll have overcome your most difficult hurdle. Have a look at existing apps, or find a 'Mess Buddy' who got mostly As. What rewards would give you the incentive to get past first base?

I need to work first on

....

I should find it easier to

....

Rewards for progress

....

Mostly C

I won't pretend this will be easy but a step-by-step approach will help you gradually pick up the skills you need to move down the Mess Spectrum. Make sure you break down your changes into small units and give yourself lots of rewards and pats on the back as you go. Focus on not backsliding and don't be over-enthusiastic and try to change too much at once.

I need to work first on

....

I should find it easier to

....

Rewards for progress

....

Thinking it through

There are a number of things that organized people have in common, so let's look at those qualities and borrow a few to put into practice.

Who is my role model?

Everyone knows someone – or perhaps several people – who are naturally organized. When you are trying to decide what to do about a particular issue, ask yourself 'What would X do?' At first you may have to ignore the obvious answer that they wouldn't get themselves into this mess in the first place, but that will crop up less frequently as you proceed. There are bound to be one or two things that stand out and help nudge you in the right direction.

My role model is

....

....

....

....

....

....

....

....

Because

....

....

....

....

....

....

....

....

Problem solving

When you think about organizing your affairs or solving a problem, try to look at the best way to make things happen as efficiently as possible. Working out a solution can go in many different ways.

- The 'charge at it and hope for the best' solution: More often than not this will just leave you with a sore head.

- The 'ignore it and it'll go away' option: Does it ever? Rarely in my experience.

- The confrontational approach: Getting angry just makes everyone else angry and that helps nothing.

- The 'pull it apart to see how it works' solution: Can be useful but is only a stepping stone to a result and you do need to be sure you can put it back together again.

- The 'James T Kirk' solution: So called because in one of the Star Trek movies, the said Captain (or he may have been an Admiral by then) denied being brave and facing up to death because he said he had always found a way round it. Good call.

- The obvious solution: This almost always seems to involve doing something you really don't want to do.

The thinking it through solution

Ultimately that leaves the option that:

- gives the best outcome;
- involves the least amount of work;
- upsets the fewest number of people;
- is done in the least amount of time;
- and generally keeps most of the people happy most of the time.

That is what organized people do. They achieve it by taking the time to think about the impact of what they are going to doing and testing the consequences of each stage before embarking on it.

2

Planning

Start with the structure

Some people like to rush ahead and get stuck into whatever they are doing, with the risk of having to change it later. Good organizers tend to set up a framework and foundations first, then build on them and road test them as they go along. That way, you can identify problem areas before you start. The plan almost tests itself as it is developed.

Remember to put some idea of timescale into your plan, and that needs to take account of your everyday commitments. If you can only allocate an hour a day to your plan, that's fine, but don't expect to complete everything in three weeks.

My plan to organize my life

Main objective ....

Priorities ....

I am good at ....

So the first thing I will do is ....

I am weak at ....

....

So I will practise ....

....

I want to tidy and organize these areas. Keep to the basics and you can add to it later on.

Area	Declutter notes	Date to complete

Area	Organization notes	Date to complete

Priorities

....

....

....

....

....

....

....

....

....

....

....

....

....

....

....

Schedule

....

....

....

....

....

....

....

....

....

....

....

....

....

....

....

Reason for wanting to be organized

....

....

....

....

Benefits of planning

....

....

....

....

What I'll find most difficult

....

....

....

....

Computer politics

No doubt you will be using your computer to help you in organizing your life. If not, why not? The computer is perfect at remembering and manipulating data so you don't have to.

But there are downsides. There are more programs and apps out there for more models and makes of device than you would think possible. They range from life-changingly brilliant to maddeningly rubbish; some liaise with other operating systems better than others; some are all part of the same stable and like to talk to their own family rather than anyone else. Minefield? Pretty much.

You may also have a laptop, tablet, PC or iMac, Android or iPhone. Depending how you use the items, you need to make sure you have access to your information on the right device at the right time, and that the data is co-ordinated across your devices, so a change in one is reflected in the others.

The objective here is to make a selection of the programs you are going to use so that you avoid getting entangled in the politics of the internet and can co-ordinate everything across your devices, if necessary.

Device	Operating system	I use it for	Account name

The power dynasties

There's no doubt that the big tech corporations want to link together all their products so that you remain loyal to them. That means, although it's not essential, it is easier to use programs just from one family, so if you like the way Google does things, keep to Google; if you prefer Microsoft, go for them.

I have chosen

....

....

Browser

....

....

Photos

....

....

Mail, contacts and calendar

....

....

....

....

Co-ordinate your devices

Once you have decided which programs you are going to use, make sure you register your account on all your devices, so that they co-ordinate your activity.

If you are techy-minded, you might want to spend a day sorting everything out in one go. More likely, you will want to cut it down into manageable chunks.

You will need to refer to the web for detailed instructions, but generally if you use the format recommended by or defaulted to by your device, you'll keep things simpler. The fewer accounts you have, the easier it is to structure them.

You will find the portal to the help pages for all the major organizations at support.[companyname].com

Device	Account	Date added

Your unique blueprint

This is your constant point of reference. If you lose focus, lack motivation, or if things go wrong, come back here and fortify yourself by looking at all the positives you can achieve if you persevere in organizing your life more effectively.

Fill in whatever is important to you and start putting in some detail. Write in the sequence of tasks that you need to do. For example, you may choose to focus on your clothes first. How are you going to go about it? You could:

- Empty the cupboards.
- Clean the furniture.
- Divide into groups – shirts, trousers, socks, etc.
- Decide on where you are going to store each group.
- Sort into keep and what to get rid of.
- Take the second lot to the charity shop.
- Restore the remaining clothes to their places.

Area	Main problems	Objective

If they involve a redirection of other jobs, change and adapt your plan. If it works towards your objective, it's in; if not, it's out.

Are you on a schedule to complete your objectives? It's not generally a good idea to focus on this and nothing else, but that's not an excuse to let it drag on and pretend you are still thinking about it.

	Task 1	Task 2	Task 3	Task 4	Task 5

Looking out for the potholes

Testing is very important when you are setting up a system. Think through the processes you have come up with and look out for the instances where you can see things are not going to work in practice. How can you make effective changes? Perhaps you can't see how to just now; mark it as an issue to be addressed and come back to it later.

Similarly, if problems arise while you are working on something, try to think through a practical solution. If you can't, try to complete the job to that point, make a note of where you are and let the problem settle at the back of your mind. A solution may present itself at an unlikely moment.

Google is a great asset in finding solutions to problems. You may be able to go straight to some relevant help pages but if not, don't give up. Just type in your question. Try phrasing it different ways until you find a useful solution.

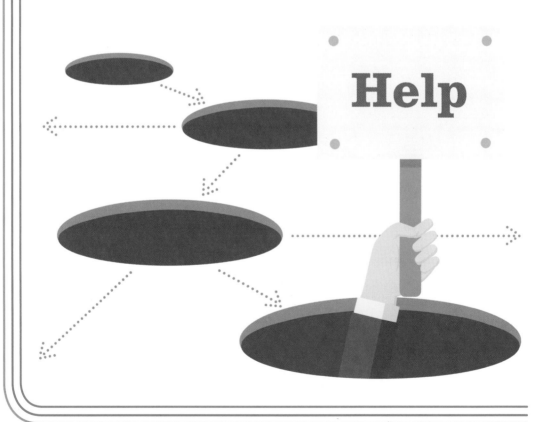

Problem

....

Solution

....

Problem

....

Solution

....

Problem

....

Solution

....

Problem

....

Solution

....

Adapting and improving

As long as you keep your primary objective in focus, don't think that being organized means that you cannot make changes and adapt things as you go along – that is far the best way of making sure it all works right in the end.

If one of your systems seems clunky, or you spend too much time on a helpline, you need to take action. Try to imagine you are coming at the system for the first time and look objectively at each stage. When it stops flowing smoothly, ask yourself why? Is the sequence wrong? Are you missing something? Once that becomes clear, you should be able to adapt the process to make it work more efficiently.

Notes

....

....

....

....

....

....

....

....

....

3

Your decluttering programme

Rooms to clear out

☐ Lounge

☐ Dining room

☐ Bedroom

☐ Bedroom

☐ Bathroom

☐ Kitchen

Local charity shops

....

....

....

....

....

Charity collection phone numbers

....

....

....

....

....

....

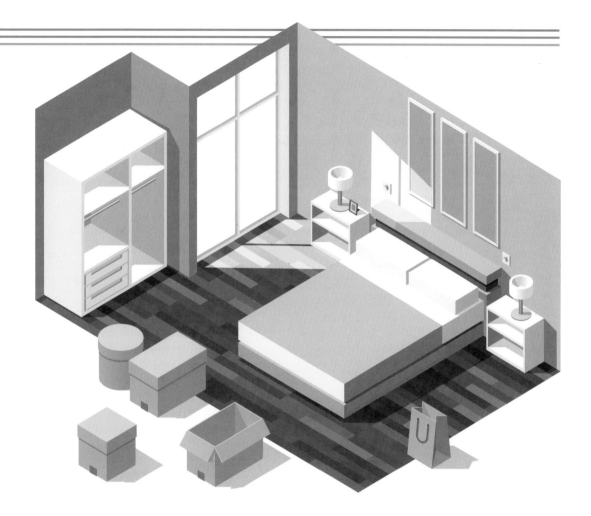

Speculate on what you've accumulated

Another downside of being busy is that we don't make the time to pay attention to how we accumulate 'stuff.' We purchase utensils for the kitchen but don't throw out the old ones; we buy new clothes but the old ones seem too good to throw away; we receive gifts; we frame photographs. There's nothing wrong with that until the quantity of stuff begins to clog your energies and you feel weighed down by things that aren't doing any useful service. Then it's time for a clear out.

There are many theories and techniques for decluttering. If you find any of them strike a chord with you, go for it. If you get a frisson of happiness when you hug an old jumper, who am I to argue with that? Especially since my approach is very similar.

One area at a time

You might decide to put aside a weekend to get it all done, or divide the task into manageable sections. You might do:

- a room at a time;

- clothes first, then books, paperwork, favourite things;

- upstairs, downstairs.

It only matters that it suits you and your mess, and it cuts down the task into manageable chunks if you can't face it all in one go. For the sake of this example, let's assume we'll work a room at a time.

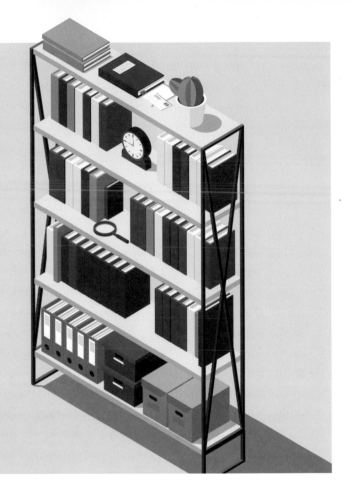

The difference between want and need

We all need sufficient clothing to stay warm and smart, do our jobs, and so on. Most people have far more than that because they like variety, it saves washing so often, and because they can. It makes you feel good if you are looking your best for a special occasion, or comfortable in old jeans for lounging around. So you will have things you absolutely need and things that you want. You don't have to throw out things you want just because you don't use them very often. If you have things you need but really don't like, then you have to decide whether you can get rid of them now or you need to wait until your cash flow improves and you can get better versions.

Yes or no – there's no maybe

Just like when you are learning to drive and there's no 'maybe' about whether to pull out of a side road, it's either 'yes, I have room' or 'no, I don't', try not to confuse the issue with 'maybe it'll come in handy.' You are making your decision now, and right now, the item is either:

- useful;
- beautiful;
- or surplus to requirements.

So you don't have to worry about feeling pressured to get rid of things you use all the time, or things that are beautiful, or valuable either in monetary or sentimental terms. Anything that lands on the surplus pile can then be divided into:

- charity shop;
- upcycling or recycling;
- selling;
- rubbish.

Some decisions will be obvious. For the ones that aren't, keep asking yourself questions until you get to a decision point.

- How long have you had it?
- When was the last time you used it?
- Is it working or broken/damaged?
- Can it be repaired? Would it be any more useful if it was mended?
- Was it a gift?
- Does it have sentimental value?
- What is its monetary value?
- Do you like it?

Act immediately

Don't leave things lying around. Deal with each pile straightaway.

- If it is useful and you have already established its place, put it away.

- If it is useful but has not yet found a home, find it one.

- Recycling can be grouped ready for a run to the recycling centre.

- Rubbish can go in the bag or bin, ready for collection.

- If you need a trip to the recycling centre, get it over and done with.

- Anything you may be able to sell needs to be photographed, if selling online, or priced up for a second-hand garage or yard sale.

Let's go round again

You will find that what you define as essential (or at least you want to hang on to) now may not feel as essential two months or even two weeks down the line. Decluttering just the once doesn't seem logical to me unless you decide not to buy or otherwise obtain anything else ever again, or view things in the same way, so set a date in your diary for the next declutter of this first room in three or six months' time.

For many people, circling round your mess and working in from the edges is the most efficient way to go because:

- it's easier to be decisive;

- the second time you look at something, it is in a different context – you have already discarded a lot of stuff – which could make the item easier to throw out, or it will confirm your decision that this is a keeper;

- you won't have to deal with everything at once.

Once you have done the next room, you can add that to your diary, too, but you don't need to do them all at the same time or even hot on each other's heels. Start to spread them out, then they'll be quicker and more interesting.

Schedule for decluttering

Room/area	Notes	Date scheduled	Date completed

What are you going to do with it?

If, like me, you hate to see things wasted, you won't need any prompting to avoid just putting everything in a black sack and throwing it away, to end up in landfill. For me, that's a last resort. Fortunately, most recycling centres discourage this approach, so you will need to separate your items so that as many as possible can be re-used or recycled. Keep this, and the layout of the centre, in mind not only when you put things in bags or boxes but also when you pack the car.

Upcycling

Finding a new use for an item or adapting it to another use can be very rewarding. It's particularly useful for those of a practical bent, who can turn their hand to a bit of sewing or DIY. A shoe rack becomes a bookcase, a coat stand becomes a spot for hanging baskets in the garden, an old tent becomes a barbecue cover, some spare wood from a cabin bed and half an old wallpaper pasting table become a raised veggie bed. Be imaginative.

Charity

By taking items to a charity shop or having them collected either by a special collection (ring the charity) or by putting them in the bags that are regularly dropped off in some locations can earn money for the charity. If you are a UK taxpayer, the government will add the value of the tax to the price received for the item, so do agree to gift aid your donations if you can.

Again, locate the most accessible shop in advance, consider whether you have to carry anything any distance, bag or box up your donations and take them straight round to the store.

Trash

Bag it up and put it out for the recycling or the refuse collection.

Bigger items may need a trip to the recycling centre or a special collection. You can find out details for your local area on the local government website.

Local government website

....

Refuse collection day

....

Contact for special collections

....

Date booked for special collection

....

Details

....

....

....

....

Making some cash

It is sometimes possible to recoup money by selling items you no longer need. You probably need to be prepared to sell them for a fraction of their former value, and remember that you are not costing in your time at a professional rate.

Where to advertise

There are many options you can try, and a quick search online will soon reveal the best opportunities for you. The most obvious are eBay, Facebook marketplace and Gumtree but there are many more.

Open a PayPal account if you don't have one already, to make payments easier to manage.

Do a search for a similar item and see how many are available and what kind of prices people are asking. Also what are they doing about delivery/collection? Don't get drawn into delivering an item if it is really not convenient, especially if you are offering the item free or at a bargain price. It is worth reiterating in your description that you don't (or do) deliver.

Think about search engine optimization (or metadata) when you write the copy so you use the words that people are most likely to use when they are searching for a similar item. This will ensure that your item appears in as many searches as possible.

How to place the ad

- Choose where you are going to advertise.

- Look at similar items and decide on
  - an appropriate price;
  - words to use in your title so it comes up in as many searches as possible;
  - words to use in your description for the same reason and also to describe the item as accurately as possible;
  - postage costs.

- Take a few photos showing
  - the whole item;
  - close-ups of particular features;
  - any damage.

- If ads run for seven days, choose a good time of day to place, and therefore finish, your ad when people are likely to be available for any last-minute competitive bidding.

- Write, check and place the ad.

- Keep an eye on your ad and make any adjustments you feel (price, description, additional photos) are needed based on the response.

- If the item does not sell, it is usually relisted several times.

- If it does sell, pack it up and dispatch it as soon as possible after you receive payment.

- Mark it as dispatched.

- Leave feedback.

Item to sell	Date advert placed	Advertised in	Price	Sold

Give it away to a new home

If all else fails, you can advertise on sites like Freecycle.org or Preloved.co.uk and someone who sees your ad can come and take the item away. Be quite specific about what you have on offer. Include close up photos and be clear in your descriptions if there is any wear or damage.

Item to give away	Date advert placed	Advertised in	Collected

Safety when trading online

If you are selling items online, take note of the website's security information and use your common sense. Here are a few pointers, but it is worth looking at the latest eBay or Amazon tips for a thorough review of safety issues.

- Remember there are scammers out there. If in doubt, don't follow it, delete it. If it is important one side or other will get in touch.

- Don't send sensitive information by email.

- Don't disclose bank details unless you are absolutely sure you know what you are doing. If in doubt, don't.

- No reputable organization will ever ask you for your password.

- Take the usual precautions about giving out your address or details for collection.

- Check your potential buyers' account records.

- Look out for very poor grammar and spelling, which can be an indicator of an unreliable buyer.

- Be clear about whether or not you will deliver and how much it will cost. Some people will ask you to deliver even if you are giving something away, which I happen to think is a bit of a nerve.

- Use PayPal for secure payments.

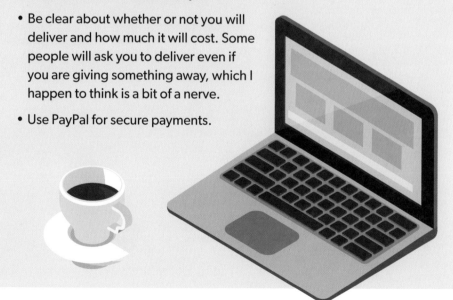

Value your space

Once you have divested yourself of all this extraneous stuff, you will hopefully feel a great sense of relief. It will also be easier to organize the things you have kept as you will have more space.

Remember how good that feels and resist the temptation to undo your hard work and clog everything up by buying unnecessary things. You may well need to do another major declutter in the future, but if you remind yourself constantly of that lovely 'cleared-out' feeling, then you'll be less likely to let it the stuff accumulate again.

How it feels to be organized

....

....

....

....

....

....

....

....

....

Advantages I've already noticed

....

....

....

....

....

....

....

....

....

....

....

....

....

....

Benefits I'd like to achieve

....

....

....

....

....

....

....

....

....

....

....

....

....

....

How to organize at home

How to organize a room

There is no big secret to organizing things at home and keeping them tidy, just three simple principles:

- Organize your space so that the arrangement of the space complements the flow of your daily routines.

- Make sure each area or storage unit is large enough to house the contents comfortably.

- Put things away in the right place.

Of course, it's not always quite so easy in practice but don't let that put you off. Solutions are always to be found.

- Draw up a rough sketch of the rooms you are working on and the position of the furniture.

- Mark in what you keep in each of the drawers and cupboards.

- Now draw in your sequence of movement through the room – where you sit, what you do first.

- Assess the space you have available and how it is currently deployed. Is it fit for purpose? Would somewhere else be better? Is there too little space? Too much?

- Can you reposition it elsewhere?

Play around with ideas, then test them out in practice and you should find it much easier and quicker to get around and get things done.

Use this system to map out how your rooms should flow in terms of how you use them and position your furniture accordingly.

For example, look at the following three arrangements of the same bedroom. One opens up a larger space in the room and gives a view out of the window from the bed, but no way of getting into the bed from both sides – fine if the bedroom is used by only one person. The second divides the space into smaller blocks but means you can get into the bed from either side. The third is perhaps the happy medium, although it does have to suit the way you use the room.

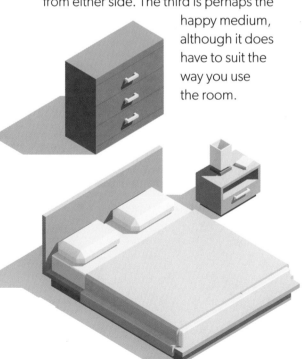

Layout 1

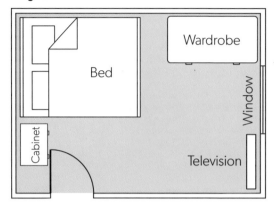

Layout 2

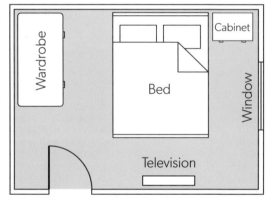

Layout 3

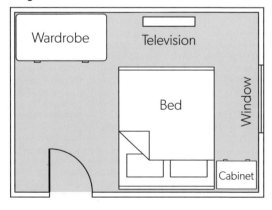

A place for everything

Now see if there is enough space for the items you want to put in that position. If there is, fine, it can stay there. If not, can you exchange two pieces of furniture? Or can you get rid of the existing item and get something that fits? Or could you look at the plan again and reorganize so you create an appropriate space for what you want to put in it. For example, socks are best in a drawer, shirts on hangers or folded on shelves. Are yours in a logical place?

As you live with the new arrangement, you'll spot improvements you can make as you go along.

So now you have a place for everything.

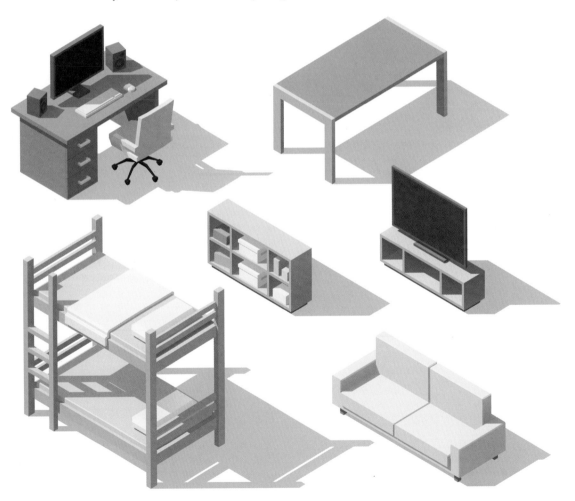

Where are you going to keep your things?

Room/area	Item	Furniture	Position
Living room			
Dining room			
Kitchen			
Bathroom			
Hall and landing			
Bedroom 1			
Bedroom 2			
Bedroom 3			

Floor plans

Lounge

Dining Room

Bedroom

Bedroom

Kitchen

What's in the wardrobe?

Because it is the area most likely to be full, I am going to make an example of the wardrobe so you can use it as a pattern for other areas of the house.

By now, some of you may be crying 'Enough – I get the picture!' while those at the other end of the Mess Spectrum may be groaning 'Too much!'. Either way, that's fine. If you have picked up only a few ideas, they can still be of benefit. This is all about organizing your life, so you can do exactly how much or how little you want.

I am assuming that you have already decluttered and got rid of your bags of worn-outs, scarcely-worn-its, doesn't-fit-any-mores and never-suited-me-anyways. Now you are working on organizing what you do need or want. You have looked at where the furniture should be positioned and what should be in it for maximum convenience.

Organizational options

There are several ways to organize your wardrobe so you know where things are. Choose the one that seems the most logical to you. These are a few options:

- by colour;

- in complete outfits;

- with all the same type of thing together, so jeans, shirts, and so on;

- smart and casual.

....

....

....

....

....

....

....

....

....

The most important point is that when you go looking for something you know exactly where it will be. You can apply the same principles to other storage areas in the home, always aiming to find the easiest and most convenient solutions.

Everything in its place

Of course, it's no use having a sock drawer if it's not full of socks, so if you want to stay tidy and know where things are, then you need to put them away in the correct place. That's not actually as difficult as it sounds. There are two simple rules to follow:

- **finish what you started;**

- **slow down.**

Remember, though, that – especially if you are someone who finds it difficult to stay neat – you need to keep reminding yourself to put things away in the right place. Temporarily, try a few post-it notes in strategic places, and also try to allow yourself a little more time to keep things organized.

Many people – myself included – have a tendency to 'butterfly.' You might start doing some sewing in the dining room, then find that you need the scissors from the kitchen, but when you go into the kitchen, you realize you didn't finish washing up so you start washing up but you need a fresh tea towel from the airing cupboard … you get the idea.

If you keep reminding yourself to finish one job before you start the next, you will use your time more efficiently, and you will gradually find you have fewer reasons to butterfly as there won't be so many unfinished jobs around.

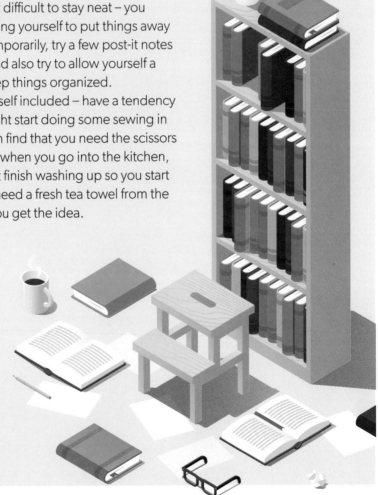

Still struggling?

If you are still finding it impossible to keep your home tidy, you may need some more support. On a sliding scale of 0 to 5, those who are at 5 have probably got it sorted by now, but if you are at 0 (lousy) up to 3 (mediocre) it may not be so easy. Perhaps you are one of the 'starters' who like to put together a system but rarely uses it. If you always seem to be clearing up but are never tidy, then here are some solutions.

The trick is that you need to find a pressing reason why you should bother to overcome your instinct to leave things where they drop. That could be trivial or serious, highlighting a negative if you don't change but preferably a positive if you do – it doesn't really matter as long as it works.

- If there was a fire, I'd never get out for all the burning rubbish on the floor.

- If I tread on that piece of Lego once more, I'll scream.

- I'm not going to miss another call from the recruitment agency because I can't find the phone.

- I'd really like to impress that new girl/guy when they come round.

- I think my kitchen/bathroom could be a health hazard.

- My Mum is coming to visit.

Allocate a tidy-up time that suits your routine and when you feel most like making a positive impression. That may be as soon as you get up so you can get it over with, when you get home from work or at the end of the day. Don't change it and don't make excuses. Make it a habit.

Make it a habit

At the heart of organization – and therefore of this little book – is one apparently insignificant word: habit. Whoever said 'habits are harder to break than principles' was wise indeed. Put it to the test. How often have you said 'I'm going to be more organized/lose weight/not miss my girlfriend's birthday again …?' But, by comparison, how many times have you set off on a route home, because you were on regular autopilot when, in fact, you had changed your plans and you should have been going somewhere else?

The only way to turn a principle in to a habit is to make it one of the principal things you do every day. Keep repeating until you no longer think about it, but you simply get up, tidy up, throw your washing in the wash bin, then head for the shower, instead of missing out the middle two stages.

Establishing habits

Take one or two task at a time – usually the dull ones that you don't want to do – and drum them into your routine. Jotting down what you are focusing on and how you plan to make these changes should help you focus on the task.

Current action	New habit	Date started	Habit established

Going digital

What's the difference?

Many people of more mature years who have grown up with pens, paper and filing cabinets find it hard to adapt to the digital universe that is second nature to the young because they feel it is alien. But if you think about it in comparative terms, the same logic applies in both the tangible and the virtual worlds. True, the virtual demands a different perspective to fully embrace its possibilities, but as a starting point, organizing a computer is not very different to how you would organize a desk.

- The things you need regularly should be easily accessible.

- Everything should be clearly labelled so you know what it is.

- Items should be organized so similar things are grouped together.

- Files and folders should be logically organized, not just in a random pile.

- You need enough space to keep things tidy.

- A regular clear-out is a good idea.

Backing up

You only realize how important things are when you lose them. Do not make the mistake of thinking you don't need a backup system on your computer – you do. You can back up on to a memory stick, CDs or external hard drives. You can also back up to a cloud system, which simply means that your data is stored on another computer via the internet and you can access it if your computer fails.

Search 'backup' on your computer for options and how to do it.

Date established	Backup frequency	Back-up to

My devices

Computer

....

....

....

....

....

....

Tablet

....

....

....

....

....

....

Phone

....

....

....

....

....

....

Program family

....

....

....

....

....

....

The jargon jungle

The digital world is a minefield of obscure terminology and acronyms but you'll never master all of them.

- You only have to know what an acronym means to you and how you can use it, not actually what it stands for – unless you want to.

- For example, knowing that a pdf is a Portable Document Format is not important but might help you remember it. Who cares that a jpeg stands for Joint Photographic Experts Group – it's just a picture.

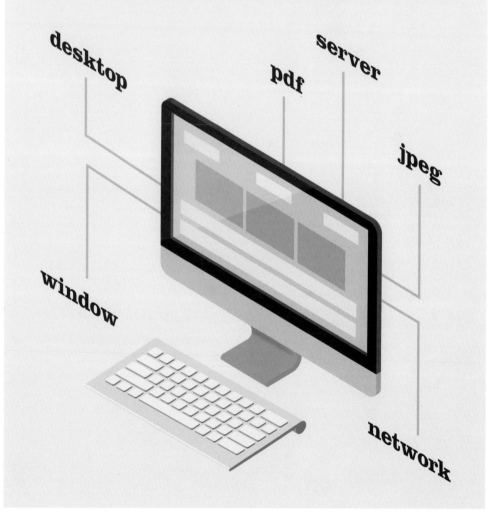

Clues to finding your way around

Those less familiar with the digital world can use the parallels between physical and digital to help understand the terminology. Using similar words and concepts to compare digital and physical things and ways of working can help familiarize you with new options.

PHYSICAL WORLD MEMORY JOGGER	VIRTUAL WORLD
Blue is the computer's favourite colour.	Anything blue or outlined in blue is what the computer expects you to press.
Theatre exits are usually in the corners.	Want to escape? Try the corners first.
Exits includes the letter X.	X means exit.
You keep everything handy on your desktop.	The desktop is the main screen where you keep the things you are working on.
A folder is useful for keeping documents together.	Ditto.
A network is a group of items joined together.	Ditto.

Need to know

There are always several ways to do things on a computer. Some people use keyboard shortcuts, others prefer touch screen, a mouse or trackpad. In the same way that you can get to the pub using two different routes, there are also options on your computer. One may be quicker or easier but neither is necessarily wrong. Just use the method you prefer. If you find useful shortcuts and tips, ways to do things that you might not use often enough to commit reliably to memory, making a note of them can be a good idea.

Date	How to	Process

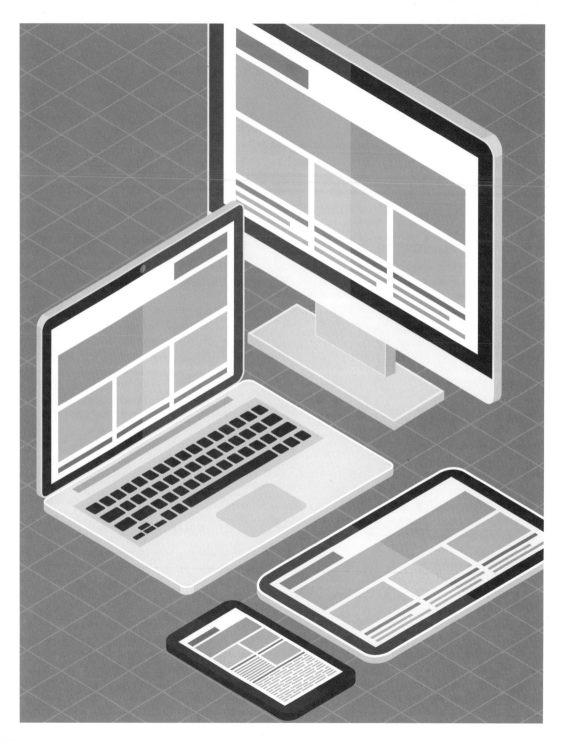

The desktop

The desktop is the place to keep the things you are using now and which are urgent or to be dealt with – the top of your 'in' tray, if you like.

- Choose a background image that is plain or does not obscure the items on top and make them hard to find (right-click for options).

- Use folders to group documents on the same project.

- Label folders in line with your document filing system so they can be transferred easily (Right-click > Rename).

- Organize the icons by name, date, last opened, and so on – whatever is convenient (Finder > View > Sort by).

- Adjust the size of the display (Finder > View > View options).

- Regularly tidy your files into the main documents folders when you are no longer using them.

- Make sure your Desktop is included in your backup.

- Use a program like Stickies or make notes to keep a check on your to-do list and what you are keeping on the Desktop.

- Keep your most-used apps visible so they are easy to access. Organizing them alphabetically is usually the simplest way.

The to-do list

There are many ways of keeping a to-do list. Some still like paper, most people tend to use the option in their calendar, thus automatically linking it with dates. Another way is to keep Stickies on your desktop, as many people like the flexibility of individual notes and the fact that it is similar to old systems they may have used.

If you decide this a good option for you and helps you prioritize your tasks and not forget things, just remember to keep an eye on the notes and delete or update them they are done.

Organizing documents

Your Documents folder is the most logical place to keep all the data you collect on your computer. The way you name and structure your folders should make things easier to find.

Whether you are talking about organizing documents on the computer or in a filing cabinet, the principles are pretty much the same. In fact, about the same as any organizational plan: decide on the best place to keep things so you can find them again easily, and then put things back in the right place. Where you keep them needs to be logical in relation to your work or life process. They also need to be labelled clearly.

Remember that you can use folders and sub-folders to keep your information in logical groups, so you might divide everything into personal and work-related, for example, then sub-divide into various smaller folders.

Viewing and sorting

Don't forget that you can use the View options in the Finder menu to view your folders and files and folders in the best way for that particular function: as list, icons, with details and so on. In List format, click on the header at the top of the column to reverse the sort. Use the Finder View options to display your files in the way you prefer:

- as icons (A);
- a list (B);
- columns (C).

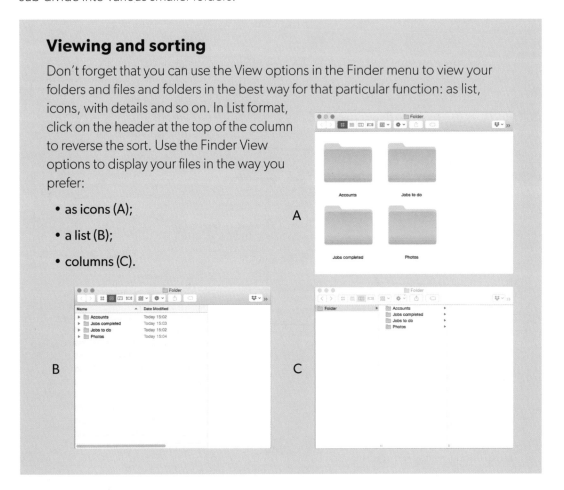

Using a search

Although you can always use the search facilities on your computer to find things, it is a bit risky. You might think you named a document '2019 holiday list' but if you made a keying error and called it '2019 holliday list' or got the date wrong, then it is not going to come up in your searches.

Using alphanumerics

If you name your folders logically, then there is no need to sort them into order as the computer will do that for you. If you use names carefully, the alphanumeric system will sort them into number then alphabetical order without any need for you to do anything. You will also be able to use the Finder Arrange option to reorganize by name, kind, dates, and so on.

A word on shredding

When you are having regular clear-outs that involve paper, remember to shred any personal documents – especially those that contain important information such as bank account details or tax codes – before you recycle the paper. Paper carrier bags or boxes are useful for containing the shreds when you put them in the bin.

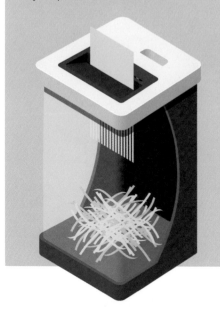

Photo bombs

Photos can be ordered in a similar way, using folders and sub-folders to group the pictures by event or time. You might, for example, have

2019
- 2019 Christmas
- 2019 Fred's 60th birthday
- 2019 Kew Gardens

2018
- 2018 Seaside holiday
- 2018 Mary and Tom's anniversary party

You can create folders manually in Finder and utilize the computer's automatic sorting prowess to place them in order.

Make sure your photos are carefully labelled so you know what they show, and that they are backed up separately.

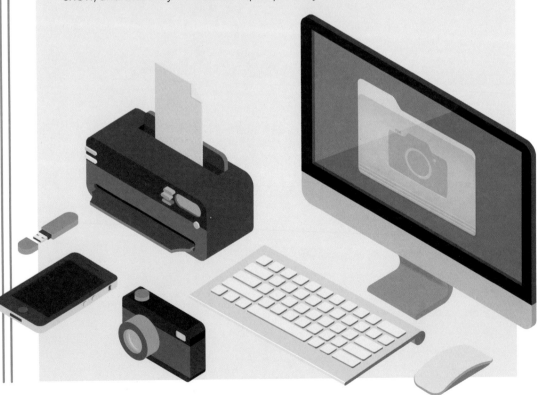

Photo organization

What's in a name?

Within the folders, the name given to each picture includes the date and time it was taken, followed by the number sequence on your camera, so the sequence 20190108-051501 reveals it was taken on 8 January 2019 and I have taken over 50,000 images on my camera. If you right-click 'Get info', it will give you plenty more details, including the latitude and longitude it was taken. I don't know about you, but I prefer to tag a name on the end of the date number with a specific location, name or event.

If you scan in or download any images, you can keep them in a separate folder within your dated folders or amalgamate them with your other images.

Culling

With digital photography making it so easy, I think it's fair to say that we all take too many photos. To keep everything well organized, it's a good idea to get into the habit of getting rid of the dross at several stages as you go along. As soon as you take photos, or soon after, run through them and delete all those that don't work – closed eyes, telegraph poles growing out of people's heads, that kind of thing.

When you upload them to your main device, go through them again. You'll find there are more that are repeats so delete them.

Uploading to your cloud could also spark another cull. You'll still have hundreds of photos and you certainly won't miss the ones that have gone.

Using a photo program

If you decide to use an online program, choose one that will co-ordinate your images across all your devices, such as Google Photos. Upload the photos from the memory card on your camera (if necessary) to your main device, then upload them to Google Photos and you will be able to access them from any device – something that will prove very useful when you just know you took a picture of Archie on your iPad and you now want access on your phone.

Upload to your online photo program via the Share option.

There's something about a photobook

Although keeping everything digitally has huge advantages, there is something about the experience of leafing through a photograph album that some of us miss. It is not difficult to create a photobook with one of the online services or apps, and some are even free to use. Allow yourself plenty of time to do the job, though, as it can be time-consuming. Look through your photos first and decide on the themes you are going to include and which images – you'll almost certainly need to be selective – and how they fit on the pages.

6

Keeping it secure

Backing up

It is of little use spending all this time organizing your digital data if you don't have a failsafe in place for if the worst happens and your phone drops in the river or your computer goes up in smoke.

If you search Backup on your device, it will guide you through the options for that device. You can back up to a memory stick, hard drive or something else physical, or you can choose which cloud to select as your backup location. As before, there is competition for your custom, so go with something that links in with as many as possible of your other apps and programs. Once they are safely on the cloud, you can view or work on them remotely, or download them back to your devices.

Backup disk information

....

....

....

....

....

....

....

....

....

....

....

....

....

....

Password clues

....

....

....

....

....

....

....

....

....

....

....

....

....

Back up location

....

....

....

....

....

....

....

....

....

....

....

....

....

....

A million passwords every day

Also on the subject of security, those dreaded but essential passwords must come high on the agenda. Here is a roundup of the usual advice.

- Passwords should be eight to twelve characters, including digits and upper and lower case letters; sometimes symbols are allowed or essential, sometimes not.

- You need to remember the passwords without writing them down but they should not be obvious.

- Don't use personal details that are easy to guess, such as names of family or pets, favourite sports teams, place of birth, and so on.

- Avoid obvious substitutions that are easy to guess, such as 'Pa55word.'

- Don't re-use the same password on multiple accounts.

- Don't write down your passwords or leave them where they are easy to find – on a note next to the screen or in a document called 'passwords.'

- Your email account is crucial so make sure you have a strong, separate password for that account.

- Using three random words can create a secure password, with a couple of numbers and capital letters. They can be loosely related to the site to help you remember them. For example: 5parcelshopChina6 for eBay.

- Use two-factor authentication where it is available.

- Make use of the fingerprint options on your devices.

- According to the UK's National Cyber Security Centre (ncsc.gov.uk), pasting your password increases rather than decreases security.

If you decide you have to write down passwords, keep them separate from your devices, don't label them clearly, and use clues or parts of the password rather than writing down the whole thing.

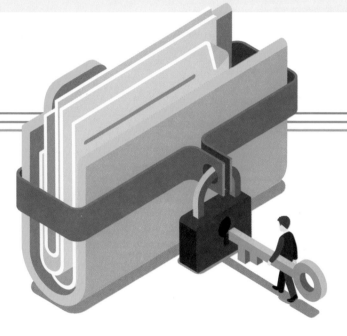

Password managers

You can get free apps that choose and store all your passwords and personal information and fills them in automatically when required. Some also encrypt your online activity on unsecured networks, and can replace weak passwords with stronger ones. It goes without saying that you need to be sure of the source and reliability of the company providing the software. They are useful because:

- you don't have to remember a huge number of passwords;

- they reduce the frustration of forgetting or mis-keying passwords;

- they make it easier to use complex, stronger passwords.

7

Money, money, money

Keep it simple

It is essential to keep tabs on your income and outgoings. However much or little you are dealing with, if there's more going out than coming in, that's a problem and you need to do something about it. If there's more coming in than going out, you could think more about savings.

The easiest way to check up on your finances is to make notes of everything coming in and everything you spend. You can easily do that on your phone or computer, or keep a notebook in your pocket or bag. You don't have to do it for very long to be able to work out how you are getting on. In fact, you probably know already but only by collating the details can you see where any issues lie, if any, and from there you can work out what to do about them.

Create a spreadsheet

You don't have to be a whizz on the computer to create a spreadsheet. If you don't have Excel, you can use the online version for free, or there are other free apps with similar and compatible programs. The fact that they are simpler is not relevant as if you only want a straightforward spreadsheet, they have more than enough functionality.

- Working on a monthly basis is convenient but whatever timespan you choose, do make sure all the figures relate correctly, so you don't list your annual car tax bill as a single large sum just because you pay it in one go – break it down into the monthly cost.

- List all sources of income, taking into account any tax commitments.

- Include all direct debits and cash spending.

- Specify the type of information in each column so that it displays correctly.

- Use the $\sum$ function to quickly add a column of figures.

Below is a rough example of a spreadsheet with arbitrary figures and a healthy balance. But note that there are no holidays included, nor any birthday and Christmas gifts, theatre tickets – all those major expenses that vary so much between individuals. They all need to be accounted for.

Financial record sheet		
Name:		
Date:		
	Monthly figures	
	INCOME	OUTGOINGS
Car insurance		£20.00
Car maintenance		£15.00
Car tax		£10.00
Fitness club		£75.00
Food		£200.00
Gas/electric		£80.00
House insurance		£16.00
Internet		£30.00
Mobile		£30.00
Net salary	£1,875.00	
Optician		£25.00
Phone		£50.00
Rent/mortgage		£800.00
Socialising		£200.00
Travel to work		£200.00
TV licence		£13.00
Water		£15.00
TOTALS	£1,875.00	£1,779.00
FUNDS REMAINING		£96.00

The more you work in a spreadsheet program, the more proficient you will become at using the options it presents.

Keeping notes

Make sure you enter spending as you pay it, or at least keep notes so you don't forget anything.

Accounting apps

There are a number of apps available if you have to present formal accounts, which include spreadsheets, automatic recording of invoices and all kinds of other options. Choose carefully to make sure they have the specific functionality you need, then let them do the organizing for you.

Where account held	Sort code	Account number	Account name

Major expenses	Supplier	Account number	Account name

Accountant (name and address)

Coping with debt

If you do get into debt, it is even more important to try to make changes in order to manage within your income, although you also have to take interest payments into account. Don't delay. Seek advice from Citizens Advice in the UK, or an equivalent organization elsewhere. Talk to the bank, mortgage provider, landlord and any other affected parties. They are likely to be able to suggest ways of managing the situation. Ignoring it is not an option.

Income

....

....

....

....

....

....

....

....

....

Outgoings

....

....

....

....

....

....

....

....

....

Interest payments

....

....

....

Debts owed to   £

....

....

....

....

....

....

Local debt advice

....

....

....

## 8

Keeping in touch

Dealing with email

It's hard to believe how many letters used to go back and forth, especially in business – and then there was the disappearing fax (disappearing not just because we don't use them any more but because if you put one in a file and went back later to check on what it said, the text had faded to invisible!).

Now emails are a great way to contact someone immediately wherever they are in the world. It is so much more efficient to just click New, write your message and Send. There are, however, a few traps for the unwary so if you want to stay organized, then watch out that you don't fall into them.

Keep it flowing

Email clients can absorb huge amounts of data so it is unlikely that you would fill your Inbox but even if your system can cope with it, it's likely to slow things down, and it's untidy and unwieldy when you are trying to access information. Check your incoming mail regularly and deal with it.

- Beware of email 'tone'. If you are too brief, it can sound rude.

- Everyone knows not to use capital letters to SHOUT.

- Check the recipient, cc and bcc recipients before pressing 'send'.

- If you are writing a difficult or important email, leave out the recipient until it is finished and checked so you can't send it by accident.

- Use a subject that will attract attention when received.

- Deal with the mail, then delete it if it does not need to be kept.

- Deal with it, then file it in a mailbox, if you need to keep it, then it is with all the other correspondence and out of your Inbox.

- Set up Smart mailboxes so the emails come into the relevant folder. The downside is that you need to make sure you check all mailboxes.

- If you can't deal with it straight away, flag it so you don't forget to go back to it.

- If you need to keep the information for some reason but are unlikely to need to access it, archive it so it takes up less space.

To organize in threads or not?

Should you choose the thread or conversation option? Whether you use threads is a matter of personal choice. Does it make it easier for you to organize your emails if you have all the conversations linked in single threads or not? Try it and see.

Pros

....

....

....

....

....

....

....

Cons

....

....

....

....

....

....

....

But I can't do it now

When we worked on paper, we could put a piece of paper into a pending tray, which would be checked regularly until we were able to deal with the issue and file the notification. With a digital system, it is easy to put a flag on something but it is also very easy to forget it once it is done. Keep a separate note or put the item in a pending folder, then get into the habit of checking through it every morning to see if you can action and file it.

When you really need to talk

Sometimes an exchange of emails becomes a conversation and would be much better carried out as such rather than typing back and forth to each other. Break the cycle. Pick up the phone.

Avoiding email 'tone'

By its very nature, email is less formal than a letter but the danger of this is that it can be misconstrued if you make it too brief – both in questions and response.

> Dear Phoebe
>
> Will you let me know soonest whether you can make a meeting at head office on Thursday 4 May at 1pm and whether you wish to add anything to the agenda.
>> Many thanks.
>> Kind regards
>> Wendy

However busy you are, unless you know the person very well, don't be tempted to say

> Yes and no! See you there.
> Phoebe

Unless you are absolutely sure it won't be mistaken as impatience or rudeness. If it is, you'll have to waste your time correcting a wrong impression – time you could much more usefully spend doing something more productive. If an extra minute or two now will save you hours down the line, then it is a good investment of time.

Sometimes an emoji can relieve an otherwise curt email but personally I don't think they have a role in business communication.

Dictation

This is a useful and quick way to get words on paper if your typing is not very fast and you are in a hurry to get something done; programs have improved immeasurably since they first came out. Do talk slowly and clearly, though, and let the device get used to your voice, as this will gradually help it become more efficient. Always check what the computer has decided you said.

Messaging

Messaging is a quick and useful way of keeping in touch. You don't have to use text speak – and you shouldn't do to someone who you are not sure will understand it.

Now there are so many apps that use wifi, you can message or voice message to and from anywhere in the world for free, which can help you organize your life much better.

Video calling and photos

If a picture paints a thousand words, snap it and send it. Speed and efficiency don't always go hand in hand, but in this case they do. Use the technology.

My landline

....

My mobile

....

Important numbers

....

....

....

....

....

....

....

....

....

Important work numbers

....

....

....

....

....

....

....

....

....

....

Email address

....

Important email addresses

....

....

....

....

....

....

....

....

....

....

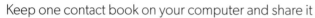

9

My friends

My contact book

Just a few pieces of common-sense advice will help you keep your contacts – family, friends, colleagues or business associates – well organized.

Keep one contact book on your computer and share it between your devices. That way, you won't have your friend's old address on your phone when you know you updated it on your laptop. You can separate personal and work-related contacts, if you wish, and make appropriate groups.

You can keep important information such as email, address and phone numbers and you can also add birthdays, children's names or whatever other information is helpful. Let the phone help you to organize your contacts – it takes the weight off you and does it very well.

Make sure it is included in your backup.

You might like to jot down a few important numbers in this book for quick reference should you be without your phone for any reason.

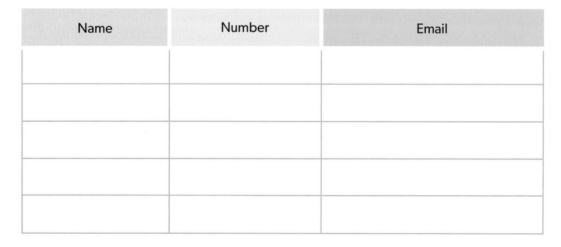

Name	Number	Email

Name	Number	Email

Birthdays and anniversaries

All the main digital contact books have the facility to record birthdays and anniversaries – or any special occasions – in the contact information. Fill it in so that you can use it in your diary.

Family birthdays

....

....

....

....

....

....

....

....

....

My contact book is

....

Important phone numbers

....

....

....

....

....

....

....

....

....

....

....

....

Important birthdays

....

....

....

....

....

....

....

....

....

....

....

....

....

....

....

....

....

....

Do not forget

....

....

....

10 My diary

Use the technology

Unless you have perfect recall, use the technology at your disposal to keep your diary organized. Keep one diary with everything in it so that overlaps will be shown up immediately. Add all events to it and keep it with you so you never jot things down on the back of an envelope or put them in a desk diary – or do neither and forget about them.

You can divide information into separate calendars if you like, then use colour coding to differentiate work from social, for example. You can then choose to show just one calendar in your display – but this is not a good idea because you are bound to miss something important.

My calendars

....

....

....

....

....

....

....

....

....

....

....

....

....

....

Events

When you set up an event, you can specify all the details in one place so nothing gets lost, you know where everything is, times, locations and people. Once again, use the technology to do the work for you. If not, you'll need to collect all that information manually and keep it all together in a designated safe place. (But don't forget where your safe place is.)

Birthdays and anniversaries

Since you have put your contacts' birthdays in your contact book, they will automatically appear in your calendar and you will be able to set up a notification so you have time to send a message or cards. Using this will save you a ton of work and gain you lots of good opinion.

My year ahead

January	February	March	April	May	June

My year ahead

July	August	September	October	November	December

## 11

My social life

Newsletters and other mailings

Signing up to mailing lists can seem a good idea – it often involves being entered for a prize, for example, or you may genuinely want to receive the information. There are times, however, when the quantity of incoming mail can be daunting and you might wish you had never joined.

To rid yourself of unwanted emails use the 'unsubscribe' option at the bottom of the email. Alternatively, create a separate email address for all such circumstances and have them go into a separate mailbox. That way you can go through them as a lower priority.

Social media

Facebook has been much in the news of late with regard to its use of users' personal information. If you do use it, make sure you review your security settings and that you are happy with how they may use your data. Read their advice to make sure you are in control and be sensible about the posts you make.

Events

If you book events online, separate out the booking information, especially if you have print-at-home tickets, to make sure you have everything safely stored where you know where they are when you need them. Cull the folder once the event is over. You can also add the events directly to your diary and include information about who else is going so that you can email reminders or arrangements. Since the computer does all this automatically once you have set it up, it makes light work of organization.

Organizing a party

If you are organizing a party or event, don't think that everything will simply fall into place. The secret of a good event of this kind is planning and organization.

- First decide on the when, where and numbers. If the location is fixed, you will soon be able to work out how many people you can invite.

- Let people know. Send out save the dates and/or invitations and ask for replies. You can generally expect a 75 per cent positive response.

- Decide whether you are going to serve food and whether it will be a meal, a buffet or nibbles. Write the menu. Calculate the quantities. Write the shopping list.

- Prepare a timetable that will allow you to be ready and waiting for your guests when they arrive. How much can you cook and freeze in advance? How much do you need to do on the day?

- Are you putting up any decorations? Buy them or make them. Work out how long they will take to put up and when you are going to do them.

- How much help do you need? If you have ten hours' worth of work on the day of the event, you need to get more hands on board.

- How much drink will you need? What about ice? Soft drinks?

- Buy or borrow enough glasses.

- Sort out, buy or borrow enough cutlery and crockery, if you need it.

- Leave as little as possible to be done on the day so you can really enjoy yourself.

Party

....

....

This year's events

....

....

....

....

....

....

....

....

....

....

....

....

....

....

....

....

....

....

....

....

....

....

Twitter handle

....

Instagram

....

Facebook

....

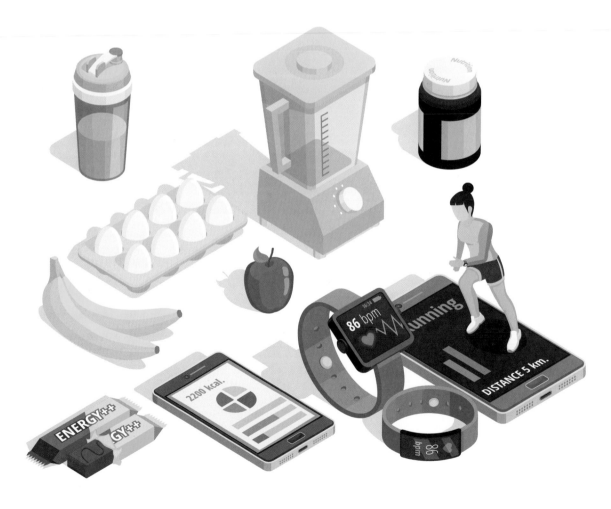

12

Looking after yourself

Height

....

....

....

....

....

Weight

....

....

....

....

....

BMI

....

....

....

....

Doctor

....

....

....

....

Surgery address

....

....

....

....

Nearest A&E

....

....

....

....

Organize your exercise

Some of us love it, some of us hate it. But the fact is that we all need to exercise, and most of us probably need to exercise more than we do. However, if we are really not enjoying what we are doing, then it then the likelihood of us doing it on a regular basis for any length of time is pretty slim, so the key is to find something that we like. First, try to narrow down what you do and don't like about it.

The advantages
of regular exercise

....

....

....

....

What I find difficult

....

....

....

....

....

What I like about exercise

....

....

....

....

What I dislike

....

....

....

....

Choosing your best options

Work your way through the chart and see if you can come up with an activity you will enjoy that will give you a bit of a workout.

Team sports are a good way to socialize, give you incentive to go rather than let the side down, and there are plenty on offer in most locations. Try basketball, netball, rugby, soccer, hockey.

Group activities are also plentiful and suitable for all levels of fitness. There are many classes at leisure centres that you can enjoy: aerobics, aquaerobics, body pump, Pilates, yoga.

Paired options are good for competitive people who like to go for a one-on-one: badminton, squash, tennis.

Individual sports also offer plenty of choice: cycling, running.

Classes of any kind from yoga to body pump or Boxercise are a good way to encourage yourself. If you pay in advance for a term for example, you won't want to waste your money. If you find that you are missing too many to make it economic then it's time to try something else.

Going it alone. Some people just love to run – I can't think of anything worse – but if you have the will power to go out running regularly and you get a buzz out of it then that's your thing.

Exercising at home is probably the most difficult because you really have to be motivated to keep it going for very long. Get it in into your general routine: for example, a session on the exercise bike, while you watch the early morning news.

Not into sport? There are other options, such as walking, dancing or physically active conservation work.

Sports/activities to try

....

....

....

....

Organizing your diet

The first thing to say about your diet is that it's a good idea to try to use the word correctly! The kind of diet referred to here is not a slimming diet, which is the shorthand we usually use. If slimming diets were successful then there wouldn't be a huge industry surrounding them and we would all be an ideal weight. Slimming diets that do succeed are focussed on changing your everyday diet to a healthier model.

What you should aim for is a healthy balanced diet. No one food stuff is bad or good, they all combine into a healthy mix if eaten them in the right quantities and proportions. The healthy eating plate below, is a straightforward way of making sure you are eating enough of each of the main food groups. Of course, if you eat a balanced diet but twice as much as you need, then it's not going to work.

Jot down details about your health and diet and where you would like to and are able to make changes. Try to apply them gradually and by eating foods you actually like and savouring them. Try not to make food a big issue. If you need help, there are books, support groups, videos, apps and all many other tools you can use to help you. If changing your diet were easy it wouldn't be a topic in this book but unfortunately nobody else can do it for you.

Current weight

Target weight

....

....

Diets I've tried

....

....

....

What I find difficult about
maintaining the right weight

What I am going to do about it

....

....

....

....

....

....

....

....

....

....

....

....

....

....

....

....

Your well-being

Fortunately it is becoming more acceptable to talk about our mental health. One big step forward is that many celebrities have discussed their experiences of mental health issues, which has helped to break down some of the attached stigma.

Mental health problems can play just as much havoc with the smooth organization of your life as a broken leg, a serious physical illness or an operation. What's clear is that you need to seek help as soon as possible and not be afraid to talk about it. This is neither pleasant nor easy, but is something many of us will have to face up to at some time in our lives.

Start by making some notes on how you feel about yourself and your circumstances. It may be a starting point for professional discussion or therapy.

How I feel about myself

....

....

....

....

How I feel about my family and friends

....

....

....

....

My work situation

....

....

....

My social situation

....

....

....

How can help myself?

....

....

....

....

....

....

Finding a life-work balance

At the beginning of this book, we talked about learning to say no, about being self-aware but not selfish, and about valuing ourselves as much as other people. So many of us – especially the young and ambitious – work far longer hours than they are contracted or paid for, and they do it because there is a culture of expectation. Even if you were at your desk at eight and worked through lunch, if you leave at five on the dot there is often a literal or metaphorical tutting and your card is effectively marked.

This can lead to a serious disorganization at the core of your life.

We are not talking about occasional extra-long days or weekend catch-ups but systematic over-working. You'll know if you have fallen into the trap of letting your work take over but just to show how much, fill in the chart for at least one week and preferably a few, making sure they are fairly representative. (By the way, I don't think I've ever heard of life taking over; if it did, you'd find a job that you could do as easily as possible for as few hours as possible.)

Time spent at work

Contracted hours ....

Day	Started at	Stopped for lunch at	Started at	Finished at	Additional hours at home	Total hours
Monday						
Tuesday						
Wednesday						
Thursday						
Friday						
Saturday						
Sunday						
TOTAL						

If you also add travelling time, that will leave even less time for yourself. The mantra to repeat is: quantity of work does not necessarily result in quality. 'Over-worked' already has negative connotations; so should 'over-working.' Think hard about how the balance of your life is disorganized.

How is my life out of balance?

....

....

....

Are there any advantages?

....

....

....

What are the downsides?

....

....

....

What are you going to do about it?

The problem is that resolving the situation is unlikely to be within your control. Start by writing down what you do now and the pros and cons of your current situation. Then write down what you think is reasonable on a regular basis. If you can implement that yourself, do so.

Contracted hours

....

....

Advantages

....

....

....

....

....

Actual hours worked

....

....

Disadvantages

....

....

....

....

....

Intention

....

If there is a culture of over-working, talk to your colleagues. It will not be an easy dialogue to open but someone has to if you are not all going to burn out. Start with close colleagues and work outwards; ask them to talk to other colleagues. You may be able to agree to cut down on over-working and solve the problem.

I have spoken with (tick their name if they agree)

.... ☐

.... ☐

.... ☐

.... ☐

.... ☐

.... ☐

.... ☐

.... ☐

.... ☐

.... ☐

.... ☐

.... ☐

.... ☐

.... ☐

.... ☐

.... ☐

If the culture goes right to the top, you need to get together and muster your arguments to take to your line manager. Think about counter-arguments to the objections that might be raised. Make sure you start by ensuring they understand you are not talking about odd half hours or extra time when it is really necessary.

Number of unpaid overtime hours per week (per employee)

....

Negative impacts

Tiredness

....

....

Potential loss of quality of work

....

....

Increases likelihood of losing staff

....

....

Resentment

....

....

Unhappy workforce

....

....

....

Counter-arguments

....

....

....

....

....

....

....

....

....

Advantages to the company

....

....

....

....

....

....

....

....

....

This is another difficult conversation. Can you discuss with your boss why this is happening, what you propose to do about it and why it will be beneficial to the company as well as the employees. What positive steps would you take to change the culture at your workplace?

....

....

....

13

Compromise and co-ordination

Living together

Whether you are living with a partner, a friend, a flatmate or a family, your circumstances will be unique. However, there are some common factors:

- everyone does things differently;
- you know how hard it is to change your own behaviour so you can be sure you can't change anyone else's.

Living with other people can challenge your ability to organize things as you would like so you will need to talk to each other about what you each expect. There will be certain standards you all want to maintain and if it is possible to agree them up front, that will be a great help in avoiding later conflict or misunderstanding. Talk about how you expect the house to be organized.

- **Who pays the bills? How do you share the finances?**
- **How will you organize the cleaning?**
- **What about food and other provisions?**
- **How will you deal with visitors?**
- **What about personal privacy?**

Discussing these topics and coming to an agreement will make for a much more organized and pleasant household.

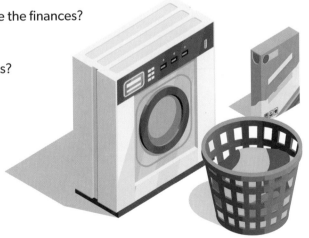

What aspects are particularly important for you to agree on?

....

....

....

....

....

....

....

....

....

....

....

....

....

....

I live with

....

....

....

....

....

....

....

....

....

....

....

....

....

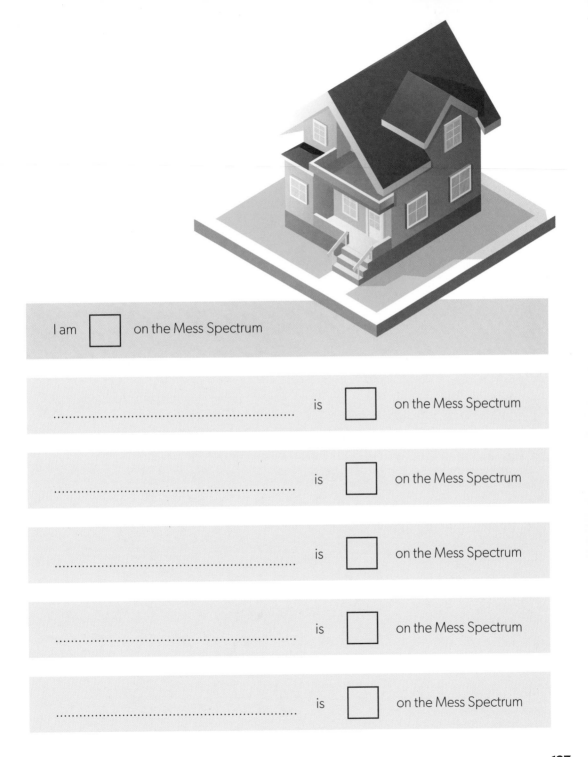

I am ☐ on the Mess Spectrum

.... is ☐ on the Mess Spectrum

.... is ☐ on the Mess Spectrum

.... is ☐ on the Mess Spectrum

.... is ☐ on the Mess Spectrum

.... is ☐ on the Mess Spectrum

House rules

You may want to draw up some house rules. They don't have to be formal but should be unambiguous. Think about the topics you might include. Sometimes it's the small things that cause friction. Don't be afraid to raise things that may seem trivial (like putting the toilet seat down or how long you spend in the shower) if they are important to you.

Money

....

....

Cleaning

....

....

Visitors

....

....

Catering

....

....

Laundry

....

....

....

Timetables

....

....

Showers

....

....

Sample house rules

- Tidy up at the end of the day and keep most of your things in your own room.

- If you are having visitors, let your flatmate know.

- No smoking in the house.

- Turn off the TV when you leave the room.

....

....

....

....

....

....

....

....

Curbing the disorganized and encouraging organization

If you are finding improvements in your ability to organize your life, then you might like to share them with your flatmates. Tell them what you find annoying about their disorganization – but be prepared for them to tell you too!

Make decisions on where you need to compromise and where each of you needs to change. You should find that you each give in at some points and stand your ground at others. The point is to find a middle way.

## 14

Keep it up

Archiving

Nothing actually tidies itself up so you need to keep on top of things. Tidy up regularly, go through each room – or each folder on your computer – and put in the charity bag, delete and otherwise get it out of your way.

There will be some things that you need or want to keep but don't need clogging up your working systems, so archive them – it's like putting things in the loft, but you must wrap and label them clearly and make sure they are easily accessible if you do need them again.

You also need to clear out your archives or loft occasionally so if they are well organized and in sequence, that will make it much easier.

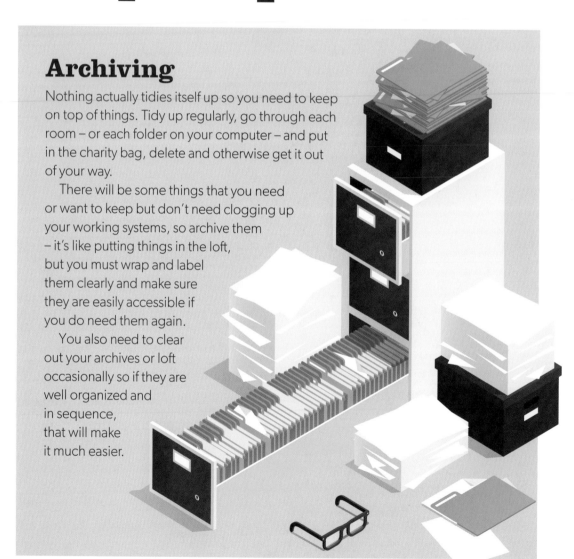

Archive record

Label	Location	Contents	Date

No backsliding

Now you have repositioned yourself at the right end of the Mess Spectrum, don't backslide. It's easier to say than do, but there are things that can help to maintain this new organized you.

Remember how it used to be

What made you angry, upset or came with serious consequences when you were at the top of the Mess Spectrum? Maybe you lost the phone number of someone you would really have liked to meet again. Or perhaps you were late for an interview and missed out on your dream job.

....

....

....

....

....

....

....

....

....

Define the advantages

What about the good bits? How much less do you shout at the computer and expect it to respond? Did you land that dream job because you were able to do such a strong presentation of your work career?

··

··

··

··

··

··

··

··

··

··

··

Write it down

There's something about the process of writing that encourages knowledge and habits to stick in your mind. So if you have not already used this book to make notes, now's the time to go back to the beginning and fill it in.

....

....

....

....

....

....

....

....

....

....

....

....

Make it public

Tell anyone who'll listen that you have turned over a new leaf and are determined to stay at the bottom of the Mess Spectrum from now on. A bit of external scrutiny can be a good motivator (but don't go on about it!).

I've told

....

Find a Mess Spectrum buddy

You might even team up with someone else for mutual support.

My Mess Spectrum buddy is

....

Evolve

Don't change for its own sake but if you find better ways of doing things, adapt, update and improve your systems. Check in regularly to see what is or is not working.

Works well	Room for improvement
....	....
....	....
....	....
....	....
....	....
....	....
....	....
....	....
....	....
....	....
....	....
....	....
....	....

Reward yourself

There's nothing like a monthly bar of chocolate, trip to the pub, meal out with friends, new music download, pair of shoes – whatever gives you a boost – both to incentivize you and pat yourself on the back to encourage you to keep going.

Month 1	Treat

Month 2	Treat

Month 3	Treat

Month 4	Treat

Month 5	Treat

Month 6	Treat

Above all, enjoy the perks of becoming the go-to organizer and moving yourself down the Mess Spectrum. Well done, you!

My notes